Bargain City

Booking, Betting, and Beating the New Las Vegas

Other Huntington Press titles:

The Theory of Blackjack: The Compleat Card Counter's Guide to the Casino Game of 21
by Peter Griffin

Extra Stuff: Gambling Ramblings
by Peter Griffin

Bargain City

Booking, Betting, and Beating the New Las Vegas

Anthony Curtis

Huntington Press

Bargain City: Booking, Betting, and Beating the New Las Vegas

Published by

Huntington Press
5280 S. Valley View Blvd., Suite B
Las Vegas, Nevada 89118
(702) 597-1884 Vox
(702) 597-5208 Fax

ISBN 0-929712-50-1

Editor: Deke Castleman
Production & Design: Bethany Coffey

Front cover photo by John Gurzinski

Cover design by Rin Hunt

Printing History

1st edition—July 1993, reprinted October 1993, December 1993

For Mom and Dad

Who gave me the tools, then the support,
to pull the whole thing off

ACKNOWLEDGEMENTS

Thanks to Arthur Flowers, Blair Rodman, and Lori Notaro for their help in reading and research, and to Karen Hunt for her work on the cover. Thanks also to Stanford Wong for providing the book's title, as well as friendship and encouragement over the years.

I'm grateful to Virginia, Adam, and Jonathan for lending me Deke; to Bobby for bringing dinner; and to Katie and Jacob for proving their mettle by hanging in there.

My thanks to June Flowers for keeping everything running smoothly and *cleanly*, despite fielding 50 reader phone calls a day; I'm sure she would do it all for nothing.

I owe Deke Castleman a deep debt of gratitude for his dedication and commitment, and an even deeper debt for his words, a great many of which appear in these pages.

And I have a special thank you for Bethany Coffey for having the foresight to recognize the potential early.

Finally, thanks to the *Las Vegas Advisor* readers, who've supported us through thick, thin, expired coupons, and 3rd class mail.

TABLE OF CONTENTS

INTRODUCTION

Can you imagine being 21 years old and telling your father, a university professor, that you want to drop out of college to become a gambler in Las Vegas? Well, that's exactly what I did. Having read a few books on card counting, I was convinced that Las Vegas was mine for the taking, and the big challenge to making a living was a simple matter of finding enough time away from Las Vegas revelry to visit the tables. After I arrived in March of 1979, it took only a few days to discover I possessed no secrets that would allow me to carry out my plan. That was the bad news. The good news? Secrets did exist, and over the years I learned them.

Coupons were the first revelation—the house edge didn't stand a chance against the power of a 2-1 lucky buck. Eating cheaply was next. Then eating cheaply and *well*.

Many more discoveries followed, and I began to realize that the same techniques that I had used, first for survival and later for profit, could be easily applied to enhance a Las Vegas vacation. That's when the *Las Vegas Advisor* was born. The *LVA* began as a basement production in 1983, just a little ahead of the desktop computer technology that was necessary to make it a viable publication. After two years of publishing for the benefit of less than 200 readers, I put the *LVA* aside to pursue serious gambling opportunities (primarily an assault on casino tournaments based on a winning model developed by Stanford Wong). I did keep the *LVA* alive, however, by scaling it back to a two-page bargain tip sheet in 1986. By 1988, gambling winnings allowed me to finance a full-scale publishing effort, and the *LVA* went into high gear, just in time to chronicle the great Las Vegas boom, which continues today.

Since 1988, 50 six-page issues and sixteen 12-page issues of the *Advisor* have been published, every month, right on schedule. Much of the information in this book is based on that research. But *Bargain City* is completely updated, therefore everything within these pages is relevant to the present.

One great dilemma that I faced was how to handle prices in the text of this book. Prices change faster around here than anywhere else in the galaxy; it's difficult to stay current even on a monthly or weekly basis. Not publishing prices would leave you completely in the dark, so I've decided to include them throughout. You'll certainly come across price discrepancies. But in Las Vegas, there's at least a chance that the price will have *decreased* rather than risen.

It is my hope that you will profit from this book. *Bargain City* doesn't contain all the information there is about Las Vegas, but it does contain the best. The recommendations within have all been used successfully at some time; they are a product of my 15 years of hand-to-hand combat with Las Vegas casinos.

1

BEST OF BARGAIN CITY

Western civilization appears in its most concentrated form in Las Vegas...an orgy of buildings, arches, fountains, statues, and ads, striking the eye with the abandon and wanton nature of the merry-making going on there. All this rolls before your eyes in a searing ball of fire, 24 hours a day.
—Pravda, Moscow

Exactly! I've been trying to convey this point for years. Rest assured, the forces that make America great are alive and well in Las Vegas. Competition, the free market, supply and demand—we've got it all, and that's good. But there's a flip side. In the great American tradition, you are bombarded with ads and come-ons from the moment you step off the plane or wheel your car within 100 miles of the Las Vegas city limits. The resultant sensory overload can leave you lost. You need direction.

This chapter is your bargain map—all you need to know to enjoy the best that Las Vegas has to offer right now. These are the tried and true values—examined, confirmed, and reaffirmed by thousands of visitors every day—the deals that have passed the test of time, and have played their part in establishing the Las Vegas value standard.

No doubt, you'll discover great deals of your own, but in the meantime here are the reigning best values in Bargain City.

Best Las Vegas Bargain

NY Steak Dinner, $2, Binion's Horseshoe

A 10-ounce New York steak, big baked potato, salad, vegetable, and roll served 10 pm-5:45 am, 365 days a year. Any way you cut it, this is the greatest Las Vegas value of the decade! Longer, really. It was the meal that everyone talked about when I first came to Las Vegas in 1979, and it's the one they still talk about today. The magic, of course, is the $2 tab. The price was raised to $3 in mid-1983, then rolled back to $2 in '85. In '87, it was again raised to $3, and rolled back only one year later, where it has remained ever since. Everyone stays up late in Las Vegas. You will too. Stay up a little later, grab a cab to the Horseshoe, and try one of these steaks—*the* Las Vegas value icon.

Best Room Rate

Free, Las Vegas Hotel-Casinos

The only other vacation scenario that includes this possibility involves a tent, sleeping bag, and a lot of wilderness. Why would casinos give rooms away?

Competition. Hotels with 3,000, 4,000, and 5,000 rooms open, and the owners of hotels with only 1,000 or 2,000 rooms get nervous.

Lulls. City-wide occupancy levels sometimes plummet below 90%, especially in December. Gasp!

But mostly, it's the gambling. Gambling winnings subsidize the room department (and the food department, and the alcohol department, and the entertainment department, and...).

This isn't hype. You want proof? Read "50 Nights, 49 Free" on page 50. As a sage *Las Vegas Advisor* subscriber once wrote: "Free is a very good price to pay for a room."

Best Loss Leader

Free Money, Four Queens

What a concept. You go to a casino, and *it gives you* money! The Four Queens is famous for dispensing special non-negotiable tokens that play like real coins in slot and video poker machines. Not promotional machines with reduced return percentages, but the best-paying machines in the casino. You can get free money by subscribing to certain periodicals (like the *Las Vegas Advisor* or *Casino Player)*, by picking up vouchers at tourist centers in Barstow, by buying a prime rib dinner in the Queens' coffee shop, and by getting your name on lists at the Four Queens—join the slot club or the great Club 55 for seniors. You want to be known by this casino in case

Free-Money Magic

An LVA subscriber from Dearborn, Mich., turned his $20 in Four Queens free slot tokens into $1,000 by hitting a royal flush on his first visit to the casino. It was almost a much bigger day. The royal came up J♥, 10♥, Q♥, K♥, A♥. Had the J and 10 been reversed, a $25,000 bonus would have been paid for a royal in sequence.

It happened again on New Year's Day 1993. A young couple popped the royal with free money. It was a great New Year's omen for the couple and their new baby.

they decide to do a mailing. A free-money infusion is an incredible way to begin a vacation.

Best Breakfast

Old Guard—Binion's Natural, $2.50, Binion's Horseshoe
New Guard—Steak & Eggs, $2.99, Rio

Though scores of others have come and gone, the Natural has held the title of "Las Vegas' best breakfast" the longest. Two eggs, a piece of ham that covers the entire plate, sliced potatoes (not hash browns), toast, and the best coffee and service in town. Quality, quality, quality.

The Rio is the most recent (and most serious) challenger for the title with its T-bone steak, two eggs, hash browns, and all the pancakes you can eat. Quantity, quantity, quantity.

Best Buffet

The Carnival World, $3.25-$7.25, Rio
The Feast, $3.95-$7.95, Palace Station

These two stand together atop the Las Vegas buffet hierarchy. The Rio's Carnival World is an incredible spectacle, a mini food city with fare ranging from cherry fritters for breakfast to a Mongolian barbecue for dinner. Palace Station's Feast is the innovative, working-man's buffet, where hamburgers and pizza coexist alongside quiche, Szechwan eggplant, and halibut with Chardonnay-caper butter.

Best Place to Drink

Nostalgic—Binion's Horseshoe
Classy—Golden Nugget
Cheap—Vacation Village
Friendly—Palace Station

The Horseshoe has been *the* Las Vegas drinking spot forever. Every visitor should grab at least one beer at one of the Horseshoe's three long wooden bars to get a feeling for the way it was in the *old* Las Vegas. Then walk across the street for the best of the new—the Golden Nugget's drinks at all bars for $1.25. You won't find cocktails or beer for ten bits at any other four-star four-diamond hotel in the world. Vacation Village is Las Vegas' lone throwback to the quarter-beer days of the '80s. Put a buck on the bar and relax. Palace Station is the favorite hangout for locals and after-shift casino workers, due in no small part to the best 99¢ margarita special in the city's history.

Best Meal

King Crab Leg Dinner, $10.95, Palace Station

No doubt. No contest. If you eat only one dinner in Las Vegas, this should be it. A full pound of king crab legs worthy of any seafood gourmet house. How good a deal is this? I took a friend from Alaska, a waiter who's served literally thousands of crab-leg covers in fine dining rooms. He was blown right out of the water. Two of his comments. "I doubt that my serving is only 16 ounces, seems like a pound and a quarter, maybe more." And, "The most amazing thing is the price. Even in Kodiak, straight off the boat, I haven't seen a price like this for over 15 years." Combine the crab legs with the Palace Station's 24-hour margarita for a cyclopean-cracked-crustacean-and-tequila combo.

Best Place For Dinner

Pasta Pirate, California Hotel-Casino

Of the 200+ casino restaurants in Las Vegas, this one will satisfy more people than any other. First, the restaurant has three specialties—seafood, steaks, and pasta—so most culinary tastes are covered. Second, the room is upscale, but you can dine in casual dress—so most aesthetic and fashion senses are appeased. Third, prices are great—so everyone *else* will be happy. The Pasta Pirate is home to one of Las Vegas' best and most consistent on-going steak dinners, a fantastic filet mignon for only $9.95. The daily specials are also highly recommended. The restaurant accepts reservations. Make them!

Best Story to Tell

59¢ Dinner at Boardwalk

It's a dark and stormy night in the summer of 1993. Two high rollers stroll into a Las Vegas Strip casino for dinner. One orders baked chicken, which comes with a side of spaghetti, two pieces of garlic bread, and a cup of red, white, or rose wine. The other orders roast beef, which comes with mashed potatoes and gravy, mixed vegetables, dinner roll, and wine. It's not fancy by any means—the dinners are served on styrofoam plates and the drinks in plastic cups. But the food is as good as home cooking and the plates are *sooo* full that one has a hard time finishing. Then the bill comes: $1.27! They fight like animals for the check. The end.

The Boardwalk's 59¢ dinners (25¢ last December) rotate on and off, and may not be available in the future. But don't worry. There'll be some other incredible special to partake of at another Las Vegas casino. It was upon such deals that the Bargain City legend was built. And that's no fairy tale.

Best Way to Remember the Best Vacation On Earth

Free Photo, Binion's Horseshoe

Take your entire group to the Horseshoe between 4 pm and midnight and get your picture taken in front of 100 $10,000 bills. That's a million dollars, the coolest mil you'll ever be photographed in front of. You'll join the countless other visitors who've taken home this ultimate Las Vegas souvenir over the 40+ years that the bills have been displayed. Indeed, regulars get their pictures snapped every time they're in Las Vegas, to keep running and accurate memories of each visit.

Other Deals You Can Count On

Drinks

Holy Cow! Micro-Brewery

Funbooks

Lady Luck
Sands
Riviera

Buffets

Bally's Big Kitchen	$6.45-$11.95
Golden Nugget	$4.75-$9.50

Sunday Brunch

Tropicana	$20.95
Bally's	$29.95

Breakfast

Frontier	$2-$3, 11 pm-11 am

Good Restaurants

Rio	All-American Bar & Grill (steaks)
Rio	Antonio's (Italian)
Palace Station	Pasta Palace (Italian)
Palace Station	Guadalajara (Mexican)
California	Redwood Bar & Grille (steaks)
Gold Coast	Cortez Room (steaks)
Horseshoe	Binion's Ranch Steakhouse (steaks)

Show Bargain

Riviera	Show (Mardis Gras Shows, choose from three) and Prime Rib Buffet, $9-$20
Tropicana	*Les Folies Bergere*, $19 (late show)
Stardust	*Enter the Night*, $25

Show Quality

The Mirage	*Siegfried & Roy*, $72.85
The Mirage (Moving to Treasure Island December 1993)	*Cirque du Soleil*, $38.50

Steaks

California	NY strip, $3, 11 pm-9 am, coffee shop
California	Porterhouse, $12.95, 5:30-11 pm, Redwood
Palace Station	16 ounce T-Bone, $6.95, 24 hours, coffee shop

Prime Rib

Horseshoe	$4.95, 5-9:45 pm, coffee shop
Sands	$4.95, 11 am-2 am, coffee shop
California	$5.95, 5:30-11 pm, coffee shop
Frontier	$5.95, 4-10 pm, coffee shop
Circus Circus	$6.95, 4-11 pm, Skyrise
Jerry's Nugget	$6.95-$17.70, 24 hours, coffee shop

Miscellaneous

Golden Gate	Shrimp Cocktail, 99¢
Flamingo	Gourmet Salad Bar, $8.95, Flamingo Room

2

THE EVOLUTION OF BARGAIN CITY

Las Vegas' recent metamorphosis has been astounding. In the past few years, more than $3 billion has gone into the construction of 20,000 hotel rooms, themed shopping malls and amusement parks, even a world-class observation tower. But a review of events of the past two decades shows that the developments we credit with the transformation of the old Las Vegas into the new only began in 1990—or more accurately in late 1989. It's hard to believe amidst today's casino-building frenzy, but prior to the opening of The Mirage in November 1989, a major new Strip hotel-casino hadn't opened in 16 years (Kirk Kerkorian's original MGM Grand, now Bally's, which opened in 1973).

Though more than 30 issues of the *Las Vegas Advisor* had been previously published, the beginning of the '90s marked the inauguration of our coverage of the news of gambling—primarily in Las Vegas and Nevada, but also around the country. We had no choice. It was obvious that gambling had become, and would remain for a while, the largest growth industry in the nation.

This chapter presents a brief synopsis of events in the mid-to-late '80s, and then an in-depth month-to-month chronology of the exploding casino scene of the '90s.

1983-1989

The '80s, specifically 1983 through 1989, marked a time of positioning and maneuvering for a place in the new Las Vegas. The city as a whole made plans to repel the challenge that was coming from the legalization of casino gambling in new jurisdictions around the country, while individual casinos expanded and remodeled in an attempt to remain competitive themselves. Major renovations took place at numerous casinos, among them: California, Desert Inn, Flamingo, Fremont, Lady Luck, Palace Station, Plaza, Riviera, Sahara, Silver City, Stardust, and Vegas World. Golden Nugget underwent the biggest change, with an expansion that propelled the resort to 4-star status. In fact, way back in 1983, visionary Steve Wynn called the

Golden Nugget's expansion a "testimony to our optimism concerning the future of gambling in Las Vegas."

This period also fostered a big move on the part of the casinos to recognize and attract the "middle roller," as slots asserted their dominance over table games. Circus Circus, which had mined this middle market for years, continued to prosper and went public during this period.

Casinos that catered to the "locals" became the rage. The Gold Coast and Arizona Charlie's opened, and the Bingo Palace took a swankier name—Palace Station. The non-gambling Alexis Park opened and survived. Wet n' Wild opened with a dual distinction: first theme park; first kid's attraction.

There were financial difficulties at Aladdin, Dunes, Landmark, Sands, and Riviera. Some things don't change.

In important gambling-related developments, Caesars Palace became the first to institute "simulcasting" (the live transmission of horse races). The collecting of Nevada gambling debts became legally enforceable. A major skimming scandal involving the Stardust, Fremont, and Sundance (now Fitzgeralds) was uncovered by the Gaming Control Board. When the dust settled, the last major underworld influence in Las Vegas had been eliminated, and the reputable Boyd Group had taken over the Fremont and Stardust.

Then, in 1989, two events occurring in rapid succession set the giant roulette ball of evolution rolling. In September, Kirk Kerkorian announced that he would build a new 5,000-room $1 billion casino, resort and theme park called MGM Grand. And in late November, The Mirage opened its doors.

The new Las Vegas had arrived.

December 1989

Signs on the Strip reading, "Please drive carefully. And for your own safety, try not to be distracted by the hotel on the right," herald the opening of The Mirage. More impressive than the casino is the publicity effort that accompanies the opening. Feature articles in *The Wall Street Journal* and *USA Today* and sports coverage generated by a Sugar Ray Leonard/ Roberto Duran title fight round out the media circus. The PR effort gets one more shot in the arm when a 76-year-old Las Vegas resident hits a $4.6 million slot jackpot on opening night. The jackpot is Las Vegas' largest ever [at that time]. Two weeks later, a $1.4 million slot jackpot is hit at the resort. The Mirage takes a full-page ad in the *Las Vegas Sun* asking for "a chance to catch our breath."

Caesars Palace reacts to its new neighbor by announcing plans to build the Forum Shops mall.

January 1990

All but ignored in the ballyhoo surrounding The Mirage is the opening of another new casino, Rio Suites. The Rio decides to go after the high end of the market with an all-suite room format and generally up-scale food, entertainment, and amenities, i.e., a pool with a sand bottom and a sandy beach.

The Silver Nugget reopens in North Las Vegas after being closed for nearly two years.

A U.S. bankruptcy court action places the Landmark in the hands of a federal trustee. The casino remains open under Chapter 7 bankruptcy status. Location, design, and questionable management are blamed for the financial difficulties.

The Ramada San Remo opens on the site that was formerly the Polynesian (prior to that the 20th Century, and prior to that the Treasury).

More plans for the MGM Grand are announced. Opening is scheduled for late 1992.

February 1990

Vegas World owner Bob Stupak seeks approval from the city of Las Vegas and the Federal Aviation Administration to begin construction on a 1,012-foot-high observation tower that will be three times taller than any existing building in the city. Stupak estimates the project could be completed in 1991.

The Landmark continues its journey through Chapter 7 bankruptcy. State gaming regulators grant the Landmark an extension of a temporary license while they examine the casino's cash position.

The Mirage reports a $40 million casino win for their first full month (December), the highest single-month win ever in either Las Vegas or Atlantic City. Crowds are so heavy at the resort that it's necessary to periodically ban minors (even those accompanied by parents) who are not registered guests of the hotel.

The Peppermill Casino closes.

The Royal Casino reopens.

A Culinary Union strike at Binion's Horseshoe turns into an all-out war.

Top Hotels

BusinessWeek *rated the top 1,000 companies in the U.S., and six of the nation's top seven hotel businesses have operations in Las Vegas. Marriott is number one (no Las Vegas casino), followed by Circus Circus, Hilton, Promus, Caesars, Mirage, and MGM Grand.*

March 1990

The Riviera christens "the world's largest casino." The new 125,000-square-foot facility is accompanied by the opening of an improved race and sports book and nine new fast-food eateries situated in the Mardi Gras Food Court. This completes phase two of what was to be a three phase, $200 million expansion at the Riviera. [The final phase never materialized.]

The Nevada Gaming Commission gives the Landmark a five-month extension on its license and concessions on state fees and taxes to keep the casino operating.

The Taj Mahal in Atlantic City opens. The crown jewel in Trump's casino empire is reported to have cost more than $1 billion (about 60% more than The Mirage). Not gigantic in terms of rooms (1,250), the casino is considered by some the last word in opulence. One suite is rumored to be outfitted with more than $1 million worth of furnishings.

Las Vegas visitor volume reaches 18.1 million in 1989, about one million more than 1988.

Rank and File

Periodic labor strikes are an unfortunate reality in Las Vegas.

The 1984 city-wide strike by the Culinary Union (bartenders, front desk clerks, and waitpeople) lasted 75 days and resulted in countless confrontations, hundreds of arrests and, depending on whose estimate you accept, anywhere from $60 million to $125 million in lost tourism revenue. In 1989, the Musician's Union succeeded in shutting down the headliner showrooms at Bally's and Caesars Palace. Major performers who either refused or were unable to appear included Dean Martin, Rodney Dangerfield, Connie Francis, Burt Bacharach, Dionne Warwick, George Carlin, and Bill Medley. In 1990, the Culinary locked horns with Binion's Horseshoe. Pickets and rallies clogged downtown streets for nine months. The Horseshoe eventually settled. The next target of the Culinary was the Frontier in September 1991 [it has yet to be settled, nearly two years later]. A large dose of negative national publicity was focused on Las Vegas when a young California couple was physically beaten outside the casino in an altercation with strikers.

The battle threatens to escalate, and possibly erupt, in 1994 when the massive MGM Grand opens without a union in the house and dozens of Las Vegas casinos' union contracts expire.

April 1990

The strike at the Horseshoe grabs national headlines.

A study by the University of Nevada indicates that Nevada gambling is adversely affected by the California lottery. Indian gambling and riverboat casinos (now legal in Iowa, Illinois, and Mississippi) pose another threat.

May 1990

Anticipating the June opening of Excalibur, Steve Wynn announces the first expansion plans for The Mirage—a "mountain range" resembling Hawaii's Diamondhead, designed by singer Michael Jackson. [It never materializes.]

June 1990

The 4,032-room Excalibur opens. The surrealistic $290 million castle-in-a-desert is the largest hotel in the world. Everything within the castle walls has an Arthurian theme, all the way down to security guards dressed as knights on horseback. Like Circus Circus, Excalibur is billed as an attraction for the whole family, though more upscale, with rooms priced about 1/3 higher than its sister property (average $45). More than 30,000 people visit within a few hours of the opening. A *Las Vegas Review-Journal* columnist describes the casino as "...a gargantuan slot machine that accepts humans as tokens."

With the addition of Excalibur's 4,000 rooms, the total Las Vegas room count rises to 75,000.

There is speculation that the vacant property at the northwest corner of Tropicana and the Strip will be developed in a joint venture between Harrah's and Universal Slot Company. [It never materializes.]

First word is heard about a Florida developer who wants to turn the downtown area into a modern entertainment and retail complex called Church Street Station. [The name is later changed to Main Street Station.] Downtown casino owners are opposed, but the developer moves forward with the blessings of the city's redevelopment agency and the financing of at least one powerful lending institution.

A local ordinance prohibiting open containers in motor vehicles goes into effect. Until now, drinking by passengers had been legal. Taxis and limos are exempt.

A new slogan, "Always on the Money," replaces the familiar "American Way to Play" in national ads promoting Las Vegas. The new campaign stresses the affordability of a Las Vegas vacation. Extra efforts are made to advertise in the southeast and other areas where there is a perceived dissatisfaction with Atlantic City.

July 1990

The incredible Las Vegas room boom continues. The Holiday [now Harrah's] completes a renovation/expansion that adds more than 700 rooms, making it the largest Holiday Inn in the world. The Stardust secures financing to begin a 1,500-room addition/renovation. And Palace Station unveils plans for the addition of nearly 600 rooms. Other properties adding rooms in 1990 include Sahara, Hacienda, Riviera, and Gold Coast.

The 2,000-room Flamingo Hilton opens in Laughlin. The new hotel accounts for a 35% increase in the Laughlin room count.

August 1990

The Landmark Casino closes. No bidders in a bankruptcy court auction forces the closure. Slot machines are sealed and guests are encouraged to find other accommodations. The Landmark's future is uncertain. There's speculation that interested buyers are waiting to purchase at a bargain price after the property goes into foreclosure. The Riviera has been mentioned as a potential buyer.

September/October 1990

Downtown's Park Casino closes to facilitate work on Main Street Station.

The Aladdin is up for sale.

November 1990

The nine-month strike at Binion's Horseshoe is settled. There are no clear-cut winners or losers.

The financial situation at the Dunes becomes tenuous. The Japanese owner threatens to close the casino if he's not granted an unlimited gaming license.

The Sands completes the 500,000-square-foot Sands Expo and Convention Center.

The MGM Marina closes so serious work may begin on the huge MGM Grand Casino-Hotel-Theme Park. The mega-property will employ 7,000. MGM Grand, Inc. puts the Desert Inn up for sale in an effort to raise money for the new project.

With no fanfare and little warning, the Nob Hill Casino closes. An unrenewed lease, not financial insolvency, is the cause of the closure.

December 1990

The Landmark is sold at auction to Lloyds Bank PLC for a mere $20 million. Lloyds buys the Landmark to protect a $25 million interest in the property resulting from loans made to the previous owner.

The Mirage celebrates its first anniversary with a glowing financial report card. The company has had no problem winning enough in the casino to service its considerable debt. In an article in the *Las Vegas Review-Journal*, owner Steve Wynn calls The Mirage "a better mousetrap."

Casino gambling is approved in the tiny Colorado cities of Central City, Blackhawk (both in the Denver area) and Cripple Creek (near Colorado Springs). As is the case in Deadwood, South Dakota, maximum bets are $5. Several major Nevada casino companies begin to look into Illinois and Mississippi riverboats where no limits will be imposed.

January 1991

The Persian Gulf crisis impacts Las Vegas. Casino security is beefed up and a slowdown in phone-in reservations is reported at some properties. The Convention and Visitors Authority suspends national advertising as a matter of propriety. Most noticeably, airport operations are slowed as increased security causes delays.

Santa Fe Hotel opens on the far northwest side of town off US Highway 95. The casino features an indoor ice rink and a state-of-the-art bowling center.

Palace Station opens a new parking garage and part of a 22-story hotel tower.

The Stardust's new 1,500-room hotel tower opens.

The Cattle Baron Casino opens in Henderson.

Nevada's population is the fastest growing in the country according to the U.S. Census Bureau. Population has grown at a rate of 50.7% since 1980.

February 1991

Several bids to buy the Aladdin are rejected, but the casino does not close.

Due to the Persian Gulf crisis, Las Vegas experiences a visitor-volume decline. Las Vegas tourism officials modify ad campaigns to target markets closer to Las Vegas. A new ad message, "Play in Your Own Back Yard," is intended to portray Las Vegas as a safer travel alternative.

Hilton Hotels Corp. files an application for a casino license in New

---

Locals Do It

You may have heard the statement, "If you live in Las Vegas, you don't gamble." Sure! A study of the gambling habits of Las Vegas locals reveals that 65% gamble "at least occasionally." Video poker is most popular, but residents will gamble on anything. For example, incredible as it may seem, thousands of Las Vegas residents travel to California when the lottery jackpot gets high. Some wait in line up to seven hours to purchase tickets.

Jersey. Rumors are rampant that Hilton wants to buy one of Donald Trump's three Atlantic City properties. Hilton was turned down on their first New Jersey license try in 1985.

Knight-Ridder News reports that Donald Trump will move the Taj Mahal into bankruptcy proceedings in April.

March 1991

MGM officials quickly deny a series of local news reports suggesting that the MGM Grand Casino-Theme Park project may have been put on temporary hold. Construction has not yet been initiated.

Nevada casinos win $5.24 billion in 1990, a 14% increase. Casino win in Clark County (Las Vegas and Laughlin) increases 17.5%, while Lake Tahoe comes in with the slowest growth, up 2%. Visitor volume in Las Vegas tops 20 million.

The Mirage sets a single-casino one-year win record of $409 million. That's better than $1.1 million per day. The previous best year was posted by Caesars Atlantic City in 1989.

The Atlantic City casino win increases 5% to approximately $3 billion, but it's not enough to keep pace with costs. Collectively, the twelve A.C. casinos lose money in 1990.

April 1991

An enormous new branch of the U.S. gambling industry sets sail as riverboat casinos begin operating on the Mississippi River off the shores of Iowa. The huge gambling ships can accommodate up to 3,000 passengers, and casinos offer slot machines, video poker, blackjack, craps, and roulette. The betting maximums are $5 per hand and there is a $200-per-person loss limit. Reports of a less than spectacular win during the first few days of operation are deceiving. Many passengers during the first week are press, dignitaries, etc. The level of publicity being afforded the riverboat casinos is incredible. The river is referred to by the media as "The Mississippi Strip."

There are news reports that Kansas is moving toward legalization of riverboat gambling, that Maryland is considering floating casinos on the Chesapeake Bay, and that Missouri is investigating the possibility of allowing blackjack, keno, and poker in bars and private clubs.

May 1991

MGM Grand officials unveil design and financing plans. The project is now scheduled for completion in 1994.

Reports indicating a slow-down in gambling win at downtown Las Vegas casinos prompt talks of redevelopment. One idea would turn Fremont Street into a canal upon which gamblers would be ferried from casino to casino in gondolas. The local media dubs it project "Las Venice."

The gambling win rises on Iowa riverboats; 85% of profits come from slots.

Omaha, Neb., implements a huge city/county operated keno game.

The big news is Indian-run gambling. A U.S. Supreme Court decision opens the door for Connecticut's Mashantucket Pequot tribe to construct a $50 million casino complex that will be the forerunner of similar enterprises across the nation. The specter of widespread Indian gaming is viewed (by Las Vegas interests) as a business threat far more serious than riverboats.

June 1991

The world's first rock 'n roll-themed casino—the Hard Rock—is announced. The project is expected to be completed by late 1992. [Ground has yet to be broken on this project.]

Circus Circus says they want to build another themed casino/resort in Las Vegas. The announcement comes on the heels of the one-year anniversary of the spectacularly successful Excalibur. Officials of Circus Circus Enterprises claim that 11 million people visited Excalibur in its first year of operation.

Two casinos, the Royal and the Cattle Baron, close due to financial problems.

The Aladdin fails to attract a buyer in a bankruptcy court auction.

Colorado decides to allow video poker when gambling commences later in the year.

The state of Oregon seeks legislative approval to install up to 10,000 video poker machines throughout the state as "an extension of the state lottery." The proposed video poker machines are called video lottery terminals. A VLT dispenses tickets that are later exchanged for coins, rather than dispensing coins into a hopper on the spot. The devices are also legal in Montana and South Dakota and are expected to proliferate under the protection of state lottery laws.

Excalibur

One of the more interesting aspects of the operation concerns the casino's financial status. The Excalibur's $290 million price tag was low compared with $650 million for The Mirage and $1 billion for Atlantic City's Taj Mahal. Unlike its two debt-ridden predecessors, two thirds of Excalibur's financing came from company cash reserves. While The Mirage and the Taj were said to need a $1 million per day casino win to pay their bills, the figure for Excalibur was a scant $200,000.

July 1991

Major developments in Atlantic City: 24-hour gambling is approved for weekends and major holidays through the end of the summer after a successful July 4 weekend test; three new table games—red dog, pai gow poker and sic bo—are granted approval; and the maximum allowable area designated for slot machines is enlarged. All measures are designed to stimulate gambling activity in the sluggish A.C. market.

Hilton Hotels Corp. is approved for a New Jersey gaming license.

Early progress reports from Iowa indicate that the riverboat win is 30% above projections. A bill legalizing riverboat gambling in Louisiana passes the state legislature. The bill is accompanied by another that legalizes video poker in non-riverboat venues.

California lifts a 106-year-old ban on the play of "stud-horse" poker. Although no one knows exactly what stud-horse is, anti-gambling factions had used the law to stop card rooms from dealing any form of stud poker.

August 1991

Nevada posts a record $5.4 billion casino win for the fiscal year ending June 30. The figure represents a healthy 10% increase over the previous year's total. Clark County (Las Vegas and Laughlin) lead the way with a 13% increase. Laughlin by itself had an almost 20% increase.

Main Street Station opens its doors onto one of the most beautiful casinos in the United States. It houses a large collection of antiques and authentic turn-of-the-century artifacts including a set of doors from the Royal Bank of London, a carved oak fireplace from the Preswick Castle in Scotland, and a massive snooker table from England's Windsor Castle. A chunk of the Berlin Wall occupies a spot in one of the men's restrooms. The casino features a coin-flipping game of Australian origin called Two Up.

There is talk of a "Lake Las Vegas Resort" development near Lake Mead with a man-made lake bordered by up to six casinos, a total of 9,000 rooms, and another 3,500 luxury homes and condominiums. [This is the third such lakeside project that doesn't materialize.]

It's the old "good news, bad news" scenario for an Iowa man at the Lady Luck. The good news is he hits a Quartermania progressive jackpot for $509,984. The bad news is he is only 19 years old, and ineligible to collect. The incident is reminiscent of another in 1987 when a 19-year-old from Arkansas hit a $1 million jackpot at Caesars Palace. When not allowed to collect, the family sued, lost, and appealed all the way to the 9th U.S. Circuit Court of Appeals without success.

Las Vegas casinos begin to look beyond Nevada. Caesars World expresses interest in riverboats in Louisiana and Illinois, and casinos in Colorado, Australia, and Uruguay. Hilton is interested in Louisiana, Illinois, New Zealand, Egypt, and Australia.

September 1991

A full-scale strike is called by the Culinary Union against the Frontier.

Dan's Royal Flush, a new all-slots casino, opens on the Strip across from the Stardust on the site of the former Peppermill.

Illinois riverboat gambling begins. A typical cruise lasts about 1-1/2 hours but gambling commences upon boarding which translates to about 2-1/2 hours of playing time. Patrons must pay a fee of $15-$20 to board.

Indian casinos in Minnesota and the Midwest now have coupon books, blackjack mini-tournaments, and 24-hour coffee shops with $3.99 buffets. A two-month entertainment schedule at the Jackpot Junction Casino in Morton, Minn., includes Kris Kristofferson, Donna Fargo, Helen Reddy, Chubby Checker, and Jerry Lee Lewis.

October 1991

Ground is broken for the MGM Grand Hotel & Theme Park. The project and its developer, Kirk Kerkorian, receive national media attention. The *Wall Street Journal* dubs Kerkorian the "Wizard of Vegas"; the *L.A. Times* calls him a "Rainmaker."

Main Street Station shows immediate signs of financial stress. Budget miscalculations result in delayed payments to building contractors and there are employee lay-offs.

Colorado gambling—blackjack, poker, and slots with $5 max bets—in the historic mining towns of Central City, Blackhawk, and Cripple Creek begins.

November 1991

Steve Wynn announces the 3,000-room Treasure Island. The casino will be designed to attract the family market with a pirate theme and rooms priced in the $40 range. Completion is projected for 1994. Estimated cost of the project is $300 million.

Circus Circus unveils plans for a 2,500-room pyramid-shaped casino it calls Project X. The estimated cost is $290 million, and completion is projected for late 1993. Circus Circus spokespeople indicate that the new casino will market to a slightly more affluent customer. This is an interesting flip-flop: The Mirage goes for families, Circus Circus seeks the higher end.

Silver City institutes a complete ban on smoking, including casino, restrooms, restaurants and bar. The story is picked up by important media throughout the country. Although the policy represents a Las Vegas first, the concept is not original. Reno's Ponderosa tried to market the industry's first "no smoking" hotel-casino in the late '80s.

The Louisiana gubernatorial election is watched closely by the Nevada casino industry. Winner Edwin Edwards' advocacy of land-based gambling worries many casino people.

December 1991

Nevada casinos suffer their worst year to year revenue decline (for a single month) in history in October. The state's total win is off 6.3%, the "worst in 60 years of gaming." Although it sounds serious, the big drop is easily explained by a series of events that include a scheduling change of a giant convention. The slow national economy is partially to blame, however, and the country's economic dilemma remains a matter of concern to the gambling industry. Incredibly, the Laughlin juggernaut keeps rolling along. Laughlin's casinos post an 11.7% increase.

Downtown goes topless. The Golden Goose slot arcade is transformed into a topless bar called the Gentlemen's Club.

The old Nob Hill casino reopens under the new name Casino Royale. The casino is owned by the Elardi family, owners of the strike-embroiled Frontier.

Bally's and the Riviera scare some people by filing for Chapter 11 bankruptcy status. Both moves are business maneuvers that allow them to restructure a heavy debt load. Neither casino closes.

Main Street Station has the most serious problems of all. Trouble with creditors aside (bankruptcy is imminent), the casino's marketing concept is completely wrong. They fail in an effort to match food specials with the likes of the nearby Horseshoe and California hotels.

California tries to halt a steep drop in lottery sales caused by the change from a 6/49 format (choose six out of 49 numbers) to 6/53. The change was designed to increase the likelihood of large jackpots, which was expected to stimulate increased ticket buying. But California Lotto players bought fewer tickets, indicating dissatisfaction with the longer odds. The new game is 6/51. The odds of hitting six out of six numbers in each version are: one in 14 million for 6/49; one in 18 million for 6/51; and one in 23 million for 6/53.

January 1992

Main Street Station limps along by the grace of a last-minute $1.5 million bank loan. More than 200 employees are laid off and all but one restaurant is now closed. The casino makes a desperate effort to turn things around by offering half price meals and nickel draft beer.

A small slots-only casino called the Aztec Inn opens near Vegas World.

The Union Plaza officially changes its name to Jackie Gaughan's Plaza.

USA Today reports that U.S. lotteries grew at a rate of only 2.7% in fiscal 1991 with ten states reporting double-digit declines.

Reports indicate that Southern California card rooms had their best year ever in 1991. Asian games like pai gow poker and super pan nine are booming.

February 1992

Despite the Gulf war, a national recession, and increased competition from Indian and riverboat gambling, the Nevada gaming industry reports a record $5.57 billion win for 1991. Although the figure represents a 2% annual increase, it's the lowest in the last nine years.

The Tropicana Golf Course is cleared so construction may begin on the MGM Grand Hotel & Theme Park.

Downtown casino executives use the specter of competition from the three megaresorts to push a revitalization of Fremont Street. Theme possibilities include: Wizard of Odds, the Starship Enterprise, a medieval castle and village, and Venetian canals.

The 260-member Mashantucket Pequot tribe opens a $58 million casino complex (Foxwoods) in Ledyard, Connecticut. Slot machines are illegal, but all major table games are offered. Some industry observers believe the new casino will hurt Atlantic City's bottom line.

Steve Wynn's Mirage Resorts signs casino-development agreements with Indian tribes in Kansas and Washington. There's talk of a $75 million project in Kansas City that will feature a casino, entertainment complex, shops and restaurants. [It never materializes.]

The New Jersey Casino Control Commission rescinds a regulation requiring that one out of every 20 slots be a nickel machine. Though casino officials indicate that they will continue to offer the low-stake slots, nickel slots are not long for Atlantic City.

March 1992

Ground is officially broken on the $400 million Treasure Island Hotel-Casino. The new estimated date of completion is Christmas 1993.

U.S. Interior Secretary Manual Lujan predicts that "ten years from now Indian tribes will have gaming in every major city in the country."

Steve Wynn proposes a $350 million hotel-casino-convention center in Hartford, Connecticut.

The number of Atlantic City visitors declines for the third straight year. A drop of 3.2% lowers the 1991 total to 30.8 million. Revenues rise a point or so to just under $3 billion.

April 1992

The recession and the Gulf war fail to depress Las Vegas visitation figures. More than 21.3 million people visited Las Vegas in 1991, a 1.7% increase. Convention attendance increased by 3% while decreasing nationally by 3%. Clark County casinos won $4.1 billion in 1991, a 6.2% rise over 1990.

Circus Circus announces that they will name their new casino Luxor.

The famous Harrah's logo finally occupies a spot on the Las Vegas skyline as Holiday Casino formally changes its name.

Hilton, Caesars Palace, and Circus Circus announce they will seek legal permission to build a $2 billion casino complex in Chicago.

A full-scale casino is proposed for Windsor, Ontario, Canada.

The city of New Orleans runs ads in the *Wall Street Journal* soliciting developers of a land-based casino.

May 1992

The Flamingo Hilton begins a $104 million expansion.

Reno begins to heat up with expansions announced at Sands Regency

Rest In Peace

The following casinos either closed, merged, or underwent a name change in Las Vegas within the past ten years.

Royal Americana (became Paddlewheel)
Paddlewheel (became Debbie Reynold's Hollywood Hotel)
Club Bingo (merged into Pioneer)
Sundance (became Fitzgeralds)
Friendly (became Golden Nugget's new tower)
Tommy B's
Swanky Club
Shenandoah (became Bourbon St.)
Mint (merged with Horseshoe)
MGM Grand (became Bally's)
Union Plaza (name changed to Jackie Gaughan's Plaza)
Silver Star
Golden Goose
Slot Joynt (became Boardwalk)
Orbit Inn (became Franklin Bros.)
Franklin Brothers (became Reel Deal)
Reel Deal
Jolly Trolley
Silver Slipper
Foxy's Firehouse (became Holy Cow!)
Holiday (became Harrah's)
Castaways
El Morocco
Ambassador (became La Mirage)
Ambassador East
Las Vegas Inn
Winner's Circle (became Silver Spur)
Bingo Palace (became Palace Station)
El Rancho
Marina (became MGM Grand)
Peppermill (became Dan's)
La Mirage (became Anthony's)
Coin Castle
Old Vegas
Park (became Main Street Station)
Main Street Station
Nob Hill (became Casino Royale)
Dunes

and John Ascuaga's Nugget [neither materializes], and plans to build the country's first National Bowling Stadium downtown [completion scheduled for January 1995].

Three major Indian-owned casinos open in Minnesota. The $15 million Mystic Lake Casino is hailed as the largest casino between Nevada and the East Coast. The Grand Casino in Hinckley boasts 1,400 slot machines, 50 blackjack tables, and a day-care center. And Shooting Star Casino, 200 miles northwest of Minneapolis, has 70,000 square feet of gaming floor space.

The battle lines are formed in the fight over the future of Chicago casinos. Mayor Daley and a 2-1 margin of residents are in favor. Governor Edgar and the state police are opposed.

June 1992

Main Street Station closes.

The Louisiana Legislature passes a bill permitting a single land-based casino to open on the New Orleans riverfront. Several Nevada casino operators submit proposals to build and operate the facility despite an enormous tax on the gross gambling win—18.5% or $100 million a year, whichever is larger. To hit the $100 million ceiling, the casino would have to win more than $600 million. By comparison, the Mirage generates about a $400 million annual profit.

Hilton outbids Harvey's for the 2,001-room Bally's Reno. The sales price is a scant $83 million. The acquisition makes Hilton the largest hotel company in Nevada with five hotels and 11,300 rooms.

Two of the four riverboat casinos operating in Iowa suddenly weigh anchor and sail off for Mississippi. The boat owners cite Mississippi's much less restrictive gambling policies and taxes.

About 900 bars and taverns throughout the state of Oregon house operational video poker machines.

The Las Vegas News Bureau, Las Vegas' most famous publicity machine, loses its funding, after 43 years of sharing all the virtues (and none of the sins) of southern Nevada with the world.

July 1992

The El Rancho closes. The casino was formerly the Silverbird and originally the Thunderbird. It was the fourth hotel to open on the early Strip, in 1948.

The Reel Deal Casino opens downtown in a spot previously occupied by the Franklin Brothers Casino, and by the Orbit Inn before that.

The Fremont Street Experience is announced. This latest in a list of downtown revitalization ideas calls for a giant, fine-mesh, 100-foot-high, arched awning to be installed over Glitter Gulch between Main and Fourth streets. The venue would be equipped to handle events like championship fights and major (or minor) concerts. The $52 million Experience would unify Fremont Street into a single attraction, designed to compete with the Strip and its new megaresorts.

Mississippi becomes the "foreign" (non-Nevadan) locale of choice, partially because its gaming laws are nearly identical to Nevada's. Hot areas are Tunica, a short drive from Memphis in the northwest corner of the state, historic Natchez, and the Gulf resort towns of Gulfport and Biloxi, both less than 75 miles from New Orleans.

August 1992

Foxwood's Casino in Ledyard, Conn., is a rousing success. A $140 million expansion is announced.

Detroit looks into possible riverboat gambling on the Detroit River. The *Detroit Free Press* calls it "the Terminator issue—no matter how many times you kill it, it springs back." [Detroit voters rejected gambling proposals in 1976, 1981 and 1988.]

September 1992

Circus Circus announces the $75 million high-tech, climate-controlled water theme park Grand Slam Canyon. Completion is scheduled for July 1993.

MGM Grand officials move quickly to put the Circus Circus announcement into perspective. The entire five-acre Grand Slam Canyon, they note, will be smaller than MGM's Grand Canyon Rapids ride, only one of a dozen attractions at their own theme park.

Overhead walkways and underground tunnels are proposed for foot-traffic control at the soon-to-be very busy intersection of Tropicana and the Strip. Hotel owners at the Flamingo Rd. intersection also consider walkway options.

The *Empress* riverboat in Joliet, Illinois (the most profitable of five boats in operation), attracts nearly 1,000 gamblers per cruise in its first month. The pretax profit is $11.5 million, or $67 per passenger. Illinois collects just under $2 million in taxes; Joliet gets $745,000.

More People

The state demographer predicts that Clark County's population, now at 850,000, will reach the one-million mark by 1997. This reflects an estimated growth rate of 4% a year. The figures are based on a series of statistical projections, one of which indicates that 10 permanent residents are gained for every new hotel room that opens (11,500 new hotel rooms will open within the year).

The fate of the Chicago casino complex looks grim. The Hilton-Caesars-Circus consortium hints it might look to Gary, Indiana, to host the $2 billion complex.

Themeparkmania officially hits Las Vegas. The Fremont Street Experience gears up for construction. Chinese investors from the People's Republic want to buy and level the Dunes, then build a replica of Beijing's Forbidden City. Bally's indicates they will explore a theme park idea for their Las Vegas property. The owners (Primm family) of Whiskey Pete's and Primadonna at Stateline on I-15 also explore amusement park possibilities. Word leaks out that the Bureau of Land Management has recently taken Disney representatives on a flight-seeing tour of southern Nevada. The news prompts a flurry of denials from Disney spokespeople who say the company has no plans to build a new theme park in Clark County at this time. [Las Vegas, with 22 million annual visitors, seems to be casting its shark's gaze toward Disney World and its 28 million visitors. Disney World may not stand a chance. It's a matter of simple economics. Accommodations, food, and transportation are at least five times less expensive in Las Vegas. And Disney World can't offer even a remote illusion that any money is coming back, as can Las Vegas with its legalized gambling advantage.]

October 1992

Steve Wynn purchases the 164-acre Dunes property from Masao Nangaku for $75 million.

Debbie Reynolds and her husband buy the Paddlewheel Hotel on Convention Center Drive for $3 million.

The Rio embarks on an $8 million expansion of its casino and restaurants, and announces a 430-room, $37 million tower (its second) to be completed in January 1994.

Colorado begins to have second thoughts about its mountain-town-casino experiment. Though the Colorado gambling industry generated $100 million in revenue in its first ten months from 48 casinos in three small mining towns, residents complain that legalized gambling has done more harm than good. Voters overwhelmingly oppose five initiatives that would spread gambling to other areas of Colorado.

November 1992

MGM owner Kirk Kerkorian purchases the 18-acre vacant lot across from Excalibur on the corner of Tropicana and the Strip from Universal Distributing. The $31.5 million price tag is the highest ever paid [up till then] for land on the Strip: $1.7 million an acre, or $39.50 a square foot. An overhead walkway is expected to connect the MGM Grand with whatever is built on the property, which will be determined by the future needs of the gargantuan Grand.

The Backlash

I. Nelson Rose, considered one of the country's foremost experts on gambling and the law, predicts that "a major anti-gambling backlash is building in the country," due to the "proliferation of riverboat and mountain-town casinos and video lottery terminals, because they rely on local customers." Rose explains that throughout history, "Every society that has allowed casinos to cater to locals has eventually outlawed gambling," which siphons all the money from the local economy.

Within the past year, one jurisdiction, Nova Scotia in eastern Canada, has rescinded legalized gambling. Colorado voters overwhelmingly repudiated a bill that would have expanded casino gambling to more historic mining towns. Iowa's riverboat experiment, first in the country, has failed. And voters around the country, notably in Connecticut, Detroit, Idaho and New Mexico, continue to kill all gambling initiatives.

Gambling initiatives in 13 states are decided on Election Day. State lotteries are approved in Georgia and Nebraska; Mississippians repeal a long-standing ban on lotteries. Riverboat gambling is approved in Missouri. Gambling sponsored by charities is approved in Oklahoma and Kentucky. Idaho and the U.S. Virgin Islands defeat casino gambling. A repeal provision in South Dakota for video lottery terminals is defeated. In the three most hotly contested issues: pari-mutuel betting at horse race tracks is defeated in Utah, limited-stakes gambling is defeated throughout Colorado by an enormous margin, and card clubs in seven Southern California towns are defeated.

The California lottery introduces a new statewide keno game. Tickets are sold at regular lottery outlets for $2 to $20 between 6 am and 11 pm. Winning numbers are selected at lottery headquarters every five minutes and displayed on video monitors at the outlets. The payoff for matching ten out of ten spots is $250,000; on a $20 ticket the prize is $5 million. Winnings of $599 or less are paid off on the spot. California's house advantage averages a crushing 51%.

The partnership of Caesars World and Hemmeter-Woodmont is chosen by the mayor of New Orleans to develop the big 250,000-square-foot casino and adjoining recreation complex. The Caesars-Hemmeter team beats out a Mirage-Harrah's partnership.

Mirage Resorts unveils its plans for the $250 million Bridgeport Sporting Club, a casino complex in Bridgeport, Connecticut. [Connecticut doesn't go for it.]

December 1992

The singing Jackson family announces their intention to build the Desert Winds Hotel-Casino on West Flamingo Road (near the Gold Coast). Completion is expected by 1995. [Ground has not yet been broken.]

January 1993

The Dunes closes, ending the hotel-casino's 38 eventful years on the corner of the Strip and Flamingo.

The Foxwoods Casino in Ledyard, Conn., grosses approximately $140 million in its first year. Video slot machines are approved and attendance jumps from an average of 12,500 a day to 17,500 a day.

Maryland becomes the sixth state in the country to offer a centralized keno game.

February 1993

John Giovenco resigns as president of Hilton's Nevada division to become president and CEO of ITT Sheraton Corporation. The huge international hotel company will surely become a player in the casino industry.

The Reel Deal closes. The closure isn't even mentioned in the local media.

Steve Wynn offers the first glimpse of his vision for the Dunes property. He describes a $400 million, 3,000-room hotel facility surrounding a 14-acre lake. Always the dealmaker, Wynn wants to charge Hollywood moviemakers for filming the dynamiting of the Dunes.

Elsinore Corporation, which owns the Four Queens in downtown Las Vegas, enters into an agreement with the Twentynine Palms Band of Mission Indians to operate a casino in Southern California. Twentynine Palms is 25 miles north of Palm Springs, where the Agua Caliente Indians and Caesars World also plan to open a casino. Both projects hinge on state approval [yet to be granted].

Mexico opens its fourth sports book in as many months. A direct satellite link connects the El Cid resort in Mazatlan, Sinaloa, with Las Vegas bookmakers and American television networks.

Political Gamble

The Associated Press reports that a candidate for the Arizona House of Representatives has a seven of hearts and a seven of clubs to thank for his spot on the ballot. The primary election ended in a tie, and Arizona law dictates that ties be broken by a game of chance. The two hopefuls played a single hand of five-card-stud. The winner's pair of sevens held up.

March 1993

Boomtown, a casino truck stop 10 miles west of Reno, announces that a $60 million, 300-room hotel, casino, RV park, and supermarket will be built in Las Vegas at the intersection of Interstate 15 and Blue Diamond Road (five miles south of the Strip). The project will take a year to complete.

April 1993

The Landmark Hotel is offered in a closed-bid auction in Boston. Lloyds Bank of New York wants $22 million for the property. The Convention and Visitor Authority offers $18 million. There are no other bids.

The Triple J Bingo Hall and Casino opens on Boulder Highway. It has a 1,500-seat bingo hall. This marks the debut of high-stakes "Indian-style" bingo in southern Nevada, which is characterized by longer sessions and higher jackpots, including a big progressive.

1992 Gambling Statistics

Official numbers for 1992 were released in March 1993, most notably visitor totals and demographics. Just under 22 million people were counted as visitors in 1992, up from just over 21 million in 1991. All told, they spent $14.7 billion. Fully 90% of visitors gamble while in Las Vegas. The average gambling time is five hours a day. Fifty-one percent play slot machines, 23% blackjack, 12% video poker, and 5% craps. The average bankroll is $454, and 90% of players make minimum bets of $5 or less.

Statewide, 192 Nevada casinos grossed a total of $5.6 billion in gambling revenue (and $3.6 billion in non-gambling receipts); 141 casinos showed a profit, while 51 wound up in the red. The 14 largest Strip hotel-casinos (those with annual gambling revenues of $72 million or more) reported a pre-federal-tax profit of 12.7%, up 1.1% over 1991. For the first time ever, slot machines generated more income than tables games on the Strip: $958 million compared to $930 million at the 14 major Strip casinos. One very interesting footnote from the profit-and-loss statement for these 14 clubs is that out of the $450 million net gambling win, $260 million (just under 58% of the profits) was returned to gamblers via complimentaries!

Visitor totals are expected to reach 25 million in 1994, after the three new megaresorts have opened. This will put Las Vegas on the heels of Orlando, Florida, the number-one domestic tourist destination, which claims 27 million tourists a year.

E. Parry Thomas, longtime head of Valley Bank of Las Vegas and legendary casino financier, and Lee Iacocca, ex-auto industry giant, are named to the MGM Grand Board of Directors.

A call for proposals on a casino for Windsor, Ontario, garners an enormous response from a veritable who's who in the gambling industry: Promus, Circus Circus, Hilton, Trump, Griffin, Caesars, Foxwoods, Sands, Showboat, and others.

May 1993

Bally's announces plans to construct a $12 million people mover that will run from the corner of the Strip and Flamingo Road to its front doors. Completion is scheduled for early 1995.

MGM Grand and Bally's will team up to build a $15 million mile-long monorail linking the two resorts. Construction will take 12-15 months. Clark County officials express an interest in incorporating the monorail into a long-discussed high-tech public transportation system linking the Strip, downtown, Convention Center, and airport.

A three-phase $17 million road expansion of Tropicana Avenue is scheduled to be completed by early 1994. Tropicana Avenue will be four lanes in each direction. Elevated pedestrian walkways, accessible by escalators, elevators, and stairs, will connect all four corners of the intersection.

Casino Royale is being expanded into a 250-room hotel, 20,000-square-foot-casino, and a six-story 1,000-space parking garage.

The new $37 million tower being added to the Rio will double the room count (to 850). It's scheduled for completion in December 1993.

Circus Circus and the Eldorado announce a joint venture to build a $220 million hotel in downtown Reno. A large dome is planned to cover a "family entertainment center." The hotel is scheduled to be completed by spring 1995.

June 1993

ITT Sheraton, ends its years-long search for the perfect casino property by purchasing the Desert Inn from Kirk Kerkorian for $160 million cash. Included in the deal are the golf course and a 35-acre vacant lot, which Sheraton hints it might turn into a megaresort.

Palace Station's initial public offering raises nearly $300 million. The Gaming Control Board approves a public offering by the Primm family, owners of Whiskey Pete's and the Primadonna; they plan to open an amusement park with the world's tallest and fastest rollercoaster. And the Boyd Group announces its intent to go public with a $100 million offering.

Atlantic City celebrates its 15th anniversary; it has earned $30 billion over the decade and a half.

The Great Race

By spring 1993, four mega construction projects were well underway along the Las Vegas Strip. From Vegas World to the Hacienda, the spindly mechanical arms of giant cranes rose hundreds of feet into the air, adding a dramatic and dynamic dimension to the rapidly-changing Las Vegas skyline. To track the comparative progress of the MGM Grand, Luxor, and Treasure Island, the LVA introduced a new category to news: the Great Race. Soon thereafter, the Vegas World Stratosphere Tower and Circus Circus' Grand Slam Canyon entered the fray. This category could conceivably continue into the indefinite future, eventually tracking the announced Hard Rock Casino, Jackson family Desert Winds, Primadonna amusement park, Boomtown truck stop, Fremont Street Experience, Dunes demolition and new hotel, the MGM Grand-Bally's monorail, Bally's people mover, MGM Grand-connected mall and movie complex, possible transformations of the Landmark and El Rancho properties, and Sheraton's megaresort next to the Desert Inn.

Below are the specs for the three projects opening now.

LUXOR HOTEL

SIZE: 47-acre site; 2.5-million total square feet, with 90,000-square-foot casino; 30-story pyramid with 2,521 rooms and suites.

COST: $300 million, financed entirely from corporation's cash flow.

OWNER: Circus Circus Enterprises, its 8th Nevada property and third "entertainment megastore."

NAME: Luxor, on the Nile, is the locus of an ancient Egyptian civilization, the religious center for its capital at Thebes. Nearby are the valleys of Kings and Queens, and Karnak. Exclusive rights to the name were purchased from the 25-room Luxor Motel in Old Orchard Beach, Maine.

UNIQUE FEATURES: The "Nile" runs through the pyramid, separating casino from hotel. Guests are transported by boat from the front desk to the elevators, which ascend the pyramid at a 39-degree angle. Also: museum of Egyptian artifacts, life-size reproduction of King Tut's tomb, FX adventures.

MGM GRAND HOTEL & THEME PARK

SIZE: 5,007 rooms and suites, 171,500-square-foot casino, 33-acre theme park and space for 9,000 cars.

COST: $1 billion, including financing; base construction cost is $825 million.

OWNER: MGM Grand Inc., whose majority stockholder is Kirk Kerkorian, the self-made billionaire who started as the son of a California raisin

farmer and never graduated from high school.
OPENING: *December 1993* ***NEW JOBS:*** *7,500 to 8,000*
THEME PARK PREMISE: *Over a few hours, visitors wander through Hollywood-style sets posing as streets from Casablanca, the Wild West, New Orleans, Salem, Mass., historic England, France, the Netherlands, Asia and old New York. Shops, restaurants and a crafts area are included.*
THEME PARK ADMISSION: *$25 a day*
THEME PARK ATTRACTIONS: *Grand Canyon Rapids (raft ride); Over the Edge (water ride in a two-person log); Ghost Coaster (roller-coaster ride in the dark with special effects); Deep Earth Exploration (ride simulating adventures, including earthquakes and explosions under the earth's surface); River Studio Tour (boat ride through movie sets such as "Apocalypse Now" and simulating various adventures); Haunted Mine Ride (chills and thrills in an abandoned mining town); Bumper Cars (using the style of Parisian taxis); Walk the Plank (movie stunts set on a pirate ship; Cartoon Theatre (shows the creation of cartoon, using characters that "come alive"); You're in the Movies (members of the audience participate in the creation of a movie, including casting, costuming and makeup); Animal Talent Theatre (animal training is revealed with the help of real animals); Magic Screen Theatre (musical production via split screen and live actors).*

TREASURE ISLAND
SIZE: *3,000 rooms*
COST: *$450 million*
OWNER: *Steve Wynn's Mirage Resorts, Inc.*
THEME: *The front of the hotel will be transformed into a Caribbean bay, waterfront, and pirate village within a 360-foot semi-circle facing the Strip. A naval Man O' War, The Royal Brittania, will sail up to the pirate vessel, Hispaniola, docked at the village. The navy will overpower the pirates with cannonade and some hand-to-hand. The destruction and general mayhem will be ferocious; after the battle the cast will rebuild the set, with the entire drama reenacted in an hour. The edge of the action will be within four yards of the Strip.*

I

Booking

3

ACCOMMODATIONS

Lodging rates in most gambling cities are ultra-low compared with other vacation destinations. Why? Because the primary objective is not high revenue, it's high occupancy. A full hotel means a full casino. This, combined with the mega-competition factor—there are about 75,000 hotel and motel rooms in Las Vegas—virtually assures you of landing a good deal on a room, even if you employ no savings strategy at all and settle for prevailing rack rates. Of course, a little strategy can add up to even greater savings. Day of the week, time of year, convention schedules, special promotions, the slot clubs you belong to, even your geographical location can affect the price you ultimately pay for a room.

Quality

Before getting into specific price-reducing considerations, here's an important disclosure that will save you a great deal of anxiety, especially if you're a first-time visitor: in Las Vegas, the room itself is not as important as the casino it's in.

There just aren't significant physical differences in rooms of similar price. Sure, some are newer than others, but dimensions and amenities are relatively uniform. In fact, you may be surprised by the lack of luxury in even the newest facilities. Rooms are what they have to be, clean and comfortable, no more. People don't spend much time in hotel rooms in Las Vegas (management doesn't want them to), and casinos realize that the room is only a small part of the sell. If you don't have a casino preference, look at a map and choose one according to where it's located, i.e., center Strip, downtown, near MGM Grand, etc.

If you don't agree that a hotel room is "just a place to hang your hat," and are concerned about the comparative quality of your room, here's an indicator you can use as a guide. When casinos advertise rooms or room packages with a split rate, i.e., $18 "garden" room, $42 "tower" room, the prices usually reflect differences in quality. The less expensive room has probably been around since the casino was built (though certainly up-

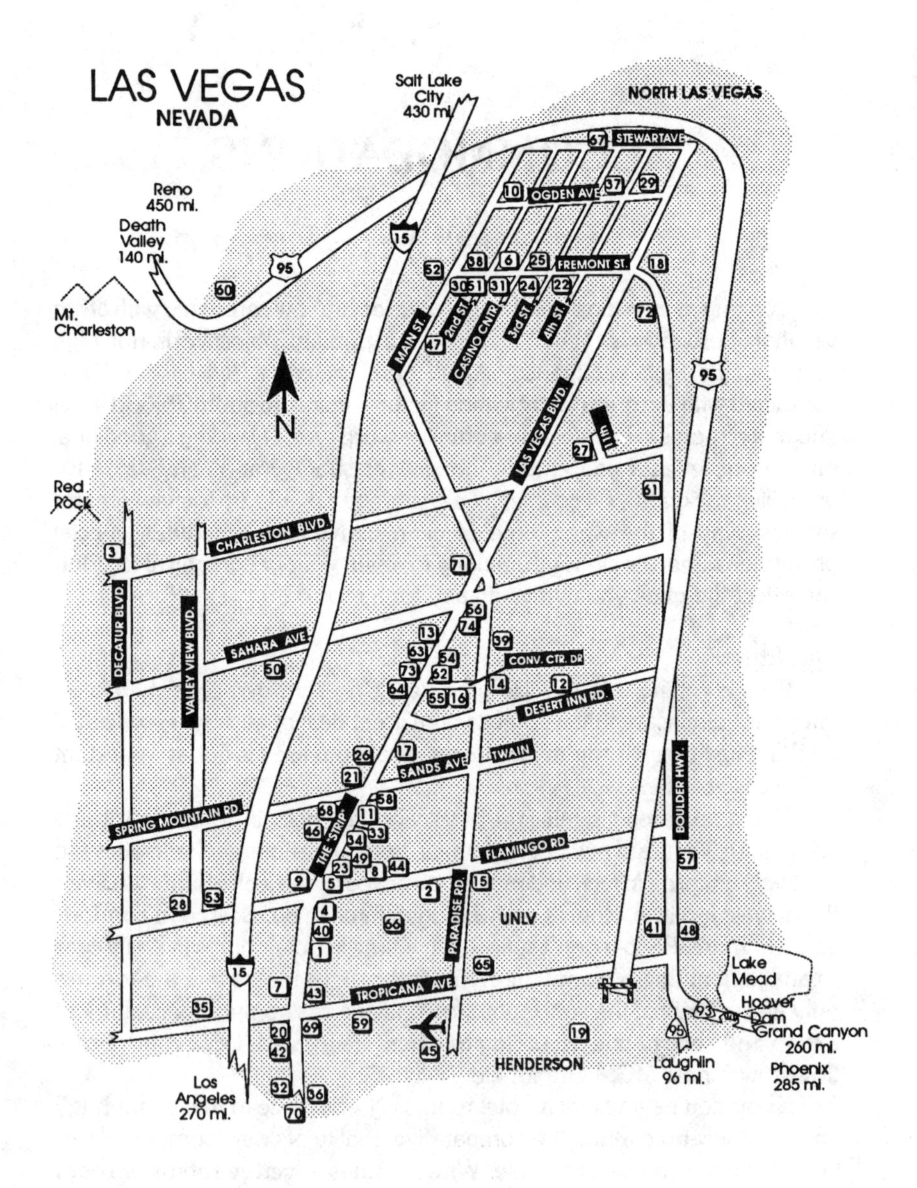
LAS VEGAS
NEVADA
Salt Lake City 430 mi.
NORTH LAS VEGAS
Reno 450 mi.
Death Valley 140 mi.
Mt. Charleston
Red Rock
STEWART AVE.
OGDEN AVE.
FREMONT ST.
MAIN ST.
2nd ST.
CASINO CNTR
3rd ST.
4th ST.
LAS VEGAS BLVD.
11th
CHARLESTON BLVD.
DECATUR BLVD.
VALLEY VIEW BLVD.
SAHARA AVE.
CONV. CTR. DR
DESERT INN RD.
SANDS AVE
TWAIN
SPRING MOUNTAIN RD.
THE STRIP
FLAMINGO RD.
PARADISE RD.
UNLV
BOULDER HWY.
TROPICANA AVE
Lake Mead
Hoover Dam
Grand Canyon 260 mi.
Phoenix 285 mi.
Laughlin 96 mi.
HENDERSON
Los Angeles 270 mi.
N

Map Directory

		1-800 #s	LOCAL #s
1	Aladdin	(634-3424)	736-0111
2	Anthony's	Closed	
3	Arizona Charlie's	(342-2695)	258-5200
4	Bally's	(634-3434)	739-4111
5	Barbary Coast	(634-6755)	737-7111
6	Binion's Horseshoe	(237-6537)	382-1600
7	Boardwalk	(635-4581)	735-1167
8	Bourbon Street	(634-6956)	737-7200
9	Caesars Palace	(634-6661)	731-7110
10	California	(634-6255)	385-1222
11	Casino Royale		737-3500
12	Chamber of Commerce		735-1616
13	Circus Circus	(634-3450)	734-0410
14	Convention Center		733-2323
15	Continental	(634-6641)	737-5555
16	D Reynold's Hollywood		
17	Desert Inn	(634-6906)	733-4444
18	El Cortez	(634-6703)	385-5200
19	Ethel M Chocolates		458-8864
20	Excalibur	(937-7777)	597-7777
21	Fashion Show Mall		369-8382
22	Fitzgeralds	(274-5825)	388-2400
23	Flamingo Hilton	(732-2111)	733-3111
24	Four Queens	(634-6045)	385-4011
25	Fremont	(634-6182)	385-3232
26	Frontier	(634-6966)	794-8200
27	Gamblers Book Club	(634-6243)	382-7555
28	Gold Coast	(331-5334)	367-7111
29	Gold Spike	(634-6703)	384-8444
30	Golden Gate	(426-0521)	382-6300
31	Golden Nugget	(634-3454)	385-7111
32	Hacienda	(634-6713)	739-8911
33	Harrah's	(634-6765)	369-5000
34	Imperial Palace	(634-6441)	731-3311
35	King 8	(634-3488)	736-8988
36	Klondike		739-9351
37	Lady Luck	(523-9582)	477-3000
38	Las Vegas Club	(634-6532)	385-1664
39	Las Vegas Hilton	(732-7117)	732-5111
40	Little Caesars		734-2827
41	Longhorn		435-9170
42	Luxor	(288-1000)	262-4000
43	MGM Grand	(929-1111)	891-1111
44	Maxim	(634-6987)	731-4300
45	McCarran International Airport		798-5410
46	Mirage	(627-6667)	791-7111
47	Nevada	(637-5777)	385-7311
48	Nevada Palace	(634-6283)	458-8810
49	O'Shea's		792-0777
50	Palace Station	(634-3101)	367-2411
51	Pioneer		386-5000
52	Plaza	(634-6575)	386-2110
53	Rio	(888-1808)	252-7777

		1-800 #s	LOCAL #s
54	Riviera	(634-6753)	734-5110
55	Royal	(634-6118)	735-6117
56	Sahara	(634-6666)	737-2111
57	Sam's Town	(634-6371)	456-7777
58	Sands	(634-6901)	733-5000
59	San Remo	(522-7366)	739-9000
60	Santa Fe	(872-6823)	658-4900
61	Showboat	(826-2800)	385-9123
62	Silver City		732-4152
63	Slots a Fun		734-0410
64	Stardust	(634-6757)	732-6111
65	Thomas & Mac		739-3900
66	Town Hall	(634-6541)	732-1499
67	Transportation Center		228-7433
68	Treasure Island	(944-7444)	894-7444
69	Tropicana	(468-9494)	739-2222
70	Vacation Village	(338-0608)	897-1700
71	Vegas World	(634-6277)	382-2000
72	Western	(634-6703)	384-4620
73	Westward Ho	(634-6651)	731-2900
74	Wet 'n Wild		737-3819

(Not located on map)

<u>NORTH LAS VEGAS</u>

Jerry's Nugget	399-3000
Mahoney's Silver Nugget	399-1111
Opera House	649-8801
Poker Palace	649-3799

<u>HENDERSON</u>

Eldorado	564-1811
Joker's Wild	
Rainbow	565-9777
Skyline	565-9116
Tom's Sunset	564-5551

graded or modernized; few hotel rooms in Las Vegas are rundown or shabby), while the more expensive room is newer, perhaps a product of a recent expansion. Newer rooms are almost always called "tower" because expansion these days occurs upwards. The older rooms may be called "garden," "motor inn," "economy," or something similar. The price difference is the important tip-off. Another giant step up can be accomplished by booking a suite at a casino that offers suites at only a slight premium over regular rooms. Lady Luck, Frontier, and the all-suite Rio are the three casinos best known for this.

Back to Value

The *Wall Street Journal* runs an interesting monthly feature where experts pick stocks, and then compare their performance against stocks chosen by throwing darts at a page of stock listings. That, in effect, is what we did in the following comparison. We chose a day (from a non-holiday period) at random: October 7, 1992. On that day, we called the 12 casinos in Atlantic City and the first 12 casinos that appeared on an alphabetical Las Vegas list. A like sample of casinos from Laughlin, Reno, and Lake Tahoe (there are only five major casinos on the lake) were also included. The results are typical of comparative rates year-round, and make it obvious where the lodging bargains are. Only Laughlin, anomalistic in many ways, has lower rates than Las Vegas.

October 7th Room Rate Survey

Atlantic City	Las Vegas	Laughlin	Reno
Trump's Castle-$56	Continental-$25	Gold River-$18	Pioneer Inn-$34
Bally's Park Place-$69	Circus Circus-$32	Ramada Express-$21	Sundowner-$40
Taj Mahal-$78	AZ Charlie's-$35	Flamingo-$22	Peppermill-$44
Showboat-$82	Aladdin-$35	Edgewater-$24	Eldorado-$49
Bally's Grand-$87	Anthony's-$35	Harrah's Del Rio-$24	Hilton-$49
Resorts-$88	Boardwalk-$35	Golden Nugget-$25	Harrah's -$75
Harrah's-$91	Excalibur-$45	Riverside-$25	Fitzgeralds-$78
Sands-$102	Barbary Coast-$50	Colorado Belle-$29	**Lake Tahoe**
Trump Plaza-$106	Binion's-$50		Harvey's-$79
Caesars-$110	Caesars Palace-$65		Caesars-$105
Claridge-$114	Bally's-$85		Harrah's-$115
TropWorld-$125	Desert Inn-$90		Hyatt-$179

PRICE-REDUCING STRATEGIES

Information and consumerism are your two primary weapons when searching for the best rate.

Information—First, you have to be aware of the various booking options and price-cutting tactics. Many are explained in this chapter. You must also know how and when to apply them. This is a matter of staying informed via newspapers, periodicals, word-of-mouth, phoning around, etc. Room rates and specials change fast and often. The more current your information, the better you'll do. This theme will come up often as you read about these strategies.

Consumerism—You must be willing to spend some time and effort making the information that you acquire work for you. Be thorough—always ask a score of questions, then double check to make sure you understand all the details of an offer. And be flexible—isn't that what traveling and gambling are all about?

General Concepts

For lowest prices and widest availability, avoid holidays, large conventions, and major events like championship boxing matches. The *Las Vegas Advisor* provides a list of these "key dates" (three months forward) in its Advance Planner section. Weekdays are always easier to book than weekends, and all the best deals run Sunday-Thursday. If you are unable to avoid the busier times, it's imperative that you begin making reservations as far in advance as possible.

Shopping With Toll-free Numbers

There's no substitute for comparison shopping. The information that follows provides you with ideas and direction, but it always comes back to

Better Book Early

The quintessential example of a night that requires early booking is New Year's Eve. Start making your arrangements in April, March, or even earlier. The longer you wait, the more difficult it gets to find accommodations.

An LVA subscriber writes:

"Tell people to be persistent when calling for room reservations for New Year's Eve. When I started calling [my favorite casino] in March, I was told they were already sold out. I kept calling back every few days, until they finally relented and gave me a room. Call early for New Years and persevere!"

the telephone. Set aside an hour and call 15 or 20 casinos. It doesn't cost anything because the casino reservations numbers are all toll free. When an operator answers, ask for "room reservations, please." At the end of the hour, you'll be an expert.

Check Your Calendar

Monitoring the *L.A. Times* "Calendar" section is the best way to keep your finger on the pulse of the room-rate cycle. The Calendar is the advertising forum of choice for many casinos, and it's well worth a trip to your out-of-town newsstand or local library to secure the latest copy before doing anything else. Use it for leads, late-breaking offers, or even "ordering codes" that will save you money (see next paragraph). Sunday sections from other major newspapers can be helpful in the same way, but the *L.A. Times* is the best.

Calling from L.A.

If asked, always tell reservations clerks that you are calling from Los Angeles. This will often get you the lowest quote. Many casinos target Southern California with their room-rate advertising because those living closest to Las Vegas are more likely to take a spur-of-the-moment trip after seeing an ad. The casinos reason that visitors calling from cities farther away have already made their decision to visit and will not be deterred by a higher rate. This play is not fool-proof. A reservations person might refuse you an advertised rate if you don't really live in California (they'll know when you provide personal data upon booking), but it's highly unlikely they'll retract an offer after it has been made. You can say you live wherever, but are calling from Los Angeles; if you've learned of the rate or deal through the L.A. papers, and can quote from the ad, or cite a code, the reservationist should be satisfied.

Knowledge Is Power

If you are quoted a rate higher than you've seen advertised somewhere else, mention the lower rate. Some casinos extend their specials only to those who have prior knowledge of them.

A few years back we were researching the best December deals and discovered a great room, meals, and matchplay package at Palace Station for $29.95. After confirming the deal, we called again and asked for the best rate (without mentioning the package). The quote was $35, no meals, no matchplay. Our next call was to the hotel manager to find out why. He was candid: "Call-ins who don't specifically request the special are given the standard rate." There's nothing unethical about this. It's just the way business is done in the hotel industry.

Lock Them In—If you see something you like, book it. Liberal cancellation policies protect you in case you find something better.

Packages

The Wholesaler Option

Locating a good wholesaler may be the only move you have to make. Today's wholesale package deals are getting better and better, and often represent the quickest, easiest, and most economical route to booking accommodations. Wholesalers are specialized travel agents who, through high-volume dealings, are able to combine discounted rates for rooms and airfare into low-priced all-inclusive packages. This option becomes increasingly valuable as you become more and more familiar with Las Vegas. Savvy travelers often fashion their own bargain vacation by combining a portion of a wholesale package—i.e., "air-only" or "room-only"—with arrangements they make on their own. The specific area of the country you live in and your proximity to a major city are two factors that will determine whether or not wholesalers are an option for you. Local travel agents are your best connection to reputable wholesalers. The travel section or classifieds in your local newspaper will direct you to travel agencies that specialize in Las Vegas business. Don't circumvent travel agents by going directly to the wholesaler. The travel agent's commission comes from the wholesaler, not you, and every wholesaler I've ever spoken to has indicated that they are happy to pay the travel-agent commission in exchange for the TA handling the individual details. An insightful treatment of the travel agent and wholesaler scene can be found in *The Unofficial Guide to Las Vegas* (Prentice Hall) by Bob Sehlinger.

If you don't use a wholesaler or travel agent, you'll be making your own arrangements. That's fine. Doing it yourself is a great way to book a bargain.

Casino Packages (Advertised)

Here again, newspapers and periodicals are the best source for finding hot deals. One of the best packages in recent memory was the Stardust's "Lido Package." For $25 you got a room for two and two tickets to the *Lido de Paris* show. The tickets were worth $43 by themselves. This was a 200% savings on a room and tickets secured individually. The Stardust continues to offer variations on this package, combining a room and discounts on their new show, *Enter the Night*. Bally's, Palace Station, Las Vegas Hilton, Flamingo Hilton, and Riviera are other frequent package advertisers. Check the *L.A. Times* Calendar.

Casino Packages (Unadvertised)

Ask reservations personnel about packages that combine a room with a show and/or other amenities. These packages are offered by the casinos themselves, not wholesalers. Here's an example:

A couple of years ago, a two-night stay in a Desert Inn "mini-suite" was $222.60. Tickets for two to the Desert Inn show ran an additional $60, bringing the total cost for room and show to $282.60. Tolerable, but the DI also offered a special "Show Package" that included the same mini-suite and show for only $243.30, a $40 savings. In addition, the package included unlimited use of the health spa ($17.50 per visit), unlimited tennis and a tennis clinic ($20), $10 slot machine cash ($10), two cocktails per person (about $10) and a free keno ticket. In addition to the cash savings, the package added $75 worth of services and amenities.

Booking similar packages at other major resorts can result in savings in excess of 50% off typical prices.

A few things to know—

• Since packages are designed to fill hotels during off-peak times, most (but not all) are limited to Sunday-Thursday arrival. Many casinos allow you to roll your stay over for Friday and Saturday with some sort of discount on the regular weekend prices.

• Almost all packages are based on double occupancy. Solo travelers may not be able to save money.

• Although these programs are for real, and not come-ons that are advertised but never offered, they are based on availability and you should call well in advance of your travel dates.

• Despite the large savings, these packages may not represent your best alternative, particularly if you travel by air. Travel packages that include airfare may result in greater overall savings (see Wholesalers).

Packages come and go. Casinos that have consistently offered good packages are Caesars Palace (Roman Holiday), both Hiltons (Fling and BounceBack), and the Desert Inn (extraordinary golf packages).

Seasonality

Room rates follow a seasonal rate pattern. The two biggest bargain periods are the December holidays (including early January), and mid-summer (July and early August). The December bargain period manifests in ultra-low rates, while summer specials tend to be more creative, often taking the form of special promotions.

December

The period between Thanksgiving and Christmas is Las Vegas' slowest time of year. With the exception of a 7- to 10-day period at the beginning of December when the National Finals Rodeo brings 100,000 people to town, occupancy levels are at their lowest. The week between Christmas and New Year's heats up, then it's back to the doldrums for most of January.

How low do prices go in December? Very low! Every year new properties open. The city's room count rises and competition keeps rates dirt cheap, as you can see here:

Lowest Price On a December Room

1988 — Fitzgeralds — $12
1989 — Fitzgeralds — $12
1990 — Fitzgeralds — $12
1991 — Fitzgeralds — $18
1992 — Lady Luck — $15

Number of Casinos with Rooms for $20 or Less

1988 — 3
1989 — 10
1990 — 9
1991 — 7
1992 — 7

Number of Casinos with Rooms for $30 or Less

1988 — 13
1989 — 24
1990 — 18
1991 — 15
1992 — 22

Specifics change, but rates at the following properties have consistently fallen into the *$30 or Less* category in recent years: Arizona Charlie's, Barbary Coast, Bourbon Street, Circus Circus, El Cortez, Excalibur, Fitzgeralds, King 8, Lady Luck, Maxim, Plaza, Sands, Santa Fe, Showboat, Tropicana, Vacation Village, Westward Ho.

Even though the sub-$20 and sub-$30 rates are out there, they are becoming less important for two reasons: premier offers and slot clubs.

Premier Offers

A "premier" offer materializes when a casino decides to give away the store to attract business during the holidays. The Stardust was one of the first to do this when they sold a room and two tickets to their main show for $18.50 (complete price) from 1989 to 1991. Premier offers are well-publicized and available to the general public. When you find a good one, there's almost no reason to hunt further. Three casinos have made premier offers in each of the last two years and can probably be counted on to do so again in the future.

Palace Station Tower Room Package—Palace Station is always innovative. They like to offer combinations of matchplay, meals, drinks, free bingo, or a souvenir like a T-shirt with a room in their new tower for under $40. When you add the value of all the perks, it's like getting a free room. Watch the *L.A. Times* or call the Palace Station in late November or early December.

Bally's December Celebration—This two-night package includes a headliner show, matchplay, buffets, and other amenities and discounts at a discounted price for the holidays ($118 in 1992).

Imperial Palace Valued Guest—They've run this monster deal for three years straight. Your first night is free, then additional nights are $10 apiece. You must book at least one $10 night, but there's no restriction, other than availability, on booking more. Last year, this deal was even available during rodeo week. Be sure to ask specifically for the "Valued Guest" room rate.

The Slot Club Phenomenon

Slot clubs are changing the face of the bargain-room-rate scene, as casinos turn to their club lists to fill rooms in December. Searching out low-priced rooms is no longer necessary when you're receiving free-room offers from every casino in town.

The pace accelerated in 1992. In mid-November, a few discount offers began trickling into my own local mailbox. One was from the club of a casino I hadn't played in for more than a year. Soon, stories from *LVA* readers were streaming in. One man called to say that he was staying ten days free, compliments of various slot clubs. I'm not familiar with this individual's gambling habits—it's possible he lost a lot of money "earning" his free nights—but judging from his enthusiasm, I don't think so. Then there was a call from someone I know to be a serious bargain hunter. He works the system hard. "To date, I've been offered a total of 36 free room nights in December," he said. "Of course I've got meals and other extras. The only thing I have to pay for all month is public transportation."

For more on slot clubs, see pages 46 and 136.

Christmas in July

Las Vegas is busy during the summer. It therefore seems illogical that casinos would offer December-like values in July, but they usually do. That's because a full hotel in July is good for the casino win figure. People tend to play where they stay, especially during the hot summer months. Realizing that they have to get you before they can keep you, casinos offer especially juicy deals on rooms during the summer.

For the most part, the same ideas and concepts that apply to exploiting December rates apply in July (also June and August). The July deals seem to be a little more creative. One of the best appeared in the summer of 1991.

The Maxim ran the following ad in the *Dallas Morning News:*

Free Rooms To Texans
Must present a major credit card and a valid
Texas drivers license. Up to 3 Nights
Absolutely Free, No Hitches.

There was no gambling stipulation; the Maxim had simply decided that having a house full of Texans would be good for their casino action. They later made the same offer to Canadians and Arizonans.

Summer/Winter Deals

Most casinos are imitators, not innovators. When they see something work somewhere else, they scurry to implement the idea themselves. For example, the casinos jumped all over the latest marketing buzz-phrase, "value-added," to create the dominant pitch of the summer of '93: pay for a room (at a very low price) in the summer, and receive certificates for discounts or free stays in the winter. The Sahara, for example, required a two-day stay at $20 per day in July, August, or September in exchange for a certificate for three free nights on select dates in November and December. It worked out to five nights for $40. An even better deal was offered by Palace Station. When you booked two nights in July or August, you received $25 in matchplay chips, dinner for two in the Pasta Palace, breakfast for two in the coffee shop, two free margaritas, and two free nights in either December or January. All this for a total price of $50-$90 (depending on the quality of the room). The value of the perks alone (chips, meals, etc.) was about $50, so it was like getting four nights free. Of course, you have to be flexible in your travel plans to capitalize on these deals. But it's worth it.

Low Prices

If rock-bottom prices are what you seek, you'll have no trouble finding rooms for less than $30 in June, July, and August; and with a little investigation, you'll do much better. In 1992, the King 8 ran rooms for $12 a night. In 1993, the Stardust sold rooms for $20, and they came with two

The Fancy Joints

The holidays are a good time to book big-name casinos too. In 1992, rooms at The Mirage were $59 and rooms at Caesars Palace were $65. Both Hiltons also like to run deep discounts (usually in package form) during this time.

$7 buffet passes. Rooms were $65 again at Caesars Palace, and the best packages at Bally's and the Flamingo were discounted.

PRICE-ELIMINATING STRATEGIES: A FREE ROOM IN LAS VEGAS

Short of hitting Megabucks, scoring a free room in Las Vegas is every visitor's most ardent desire. The difference between a $25 room and one that's free is much more than $25. It has to do with the aura around the word "comp" (short for complimentary or freebie). It's also about bragging rights to your friends back home. Indeed, the free night signifies a rite of passage for the Las Vegas visitor. It's proof of arrival. Once I did an interview on the Arthur Frommer travel show in which I made a reference to free rooms. For two years, people who saw the interview called and wrote, pleading to be let in on the free-room secret.

Well, it's not a secret. Anyone willing to risk a four-figure bankroll can be assured of a free room simply by gambliing in the casino. Just put your money in the casino cage and step into the fascinating world of casino comps (see page 143). "But that's not me," you say. "I play the quarter (or maybe the nickel) slots." That's okay. You too can take steps to improve your chances of being offered free rooms.

The idea can be summed up by a single key word. Affiliate.

Join clubs. Subscribe to periodicals. Get your name in drawings and on lists. Take advantage of promotions. Use coupons. Above all, be alert—these opportunities can literally materialize out of thin air.

Balloon Payment

To celebrate the topping off of the MGM Grand, 5,009 balloons (one for each room in the hotel) were released from the top of the MGM parking structure. The balloons were filled with helium and vouchers for a free room at the MGM. The balloons were released into gusting southerly winds that swept them past North Las Vegas and out of town.

Slot Clubs

Of the many benefits of slot-club membership, preferred status in lodging is the most valuable. Simply being in a casino's slot-club database will usually qualify you for some sort of lodging consideration. Perhaps a minor discount or the casino rate is the best you will be offered, but it's more likely you'll receive at least one invitation for free nights. That's nights, plural; the offers are usually good for two- or three-night stays. In time, you'll settle on a favorite club that's structured to give you the most for your level of play. Initially though, your best strategy is to spread your action around a little. Join slot clubs at several different casinos and activate your card by playing a little. When you start receiving invitations and offers from more than one casino, you're in business. This reader's letter punctuates these points:

I arrived in Las Vegas on December 4 and returned to Chicago on December 22. My hotel bill for those 18 nights was $60. I stayed at the Stardust for seven nights, six courtesy of the slot club. The Flamingo Hilton and Westward Ho slot clubs comped me three nights each. The Westward Ho has a card reader that tells you how many points you have. I checked it when I arrived and I had 11 points. I later played 25¢ video poker for about half an hour and accumulated 75 points [enough to remain in good standing]. This is certainly proof that regardless of how much you play, these slot clubs can be worth the five minutes it takes to sign up.

Possibly even more important than free rooms is the ability to find rooms where they aren't. Slot clubs can be your best resource for securing accommodations when the city is running at high occupancy. I once called the Frontier requesting three nights over a busy weekend and was told that the hotel was sold out. I then mentioned that I had a slot card. "Oh, that makes a difference," responded the reservations clerk, who then allowed me to book the three nights. Slot clubs usually set aside blocks of rooms for use by their members during busy periods like holidays or major conventions. Call the slot club directly to inquire about rates and availability.

Take advantage of the competitiveness here. If you've been playing in a casino without getting offers and invitations from the slot club, it might be time to try another casino.

Coupons, Tournaments, and Promotions

Lady Luck Funbook—Coupons don't usually translate into free nights, but the Lady Luck's funbook contains a coupon for a free night when combined with two paid nights. The funbook is free at the casino.

Tournaments—Gambling-tournament players can schedule trips that coincide with tournament dates. Rooms at sponsoring casinos are usually free or deeply discounted.

Promotions—A special promotion that involves a free room can pop up anywhere. About a year ago Brunswick bowling balls offered free rooms at the Showboat to customers who bought their product.

Las Vegas Advisor Free Nights

Knowing how cherished free rooms are, we've made it a priority to negotiate free-room deals for *Las Vegas Advisor* subscribers. In both 1991 and 1992, all *LVA* subscribers received one free night in the Stardust Tower. In December 1992, Harrah's offered subscribers two free nights (plus parties and a gambling tournament) at a big Harrah's/*LVA* Invitational. In 1993, Harrah's again offered *LVA* subscribers two free nights, plus parties and a $5,000 raffle, and this time there were three dates to choose from in either June, July, or August. Why did the Stardust and Harrah's do this? Casino management made the offers based on their assessment of the gambling potential of *LVA* subscribers. That assessment was based on demographic information we collected and supplied to them while negotiating the deals. While it's true the majority of *LVA* subscribers did fit the profile that the Stardust and Harrah's were looking for, there were others on our roles who did not. These people benefitted by sole virtue of their affiliation with a favorable group. In other words, they got their names on the right list.

Free Rooms at the Frontier

One of the best and most innovative free-room promotions, ever, continues to run at the Frontier. Here's how it works: Play blackjack ($5 minimum bets), and receive a silver token each time you are dealt a natural (blackjack). When you've accumulated 11 tokens, you can redeem them for a free-room voucher at the Frontier, Sunday-Thursday. With 21 tokens, you get a voucher for a weekend room. Since you are dealt a blackjack about once every 21 hands, you should earn your free room after about 3-1/2 hours of $5 play. You may reserve a maximum of three nights (33-53 tokens) per seven-day period. You are further restricted only by availability: vouchers must be redeemed within 120 days from the time you accept them. Exchange tokens for vouchers (in the pit) only if you know you will be returning to Las Vegas within the 120-day time allotment. Otherwise, hold on to the tokens until you return to town.

You can use a Frontier "Casino Player's" card to earn further credits while you're winning your room. These will qualify you for free meals and other offers from the casino.

A Frontier frequenter offers the following tips:

Many players don't seem to want the tokens or know what to do with them. Mention that you are saving them, and then graciously accept any that come your way. There seems to be no requirement to have vouchers in hand when you arrive. Make sure you let them know you're paying for your room with blackjack tokens when you make your reservation and again when you check in. You'll still have to lay down a credit card, but you don't have to produce the vouchers until check-out. I saw many guests who arrived thinking they were paying for their rooms, then won tokens, bought vouchers, and got off free.

A Caveat

Be careful! Any time a gambling stipulation is attached to a promotion, you must consider the risk of pursuing the prize. The expected result for a basic-strategy blackjack player after 3-1/2 hours of single-deck play is to approximately break even.Even a poorly skilled blackjack player has an expected loss of less than $15, betting $5 a hand. Therefore, your cost of winning a room in the Frontier promotion is $0-$15, depending on your level of blackjack skill. However, *expected* results and *possible* results are two different things. Possible results take risk into account. The statistical measure for gauging risk is called standard deviation. Calculating the standard deviation for 210 hands (3-1/2 hours of blackjack) tells us that 95% of all results will fall somewhere between a win or loss of about $170. Approximately 66% of the time, your result will land in a narrower range of about plus or minus $85. This is a realistic assessment of what can happen playing the Frontier promotion. You must be mentally (and financially) prepared for a loss of this magnitude. Of course, it's possible that the loss (or win) will be greater, but those occasions will be rare.

Comps

Most free-room arrangements come about via casino complimentaries, commonly called comps. The biggest gamblers don't worry about rooms and availability. They get comped to suites during the Super Bowl. But even small- to mid-range gamblers can tap into the comp system. Comp expert Max Rubin says that in a typical Strip casino, eight hours of table play at a minimum bet of $25 (or eight hours of $1 slot-machine play) will get you two comped nights in the hotel. If you play at these stakes, make sure that you get rated (your bet-level recorded) by the pit, or that you have a slot-club card inserted in your machine. After about three to four hours of play, you can enter into negotiations with a pit boss or slot-club host for your room. See (Chapter 12) for more on the ritual.

Casino Rate

The casino rate is a preferential room rate reserved for a casino's better customers. The room isn't free, but it's usually discounted by 35% to 50%. Eight hours of $15 minimum bets should get you two nights at the casino rate. You'll need to ask for a rating here too, and it doesn't hurt to sprinkle your first 20 minutes of betting with a little bit of quarter ($25) play to make your average bet look larger.

Return Comps

A few casinos have liberal comp policies for small bettors who are willing to return at a future date. The Four Queens is one of the best in this regard. A few hours of rated red ($5) action will often get you a mailed invitation to stay in the hotel at the casino rate on a future visit. Depending on the state of their promotional push, two or three hours of $25 play might get you an invitation for a free room. Any casino with a slot-club card that also accrues points when you play table games (Frontier, Tropicana) is a great place to qualify for return comps. It's also easier to initiate a rating at these places, because all you have to do is show them your slot/table card.

Sprees

A "spree" is a short gambling excursion in which you pre-pay a low fee for airfare, two nights lodging, and usually a couple of buffet meals. You are expected to gamble four hours a day for two days at $10 minimum bets. If you do, you receive rebates in the form of cash and *funny money* (special non-negotiable gambling chips). If you fulfill the gambling requirement and receive all the rebates, your trip costs nothing, aside from potential gambling losses. Sprees, once quite common, are dying. Outside operators who coordinate sprees are having difficulty finding casinos that are still willing to sponsor them. Check your newspapers to locate spree operators. Their ads may not use the word spree, but the offer will look something like what I've just described. You can also try calling around to the casinos. The Riviera and the Four Queens have done a fair amount of spree business in recent years.

Putting It All Together

How viable are these strategies? Extremely viable. Following is the true story of a retired English teacher who was able to use these ideas to live in Las Vegas hotels for seven weeks (in '92/'93), during a period that included Christmas, New Year's, and the Super Bowl, at no cost. Granted, this is not your typical tourist (we've christened her the Queen of Ku Pon). She has the time, and the inclination, to chase down every deal she can find. She's a thinker, a planner, and somewhat of a schemer. Here, the Queen describes her coup in her own words.

50 Nights, 49 Free

I always travel to Las Vegas with my boyfriend and sign up for everything in both of our names. This ensures the doubling of every offer and invitation. We arrived on Dec. 13 and checked into the Stardust for five free nights through a slot-club invitation, three in my name and two in his; we could've had a sixth night free but didn't need it. On Dec. 18, we moved over to the Riviera for six free nights, three and three, also through the slot club. During this period, we also stayed at Harrah's the Sunday night of the big LVA party.

On Dec. 24, we moved to the Flamingo Hilton for six free nights. This was a curious comp, since we've never played there, though we must have signed up for something sometime. It was a valuable comp as well, because it was over Christmas weekend and comps were tight. Christmas is getting more popular as Las Vegas is becoming more "family."

On Dec. 30, we moved back to the Stardust for three free nights from the slot club. We had to pay for the fourth night (at the casino rate of $22) because of how New Year's fell. It was a four-day weekend and you usually only get comped for three over a weekend.

Between January 3 and 6 we participated in the Vegas World VIP Vacation, once in each of our names, and got four nights free. Then we moved back to the Stardust, a special slot-club offer for four nights, particularly valuable since it was during Comdex.

We then moved to the Frontier for 14 nights in a large studio room with wet bar, fridge, and balcony, as a result of slot-club offers and accumulating several hundred free-room-for-blackjacks tokens, half of which were given to us by other players. We had to check out of and back into the same room when we switched from slot-club to token nights. But you can do this every month! You can stay two nights free as long as you earn 400 points on your card—easy on double point days. And you can stay three free nights a week with the tokens.

On Jan. 25 we moved back to the Stardust for four free nights through the slot club. Then on Jan. 29 we went over to the Westward Ho for three free nights through the slot club and rated table play. This was very valuable since it was Super Bowl weekend and there were no free nights available anywhere else. The best we could have done was to get a room at the casino rate ($65!) at the Stardust.

We could have started another two-week cycle at the Frontier on Feb. 1, but by then we had decided to go home. All told, staying for 50 nights cost a grand total of $22.

What's impressive about this story is that it didn't require an inordinate amount of finagling to secure the 49 free nights. The two-name ploy is strong, and the Queen is more flexible than most, switching casinos several times during a visit. The essence of the strategy, however, is joining clubs and getting your name on lists, which anyone can do. The Queen's gambling acumen is also important; she knows how to keep her memberships active at minimal cost by playing an informed game of blackjack and choosing video poker machines with returns at breakeven or better (all skills that you can master with the information in Section II).

MISCELLANEOUS CONSIDERATIONS

Cancellation Policies

In a 1992 study for the *LVA*, 56 casinos were asked about their cancellation policies. Almost all allowed cancellation without penalty up to either 24 or 48 hours. The standard penalty after the cut-off is a one-night charge.

Always remember to:

- Ask about the cancellation policy up front.
- Get a "cancellation number" when you cancel prior to the deadline. That way you won't be charged for a penalty-night by mistake.

The almost universal 24- to 48-hour cancellation policy gives you a great deal of latitude when shopping for a room. Lock in the best deal you find well in advance, then keep your ear to the ground. If something better comes up, you'll almost always be able to cancel the first reservation without penalty.

New Year's Eve

It's the toughest night of the year to get a room in Las Vegas. If you do find one late, you'll have to pay inflated prices, and most of the casinos with rooms remaining require that you stay (or at least pay for) multiple nights. A late-November canvassing of more than 50 casinos in both 1991 and 1992 uncovered about a dozen casinos with rooms available for New Year's Eve. Packages ran about $125 a night, usually with 3-night minimums. Four casinos had rooms available both years: Continental, Vacation Village, Hacienda, and Sahara. The best deal was at the Santa Fe in 1991, which had New Year's Eve rooms available for $50, no minimum stay required.

Saturday-Night Arrival

Most Las Vegas hotels won't book a Saturday arrival in advance. It's a simple matter of efficiently balancing supply and demand, and selling the maximum number of rooms at the best price.

How prevalent is the Saturday arrival bias? Of 56 casinos called, only twelve had a policy of booking advance Saturday-night arrivals *all the time* (which really means: when rooms are available). They were: Boardwalk, Bourbon Street, Excalibur, Golden Gate, Las Vegas Hilton, Longhorn, Palace Station, Riviera, San Remo, Town Hall, Westward Ho, and Chaparral. Another 27 said they take Saturday arrival "sometimes." Don't count on it unless the city is very, very slow.

Also try making your reservations through a casino slot club (if you are an active member). You'll be surprised at how accommodating they can be.

Taxes

A 7% sales tax is added onto room charges around the state, and an extra 1% in Las Vegas helps finance the Las Vegas Convention and Visitors Authority. Add 8% tax when considering room costs, except where stipulated that "price includes tax."

Referral Services

Referral agencies claim that dealing in volume allows them to pass savings on to their customers who would otherwise be charged higher rates as walk-ins. They make their profit from commissions paid by casinos. It therefore seems logical that room-referral services might provide a way to save time and money while shopping for rooms. In theory, the referral agencies should be able to place their customers at the lowest possible rates thanks to volume and hotel commissions, but there's a problem. Depending on individual arrangements, the hotel pays the referral agency a commission of 10-20% on the price of each room sold. By placing customers at the lowest possible rates, referral agencies are effectively limiting themselves to the lowest possible profit. Consequently, referral agents make more money by placing customers in more expensive rooms.

To get a better grip on the situation I tried the following experiment a few years ago. First, I called 35 casino-hotels on a busy Thursday with the objective of securing a room for Thursday, Friday, and Saturday nights. Of the 35 called, 15 were completely sold out, eight had accommodations for one or two nights, and 12 had vacancies for all three nights. Rates ranged from $28-$90. I then called eight different referral agencies and asked for their best deal. The results were interesting. Referral agency #1 offered the Dunes for all three nights at $62.80 per night. Chalk one up for referrals; the Dunes had quoted me a "best rate" of $75 earlier. Still, I had been able to find five other casinos on my own with rates below $62.80. I asked for alternatives and was told that there were none. Referral agency #2 offered Fitzgeralds at $75 per night. What a crock! Fitzgeralds had already quoted me $50 for Thursday and $55 for Friday and Saturday. "Is this your best deal?" I asked. "It is," I was told.

Referral agency #3 offered the Flamingo for $102 (I had been quoted $72), but they also suggested a fairly nice non-casino motel for under $40. Referral agency #4 had the Sahara for $65. I had been quoted $55. The others produced more of the same. In this instance, I was able to do much better by making my own phone calls, although it did cost well over an hour of my time to check 35 casinos.

So, do we condemn referral services unconditionally? Not so fast. A week later I repeated the experiment. This time the city was swamped. Two world championship boxing matches were taking place and a gigantic computer convention (close to 100,000 participants) was in town. I made my calls late in the afternoon on a Friday, trying to secure a room for Friday and Saturday night. No luck anywhere.

Referral agencies to the rescue. Between the eight agencies, I was offered the Imperial Palace for $95, the Stardust for $59 (if I agreed to take three nights), the Alexis Park (an opulent non-casino hotel) for $85, and a respectable motel on Desert Inn Road for only $45 per night. In this case, the referral agencies were lifesavers.

Conclusion: While usually not the most cost effective way to book a room, there are times when a referral agency can come in handy. During semi-busy periods, you may be able to use their services to direct you to casinos with vacancies. And in a pinch, they may be your last resort.

One of the largest referral services is City Wide Reservations, 800-733-6644.

Safes and Security

In a survey of 54 Las Vegas hotels, 17 were found to have small safes in at least some rooms.

The Las Vegas Club and the Rio have safes, at no charge, in every room, an excellent deal. Caesars, Four Queens, Desert Inn, and the Maxim have safes in selected rooms, also free for the using. Circus Circus has some coin-operated safes: every time you want to open it, you insert a quarter. The other ten hotels all charge a daily rate for the use of room safes. Vegas World adds $1 a day onto your hotel room bill, Aladdin adds $2, California, Continental, Flamingo, Fremont, Hilton, Riviera, and Stardust get $3, and the Tropicana tacks on $4. Front desk clerks either supply you with the existing combination, code, or key, or instruct you how to set your own combination.

An alternative at the 37 hotels that don't have room safes is a safety deposit box at the front desk or main cage. Most hotels offer this as a free service to their guests. An advantage of main floor security is that you don't have to return to your room every time you want to make a deposit or withdrawal.

Finally, in the common-sense department, even if you don't have a room safe or use a safety-deposit box, it's wise to take some precautions concerning your bankroll and valuables. Hide them, disguise them, whatever, but don't forget them!

Pools

Every hotel on the Strip has a pool, except the Barbary Coast, whose guests have pool privileges at the Gold Coast. Bourbon Street on East Flamingo next to Barbary Coast doesn't have a pool, but guests have pool privileges next door at the Maxim. Downtown, Binion's, California, Golden

Nugget, Lady Luck, and Plaza have pools; the rest don't. There's virtually no such thing as a shabby Las Vegas hotel pool; if it has one, it's nice. But those at the Tropicana, Mirage, Caesars, Desert Inn, Bally's, Las Vegas Hilton, Frontier, Sahara, and Hacienda are especially fine. When it's completed in 1994, the pool at the Flamingo Hilton will compete with the Trop for ultimate pool honors. Note: All casino pools are outdoors.

Non-Casino

There are more than 20,000 non-casino hotel and motel rooms in Las Vegas, and most of the major lodging chains are represented. Rate comparisons have shown that the non-gambling-subsidized hotels can not compete with casinos for lowest rates, but they may be your salvation on busy weekends and holidays when the casinos are sold out. Keep these numbers in your arsenal just in case.

Best Western (800-528-1234)—Best Western maintains six properties all around Las Vegas. Don't bother trying to call individual motels. Call this

The People's Choice

The LVA Reader Survey asked respondents to choose their favorite casino. That's casino, not hotel, but remember, choosing a hotel is a matter of choosing a casino. So there is something to be learned here, since the results are a product of the experience of frequent visitors. Below are their top ten favorite casinos.

CASINO	*% Of Vote*
Mirage	*8.0*
Horseshoe	*7.3*
Flamingo	*7.3*
Golden Nugget	*6.6*
Four Queens	*6.5*
Rio	*6.3*
Caesars Palace	*6.0*
Stardust	*5.8*
Bally's	*5.5*
Harrah's	*5.2*
Total	*64.5%*

Roughly 1/3 of the respondents chose a casino not listed above.

main reservations line and let the computer do all the work.

Comfort/Quality/Rodeway/Friendship/Econolodge (800-221-2222)—All are handled by the same reservations number. Seven properties in all.

Days Inn (800-241-5050)—Three properties.
La Quinta Inn (800-531-5900)—One property.
Super 8 (800-800-8000)—Two properties.
Travelodge (800-255-3050)—Three properties.
Motel 6 (505-891-6161)—Two properties.
EZ-8 Motel (800-668-3532)—One property.

In addition to these "economy" chains, there are six non-casino luxury hotels with rates that run in the $75-$100 range.

Marriott Courtyard (800-321-2211)
Marriott Residence (800-331-3131)
Ramada Suite St. Tropez (800-666-5400)
Sheffield Inn (800-777-1700)
Alexis Park (800-582-2228)
Howard Johnson Plaza Suites (800-654-2000)

Long-Term Accommodations

Though most visitors stay in Las Vegas for 3-4 days at a time, some (winter snowbirds from the north, recent transplants, transients, and professional gamblers) settle in for weeks and even months at a time. One of the most affordable and comfortable ways to remain in Las Vegas long-term (without committing to a real apartment) is in a weekly motel room. Most motels give sizable discounts for weekly rates; many come complete with refrigerators, kitchenettes, and even complete kitchens.

Weekly rooms are often available for less than $15 a night. Recently, the DI 500 (505 Desert Inn Rd., 702-735-3160) was charging $117.50 (including tax) by the week; the rooms (though older and eminently plain) have a full-size refrigerator, four-burner oven and stove, and large kitchen sink. Other weekly rooms, like Fun City (2233 L.V. Blvd., 702-731-3155) and Glass Pool (4613 L.V. Blvd., 702-739-6636), have mini-fridges and compact stove/oven combos, though some, like the Crest (207 N. Sixth, 382-5642), have VCRs and full kitchens. Most have pools, laundries, and good security.

Perhaps the nicest and largest long-term accommodation is available at Sun Harbor Budget Suites (Stardust Rd., 702-732-1500) and Shelter Island (3770 Swenson, 702-647-2220). Suites are comprised of living room, bedroom, and kitchen with refrigerator and stove. Though not particularly spacious, the rooms are newer and very comfortable. Weekly rates begin at $159 (for the least expensive rooms on the third floor). For this price you get a bare bones set-up: no linens, blankets, or towels, and no maid service. You can rent a week's linen package for an additional $20 or get full maid service for another $25.

Places like Harbor Island (370 E. Harmon, 702-732-9111) and the Falls (3825 Cambridge, 702-702-792-9191) are larger and more residential than Budget Suites. You must bring your own linens, etc., and no phone service is provided (you arrange for it personally with the phone company). But if you're staying for several weeks, the price is right, the population is less transient, and the rooms are great.

If you're on a hotel free-night marathon courtesy of casino slot clubs or promotions, be sure to request a refrigerator. Most hotels will supply your room with a mini-fridge free of charge, which can mean the difference between enjoying regular meals (breakfast and lunch) in your room and being forced to go out to eat three times a day.

RVs

And just to make things complete, here is a list of casino RV park rates with full hookups: Nevada Palace ($9.72), Silver Nugget ($9-$10.50), Sam's Town ($10-$12), California ($12), Circus Circus ($11.88-$16.20), Hacienda ($9.68-$15).

THE VEGAS WORLD VIP VACATION

This is the deal you've seen advertised via brightly colored, full-page ads in *Parade*, *Playboy*, *USA Today*, and a host of other major print media. It's the most ambitious, longest-running, and probably most successful ad campaign in the whole business of gambling. It's clever and complicated, and therefore misunderstood by almost everyone that attempts to analyze it (including gaming authorities in Nevada). No subject has prompted more mail to the *Las Vegas Advisor* than this vacation offer. I've followed the program and its creator, the enigmatic Bob Stupak, for years, and in mid-1992, I decided to launch a full-scale investigation into this controversial subject. The *LVA* conducted a comprehensive four-part study of the entire Vegas World program. Parts I and II (reprinted here) deal with the VIP Vacation—Part I is a model for analysis, Part II is a step-by-step chronicle of an actual stay. Part III looked into an early effort to raise money for the Stratosphere Tower and is no longer applicable. Part IV is the transcript of a 2-1/2 hour interview with Bob Stupak; available from Huntington Press in the *Handicapping Stupak Special Report*. Here is everything you need to know about the Vegas World VIP Vacation.

Handicapping Stupak—Part I

A typical reader question: What is your opinion of the Vegas World VIP Vacation?

Response: Which one?

There are several versions. Surprisingly, all are relatively easy to analyze. The trick is to know what's important. It's not the "free gift." It's not the free shows. It's not the total amount of the "casino bankroll." *It is the manner in which the casino bankroll is divided!* Look for three things:

Cash—Cash means cash. You'll probably receive it in casino chips but you can redeem them without obligation.

Table Action—Table action means "funny money"—special non-negotiable chips that must be played on table games. They are picked up by the dealer after each play whether you win or lose, but winners are replaced by real chips. A good rule of thumb is to value funny chips at 50% of their face amount.

Slot Machine Action—This is not as cut and dried as the first two, and it's one of the areas where Stupak has gotten into trouble with his detractors. Vacationers assume that free-play tokens can be used on any casino machine, which suggests a 90% return. Not so. Tokens must be played in special machines with payouts far below industry averages. Based on an *LVA* study in 1989, and all the reports we've received since then, it appears that these machines pay between 8% and 12%. I'm comfortable with 10%.

When you evaluate a VIP Vacation offer:	
Multiply Cash amount by	100%
Multiply Table Action amount by	50%
Multiply Slot Machine Action amount by	10%

By plugging in the dollar amounts listed in the offer you are evaluating, you will be able to determine, fairly closely, the expected return from the casino bankroll. Here's an example taken from a recently received solicitation:

Cash	$200	X	100%	=	$200
Table	$200	X	50%	=	$100
Slots	$400	X	10%	=	$ 40
Total					$340

In this example, you can expect to recoup about $340 of the $398 package price. The package offers an additional $100 divided equally between table action and slots if you are willing to begin your stay on a Sunday or Tuesday. If you exercise this option, you can add:

Table	$50	X	50%	=	$25
Slots	$50	X	10%	=	$5
Total					$30

This brings the total return up to $370, leaving a mere $28 unaccounted for. The value of two room nights, free drinks, free meals, shows, and other extras should make up the difference.

Every version of the package that I've seen can be handicapped in this manner.

There's usually another element included in the casino bankroll. It's free entries into the "Million Dollar Slot Tournament." Although there's a fair amount of expected value here, I've not included it in the formula because it's a high-variance benefit. This means that while you could win a lot, you'll probably win nothing. It's mathematically proper to take an average of all results and include it in the computation of value, but since so few will see a return, I've decided to leave it out. For those who understand and live by the concept of expected value, we analyzed these tournaments as being worth about $16 per entry in 1989.

So there you have a method by which you can handicap a Vegas World vacation offer. There are several other considerations—the value of the free gift, the casino location, the quality of the room, the refund policy. I talk about those in Part II.

Handicapping Stupak—Part II

In Part I of this series, I showed you how to assess the dollar value of a Vegas World VIP Vacation offer. The technique is straight-forward and accurate, but it gives no information as to the overall quality of the experience. I participated in the VIP Vacation, and thoroughly investigated every aspect of the program. I didn't use my real name, so no connection with this periodical could be made by Vegas World. My findings/impressions are detailed below.

Booking/Refunds

Every VW solicitation/advertisement specifies a rapidly approaching "deadline date." Should you drop everything and rush to the phone so you don't miss the deadline? Absolutely not. Deadlines are a staple of direct-mail solicitation. Don't worry about it; operators are happy to sign you up any time you call.

The "Privileges and Provisions" section of the VIP Vacation brochure states that reservations must be made "at least 20 days before arrival." They seem to be more strict about this. Still, I called on a Tuesday and was able to secure a room for the following Sunday. One interesting point: I initially attempted to book the vacation with a Nevada driver's license and was refused. The fact that locals are excluded is a tip-off that the deal offers enough value to be exploitable.

The refund policy appears very sound. Vacations have always been postponable and transferable. Now, as a result of a 1991 agreement with the Nevada Gaming Commission, they are also refundable.

Vegas World or Thunderbird?

You usually have a choice of taking your room at either Vegas World or the Thunderbird Hotel (owned by Vegas World). Sometimes Vegas World is sold out and you are forced to stay at the Thunderbird. Here's a quick assessment of each.

Vegas World—Full-service hotel. Adequate rooms but nothing fancy. Clean. Always busy. There's an Olympic-size pool on the roof (24th floor) with a good view of Las Vegas.

Thunderbird—Readers have expressed concern about imposed lodging at the Thunderbird, so I requested a room there. I found that there's a good case for choosing the Thunderbird over the VW casino tower. The rooms aren't as nice as those in the tower, but the Thunderbird is slow-paced and you can drive your car up to your motel-room door for convenience. The lobby is adorned with a great collection of old-time Las Vegas photos. If you don't have transportation, a shuttle runs between VW and the Thunderbird on the half hour.

Transportation

It's best to have a car. If you don't drive your own or rent, you have two options for getting to and from the airport.

- Taxi—Costs about $16 each way.
- Airport shuttlebus—Vegas World says it's $3.50 per person (Strip price). Bell Trans tells us $4.50 per person (downtown price). Hmm... Vegas World remains committed to perpetuating the "on the Strip" myth... Count on paying $4.50.

Location

This is one of four problems with the VIP Vacation. Vegas World is poorly located. It's only 1/3 mile from the Sahara—walkable, but not recommended due to the neighborhood. And once you reach the Sahara, you're still another half-mile away from Circus Circus, true boundary of the Strip proper.

The location problem actually works to the advantage of Vegas World. Once in, many visitors find themselves marooned and, naturally, decide to do their gambling there. This problem is solved if you have a car. If you fly to Las Vegas to participate in the VIP program, renting a car is highly recommended. Vegas World has a large parking garage and valet service.*

Check-in/Lines in General

I'd heard horror stories about hour-long check-in lines, and our advance work told us that Sunday is the worst day of all. I used basic strategy and arrived early Sunday, about 10:30 am. Not a single person was in line at the Thunderbird and check-in took a total of two minutes. Front-desk personnel told me that afternoons are busier, especially at Vegas World.

You may encounter a long line to redeem your gift. Don't stand in it. Your vacation lasts three days. Come back when the line subsides. The same goes for any line you encounter.

Souvenirs

I walked away with two decks of cards and two pair of dice, all with the Vegas World logo. These are great souvenirs. I also received a worthless "gaming guide."

Free Gift

You are told you will win one of five valuable gifts. One is a "Zsa Zsa Gabor Original Marquis Pendant." There's no reason to list the other four. I've never heard of anyone winning a gift other than the pendant. No one I've talked to has ever heard of anyone winning a gift other than the pendant. I won the pendant. You will win the pendant.

This is VIP Vacation problem number two. Vegas World claims the pendant's "retail value" is $270. But detractors of the program contend that the value of this gift (as well as your overall free-gift prospects) are misrepresented. In 1989, I sought the opinion of a Las Vegas telemarketing expert who had purchased jewelry of this sort as a "premium" for his own business. He estimated that VW might pay as much as $50 for the piece. Perhaps.

Even if the free gift deal is something of a come-on, it doesn't cost you unless you are foolish enough to buy the vacation because you think that you'll take down a valuable gift. The value of the pendant is relative. I've talked to many people who really like it. You have the option of substituting a clock radio or a 35mm camera for the pendant. These items sell in stores for about $35 so I'm according a value of $35 to the free gift.

Slot Action

VIP Vacation problem number three. Everyone is aggravated by the low payouts on slot action. Vegas World should address this because it fuels the allegations of "rip-off."

**The neighborhood is also a factor here. Use the valet at all times.*

I cashed $63 from my $400 in free play. My additional $50 play (a bonus offered for Sunday and Tuesday arrivals) netted an extra $5. The $68 total represents a 15.1% return, but one of my payoffs was a big 20-coiner. Without that, I would have been right on the 10% I predicted in Part I. Fifteen percent is probably the amount paid out by Vegas World overall. Still, I recommend that you stay with 10% because it is the result you will achieve most often.

Table Action

I cashed $122 from my $250 Table Action stake ($200 original and $50 mid-week bonus). That's almost right on expectation (50%). This may be the best part of the program. You can break your funny money down to $1 chips if you want. At $1 per hand, your $250 will be exhausted (converted into real-money winnings) in about four hours at a full blackjack table. Breaking your funny money down this way also increases the probability that you'll land close to the 50% expected return.

Vegas World allows you to redeem your funny money at the cage for $6.25 per $25 (25% return). Don't do it.

Cash

My $200 in cash came in the form of eight $25 casino chips packaged in a stapled envelope. On the envelope was a soft solicitation to play the chips (rather than just cash them at the cage), because "The amount of play will determine if Vegas World can continue [to offer cash]" in the VIP package. I wondered how they would know; I also wondered whether there were consequences for choosing one route over the other. I tested this by combining my free chips with the $122 I won at blackjack before attempting to cash out at the casino cage. Without hesitation, the attendant separated the free $200 from the real chips and requested my VIP card before cashing the former. I was impressed; the $25 tokens from the envelope appeared identical to the casino chips. Upon closer examination, however, I noticed that there is a subtle difference in the color of the chip's inlay. My name was recorded and I was paid. What does this mean? I'm guessing that my name will be coded into a less desirable category for future VW offers. If you intend to do more gambling after using your funny money, by all means use the envelope-issued chips before breaking into new money. If not, there may be some value in trying to "wash" the free chips in some way; perhaps cashing them at a slot booth for dollars.

Slot Tournament

Whoa! The format in these daily tournaments has changed drastically. I had accorded a value of $16 per free entry in 1989. That's no longer even close. I now calculate 63¢ per entry. Let's be generous and make it 75¢.

Your expected return for playing all four free slot tournament entries is $3. They're fun to play, though. If you don't have other things to do, you may as well. Sign up as early as possible. You'll get shut out if you wait until later in the day. I played once and didn't cash.

Free Keno

This is cut and dried. You get four free plays. Total expected return $1.42. I played mine all at once to save time and didn't cash.

Guaranteed Winner

Play a slot machine that guarantees a win ranging from 50¢ to $1000. I won 50¢.

Free Pull

Free shot at $1 million. I didn't cash.

Free Drinks

This is a great benefit. Drinks are free at all VW casino bars (not Thunderbird bars) at all hours. Just show your VIP card (referred to by some as the "drinking card"). No premium beers, but plenty of top-shelf call brands. You can order any mixed drink you desire, even Long Island iced tea.

Free Shows

Two tickets to Elvis and two tickets to Allen & Rossi. Drink cards are not accepted in the showroom, but there's no requirement that you purchase a drink either. The showroom is big and impressive. The Elvis show is alright. The Allen & Rossi show is terrific, thanks mostly to the musical talents of Katie Blackwell (Marty Allen's wife).

Live music, big crowds, a true night out.

Dining

Some packages have tickets to the Moonrock buffet. Mine didn't. There's a hot dog stand tucked away near the tower elevators. They sell a "Polish hot dog." I've had my share of hot dogs and this one doesn't quite make the grade. My package included a $6 discount for Kelly & Cohen's, VW's gourmet restaurant.

Champagne

You get a coupon to pick up a free bottle of champagne from the main bar. It's Andre Extra Dry which sells at the supermarket for $3.29. Not my cup of bubbly, but a nice touch, nonetheless.

Conclusion

I had fun. No kidding. The program is well-conceived, well-balanced, and Vegas World employees are among the friendliest I've ever encountered. No way is this the "best deal in Las Vegas" as *Playboy* wrote in 1987; but it's certainly fair. If it weren't, the program would have died off years ago.

So what's wrong? Why does the package get such a bad rap? I mentioned that there are four problems with the VIP Vacation, but cited only three in the text above. The fourth may be the most serious: The VIP Vacation is hyped far too much. First-timers arrive with unrealistic expectations and leave disappointed. The real key here may be having a car. If you don't care for Vegas World, you can leave and spend your time in the city's other casinos, then enjoy some free drinks back at Vegas World at day's end.

The key to coming out ahead here is to see the program for what it is—a breakeven proposition. Re-read this report, consult the benefit chart below, and make an informed decision. Those who want to participate can sign up or get promotional material by calling 800-634-6301.

VIP BENEFITS

	Expected Value	**My Result**
Cash	$200	$200
Slot Action	45	63
Table Action	125	122
Slot Tourn.	3	0
Keno	1.42	0
Gtd Win	.75	.50
Free Pull	.01	0
Monetary	$375.18	$385.50
Gift	35	35
Souvenirs	2	2
Free Shows	6	6
Dining	6	0
Free Drinks	20	30
Champagne	3.29	3.29
Free Picture	1	1
Room	60	60
Perks	**$133.29**	**$137.29**
TOTAL	$508.47	$522.79

II

Betting

GAMBLING

This book is all about change and the new Las Vegas. But one thing never changes in this city—the odds of the games on the casino floor.

Gambling, Not Gaming

"Gambling is a primitive religious instinct," writes Mario Puzo, "that has existed since the beginning of recorded history in every society, from the most primitive to the most complex." Though today's proliferation of gambling clearly demonstrates that the public desires it (and government sanctions it), casinos continue to fight a fierce battle against the keepers of the public conscience. For more than 60 years, the challenge has been to sanitize the disreputable image of gambling and gamblers, and make it palatable to a (supposedly) reluctant national market. One of the more interesting manifestations of this effort has been to replace the unseemly word "gambling" with the innocuous euphemism "gaming." Indeed, in a recent 21-page report on gambling demographics (sponsored by Harrah's), the word "gambling" never appeared. The activity is referred to as "gaming." Players are called "gamers." And gamers either "game" or have "gamed."

In this book, the word is gambling.

The Focus

Some might call this section incomplete, as limited treatment is afforded several of the major games. Indeed, the treatment of craps encompasses only a single paragraph. But what is there to say about craps beyond "bet your money and lose at a rate of 1.4% or worse"? Craps, baccarat, roulette, and most slot machines are negative-expectation gambling games that can not be beaten with any combination of luck, aura, or *money management*. There's no point in saying much more about them. Rather, this section focuses on the potentially positive-expectation games—video poker and blackjack—and the games that provide a great deal of entertainment value relative to the casino edge, particularly sports betting.

One more thing. I know that some percentage of readers will disagree with me about the merits of the $2 steak at the Horseshoe; I'll even concede that one or two may not like Palace Station's king crab legs. That's fine. Tastes in food are subjective. The fundamentals of proper gambling strategy are not. The information presented in this section does not represent my own whimsical approach to playing the games. It represents findings from the studies of scores of capable mathematicians and computer scientists. Don't second guess them.

A New Way To Learn

The primary purpose of this section is to provide you with insight and teach you methods that will improve your play. Losing money consistently is no fun, and it can put a damper on even the best vacation. Because gambling is based on mathematics, learning gambling strategy has always been considered a chore, something to be avoided. But it's the '90s, and there's a new way to learn.

Gambling software for personal computers has made great advances in recent years. The best way to learn gambling skills like video-poker strategy, blackjack basic strategy, and blackjack card counting is via computer, and it's an option I'm going to recommend strongly throughout.

The advantage to using computers is that you can have fun while you master techniques that will benefit you financially. And because you are learning via hands-on activity, you learn faster and more thoroughly. In the end, *you'll* be programmed for near-perfect play.

4

VIDEO POKER

Video poker is a vast and complicated subject, but learning just a few key skills can go a long way toward improving your bottom line when you play.

Which Machine?

Video poker has become immensely popular. As you might expect, the decision-making aspect has a great deal to do with the game's appeal. Most players want to exert as much control over their gambling fate as possible and video poker allows you to do this. Not only do you make decisions, you make decisions that actually matter. Most players know intuitively that there is a way to beat this game, and they back their conviction with their money. Unfortunately, intuitiveness alone is not enough. A few basic facts must be fully understood before video poker can be conquered.

You might expect that playing your cards properly is the most important consideration. Not so. The most important aspect of winning (or losing less) is knowing which machine to play. Surprisingly, this determination can be made with complete accuracy in a matter of seconds. The key is in analyzing the payout schedule that is posted on the machine. The schedule printed (next page) is typical.

Reading the Schedule

First, make certain that the machine returns your bet on a pair of jacks or better—a virtual given in Las Vegas, but not always the case in other places. Once that has been confirmed, the first column of the payout schedule and the first entry in the fifth column (royal flush with 5th coin) are the two points that you must reference. In the first column you are concerned with the payouts corresponding to full house and flush. In this example, the full house pays 9 and the flush pays 6. We call this a 9/6 machine. Now check the second reference point. If the royal flush with five

25¢, 9/6, 5-COIN MAX

	1ST COIN	2ND COIN	3RD COIN	4TH COIN	5TH COIN
Royal Flush	250	500	750	1000	4000 (REFERENCE POINT #2)
Straight Flush	50				
4-of-a-Kind	25				
Full House	9 (REFERENCE POINT #1)				
Flush	6 (REFERENCE POINT #1)				
Straight	4				
3-of-a-Kind	3	6	9	12	15
2 Pair	2	4	6	8	10

Bet Returned on Pair of Jacks or Better

coins played pays at least 4,000 coins (which it almost always does on the 9/6 version), then you have found a playable machine.

That's *playable*, not *beatable*. With perfect play, a 9/6 machine with a 4,000-coin payout for a royal will return about 99.5% of the money played through it, which is one of the lowest casino advantages that you will encounter. That .5% expected loss (50¢ for every $100 wagered) can often be recouped in the form of bonuses paid by casino slot clubs. These machines are called non-progressive, because the royal flush stays fixed at 4,000 coins.

The most popular alternative to the 9/6 machine is the 8-5 progressive. On these machines, the full house and flush (reference #1) pay 8 and 5 coins respectively, while the royal-flush payout (reference #2) continually climbs upward until a royal is hit. The royal-flush payout is usually displayed on a progressive meter (electronic reader board above the machine), and always as a dollar amount. When you've checked reference #1 and discovered that you have an 8/5 machine, the dollar amount on the progressive reader board becomes important. The jackpot usually begins at $1,000, and most that you encounter will be in the $1,100 to $1,700 range. Let the less informed play these machines. The jackpot is not high enough to compensate for the reduced payout for the full house and flush. You have a better gamble on the standard 9/6 machines.

But now the good news. As you may have already surmised, the progressive jackpot does, on occasion, climb high enough to warrant play. The critical dollar amount is $2,200. At this point, perfect video poker play will render a breakeven gamble with the casino. As the jackpot progresses higher, the meter becomes *positive* (the advantage switches to the player's side). As the jackpot approaches $3,000, even a fair approximation of proper playing strategy will provide you with a substantial edge. Your chances of hitting a royal do not increase; however, the payoff now makes the gamble (investment) worthwhile.

By using these guidelines and a little common sense, you can evaluate almost any standard Jacks or Better video poker machine (these rules are not applicable on *wild card* or *10's or Better* machines). For example, if you're assessing an 8/5 $1 machine, multiply the required $2,200 figure by four (four quarters equal one dollar). The progressive on the dollar machine must be at least $8,800 for you to have a fair gamble.

Better Options

There's not much to consider with the progressives; everything else being equal, the highest meter is best. The 9/6 schedules, however, sometimes come with little extras.

9/6 and more than 4,000-coins—4,000 coins for a royal flush is standard, so 4,700 coins or 4,795 coins is better. These are breakeven games. The reason for the odd number in the latter example is that 4,795 quarters equals $1,198.75. You are required to fill out a W-2G for tax purposes when you hit a video poker jackpot of $1,200 or more, so this figure avoids the reporting requirement.

9/6 progressives—A few Las Vegas casinos [recently Frontier and Westward Ho] have quarter 9/6 machines with a progressive jackpot. These games are almost always worth playing. A $1,200 jackpot on a 9/6 machine is breakeven.

4-coin 9/6—A few casinos offer 9/6 machines with a 4,000-coin royal flush that only require four coins. This pay schedule affords video poker experts a slight edge, along with 20% less risk (4 coins per play instead of 5). The Sands was the first to offer this for a short time in 1990, but the machines were quickly removed. The reduced risk associated with four-coin play makes this the beginner's best video poker option. [Four Queens and Sahara currently have a few of these machines.]

10/6 and 9/7—Vegas World became the first casino to break the 9/6 video poker barrier when they began offering quarter 10/6 and 9/7 Jacks or Better machines in early 1993. These machines return 100.7% (10/6) and 100.8% (9/7) with perfect play.

Other Coin Denominations

Up to this point, the discussion has pertained to 25¢ machines only, which are the most popular and plentiful. Machines that accept other coin denominations are also available.

Is It Loose?

This reader's letter is representative of the misconceptions many players harbor concerning the pay rates of video poker machines.

Do you determine a "loose" video poker machine strictly by the pay schedule? For instance, are all 9/6 machines looser than 8/5 machines. Or is it possible that a casino can have two 9/6 machines side by side but one pays off at a better rate than the other? I noticed that some machines seemed to be paying off quite well for a while, then had a dry spell. Is this common with all machines? Finally, someone suggested that if the machine was not paying off well, cash out all the credits and hand feed the money back in. Does this really make a difference?

The only determinant of a "loose" video poker machine is the pay schedule. In the long run, all 9/6 machines will pay back more than 8/5 machines, assuming the payoffs for all other winning hands are equal. By the same token, one 9/6 machine can be counted on to pay back the same percentage as another 9/6 machine. The "dry spell" is the result of normal probability. Regardless of the pay schedule, there will be periods when machines pay back far less (or far more) than what is normal. Unfortunately, there is no way to recognize and exploit these streaks. And, the only advantage to hand feeding a machine is that it results in fewer hands per hour, which means you are likely to lose a little less when playing machines that don't offer a positive expected return.

1¢—The only penny video poker machines in Las Vegas are in the "Copper Mine" at the Gold Spike, downtown.

5¢—Most nickel video poker machines are 7/5 or worse. If you keep your eyes open, you'll find an 8/5 progressive from time to time. The breakeven jackpot for the 8/5, nickel progressives is $440. A 9/6 nickel machine is a rarity, but you can find them downtown at the California and the Plaza. The Plaza machines pay 4,700 coins for the royal, which means they return 99.9%. If you play 500 hands an hour, your expected loss is a mere 12.5¢ per, which is about as cheap as the gambling tax gets.

$1—Same considerations as quarters; look for 9/6, 4,000-coin schedules, or 8/5s with progressives above $8,800. You'll sometimes find 9/6, 5,000-coin machines (Las Vegas Club, Lady Luck). They return 100.067% with perfect play.

$5, $25, $100—They're out there. The same selection criteria that apply to quarters and dollars also apply to these high-roller machines.

Bad Schedules

Someone once said, "There are no bad machines, only bad pay schedules." Beware of machines in bars, grocery stores, and out-of-the-way casinos. They may be 7/6s, 7/5s, 6/5s, or worse. How important is the difference? When maximum coins are played, each point in payout reduction costs about 1.1% in return. A 9/6 machine pays 99.5%, so an 8/5 pays about 2.2% less, or about 97.3%. (The sum of 9 and 6 is 15 and the sum of 8 and 5 is 13. The difference is two points.) A 6/5 machine (total of 11 points) pays only about 95.1%. If you play video poker rapidly, playing 7/5 and 6/5 schedules can accelerate losses by $20 to $30 per hour. It pays to be particular.

Another common practice in the out-of-the-way places is to offer an 8/5 return with a progressive jackpot above $2,200 on machines that require that you play more than 5 coins (i.e., 10 coins necessary to win the progressive jackpot). Don't waste your time and money on them.

Playing Strategy

Once you've determined the optimum machines to play, your next objective is to learn to play optimally. Most video poker enthusiasts play fairly well, based on their familiarity with the standard game of poker. Many plays are intuitively obvious. For example, few players would discard a pair to draw five new cards. Still, there are differences in these two forms of poker that are not obvious.

Common (and costly) Mistakes

Most improperly played video poker hands result in only slight losses in overall expectation. There are, however, some common mistakes that *do* have a substantial adverse effect on your results. It is essential that these costly errors be eliminated from your game.

Don't hold a kicker. A kicker is an unpaired high card held with a low pair, i.e., (5,5,A) is a pair of fives with an ace kicker. In standard poker, the value in occasionally holding kickers is the effect of misrepresenting your hand to opponents. In video poker, your opponent is the machine. You can't bluff the machine; therefore, kickers are valueless. Holding a kicker will only diminish the chances of improving your hand. In this example, you should hold only the pair of fives.

Don't draw to an inside straight (3,4,_6,7). Remember grandpa telling you this when the two of you had your first beer together? His advice is sound no matter what form of poker you are playing. Video poker players love to do it. Don't! Do draw to *open end* straights (_,3,4,5,6,_) which can be completed by a card on either end.

Don't hold three cards hoping to complete a straight or flush

(6♠,9♠,Q♠,_,_). The odds against drawing two perfect cards to fill these hands are prohibitive.

Don't play low two-card connectors. There seems to be some fascination with adjacent cards, especially when they're suited. Many players hold combinations like (8♦,9♦). As you'll see below, these combinations are not among those that we ought to keep.

Basic Guidelines

The following seven rules address the most common decisions you will encounter. You'll see others misplay these hands over and over again. Rule #3 seems to be particularly confounding.

1) Any pair, high or low, is preferable to a high card. Example: You have (2♥,A♠,2♣,6♦,Q♥). You keep (2♥,2♣).

2) If you don't have a pair, keep any card above a 10 up to a maximum of two (unless all are of the same suit). Example: You have (2♥,A♠,J♣,6♦,Q♥). Hold (J♣,Q♥). Interestingly, lower high cards are preferable because they allow more ways to make a straight. In this example, the ace was the least desirable of the three high cards.

3) Hands like (K♦,K♥,Q♥,10♥,4♥), (9♣,9♠,10♣,J♥,Q♦), or (7♣,7♦,Q♦,K♦,A♦) cause all sorts of problems, because you must choose between keeping high and low pairs, drawing two to a royal, or making a one-card draw to a straight or flush. When you have a choice between a combination of these five options, choose in this order:

- high pair
- two-card royal-flush draw
- one-card flush draw
- low pair
- one card straight draw (open end)

So in example #3 above, the first play is to keep the pair of kings.The second play is to keep the low pair. In the third play, you draw two to the (Q♦,K♦,A♦).

4) Don't break a pat straight or flush to draw one card to a straight flush.

5) Do break a pat straight or flush to draw one card to a royal flush.

6) If you have neither a pair, a high card, nor a one-card draw to a flush or open-end straight (3♦,4♠,5♣,7♣,9♥), draw five new cards.

Short-Coin

Lenny Frome, author of *America's National Game of Chance: Video Poker* and *Winning Strategies for Video Poker,* says: "The general public plays about 2% below the expected return for perfect play. The shortfall comes from improper decision-making and short-coin play." Short-coin play means playing less than the maximum number of coins the machine will accept. This is usually a mistake because of the non-symmetrical progression in royal-flush payouts. Look at the pay schedule printed on page 70, a standard 9/6 video poker machine. A royal flush with one coin played pays 250 coins. Two coins pays 500, three pay 750, and four pay 1,000. You would expect five coins to pay 1,250. But due to the non-symmetrical progression, the payout jumps all the way to 4,000 coins. Playing less than the maximum number of coins necessary to qualify for the royal flush jackpot costs you about 1.2%.

So much for monetary implications. Think of the psychological trauma of hitting a royal with, say, three quarters played for a $187.50 payoff, when five coins would have returned $1,000.

Perfect Play

The strategy guidelines presented here will go a long way toward improving your video poker play; however, they won't take you all the way to where you need to go. The phrase "perfect play" pops up again and again throughout this chapter. It's not meant to be taken literally—only a computer can play perfectly—but you can get close. How? There are two ways.

The first is to read one (or several) of the books on the market that specialize in video poker. The works of Wong, Frome, and Davis are outstanding. A directory of recommended books is presented in the Appendix.

The second is via computer. Computer learning is unparalleled as a method for honing gambling skills, and nowhere is it as effective a tool as it is in learning to play video poker. Of the several software programs on the market, my preference is *Stanford Wong Video Poker.* The computer deals hands; you play. The program monitors your hold and discard choices, alerts you to errors, then tells you the proper play. You simply can't help but learn. The program is so inexpensive ($30), and the improvement in play so dramatic, a player will recoup the purchase price with savings (or winnings) in less than a day of real video poker play.

Risk

You now know how to identify video poker machines that render a player advantage. You also have a basic strategy for playing them. But, there's one more important consideration. Video poker is a game of high variance, which means there is a great deal of financial risk associated with playing. Some of the realities are explained here. [I owe a debt of gratitude to Stanford Wong for allowing me to borrow so freely from his published work on this subject.]

In situations where a large payout is associated with a rare event (hitting a royal flush), an analysis of interim risk is important. According to Stanford

Wong's *Professional Video Poker*, the facts are these (relative to 25¢, 8/5 progressive machines):

- During periods of play when you do not hit the royal flush, you expect to lose at a rate of about 5.3%. Because of the speed at which video poker is played, your expected loss is about $33 per hour! That's the equivalent of playing an hour's worth of roulette at a rate of $20 per spin.
- On average, you will hit a royal approximately once per 33,000 hands, or about one time every 65 hours. Since you will usually lose money when you don't hit the royal, you must be prepared to lose during the majority of your playing sessions, even when you have the overall advantage.

Royal Flush—How Often?

8/5 Progressives—Proper strategy for positive progressives yields a royal flush, on average, about once in 33,000 hands.

9/6 Non-progressives—The 9/6 pay schedule cuts short-term risk in half, but proper strategy yields a royal flush only about once in 40,000 hands.

Do you understand what this means? You can lose a lot of money, possibly thousands of dollars, in pursuit of a royal flush on 25¢ machines. Still, video poker is a far better option than most standard slot machines. Let's take a realistic look at what you can expect in the way of risk during a few hours of play. Since risk ceases to be a concern if you are fortunate enough to hit the royal flush, we are interested in what happens when you don't hit the royal.

Let's assume that during your vacation you play five hours of video poker. For this example we'll use an 8/5 machine with the jackpot meter at $2,500. A jackpot at this level and proper play will yield a slight advantage over the casino. After five hours of play at an average of 500 hands per hour (relatively fast), your expected win is about $25 (plus any cash or benefits accrued via the casino's slot club). There's a slight catch, however. That $25 win assumes that you hit your fair share of royal flushes. Your fair share after five hours is 1/13 of one royal. You can't collect 1/13 of a royal without hitting the whole thing, so it's necessary to calculate wins and losses under the assumption that you will not realize that 1/13 of the jackpot ($192). Here's where the $33-per-hour approximation of expected loss comes in. Multiply $33 by five hours and you see that your expected loss is $165. Add that to the $25 you expected to win and you have $190 (that 1/13 of a royal).

But what if you have "bad luck?" How much can you lose if you have a really bad run? The mathematical measurement of the boundaries of what most of us call good and bad luck is called standard deviation. This measurement tells us that 19 out of 20 times, $400 will be enough to see you through a bad five-hour session. Similarly, about $300 should tide you through an equally bad three hours and a loss of $150 is as bad as things should get in one hour of play. Obviously, it can become painful. Of course, you always have the option of stopping before losses reach these high levels.

Remember, these are outer boundaries. Few losing sessions will be this bad, and it's possible that you will experience a favorable departure from the expected result (good luck) and actually profit slightly after one, three, or even five hours of royal-less play.

Risk is an important reality in video poker. Stanford Wong estimates that video poker professionals who chase the high progressives and play on an almost daily basis need a bankroll of $10,000 to withstand the possible negative fluctuations.

Reducing Risk

If this discussion has cooled your heels a little, you may want to consider one of the following measures to help preserve your gambling stake.

9/6 Machines

You lose at a rate of only about $15 per hour when you don't hit the royal on a 9/6 machine. Why? Because the interim payoffs are higher—you tend to hold cards that result in more frequent payoffs.

Fewer Coins

I've already explained that short-coin play is inadvisable; however, the strategy of betting only one coin has some merit because it reduces risk. The price you pay is the attending reduction in your overall return rate. Play either one or five coins; playing two, three, or four coins is non-optimal in the pursuit of either objective (risk reduction or highest possible expectation).

Lower Denominations

Rather than play less than maximum quarters, drop down to a nickel machine. A few casinos have 9/6 nickel video poker, and once in a while you can find 5¢ machines with progressive meters that are positive ($600 on nickel machines paying 6 for a full house and 5 for a flush). Along these same lines, playing five coins in a quarter machine is far superior to playing one coin in a dollar machine.

Slower Play

Another way to reduce risk is to play slowly, but again, the price for reducing short-term risk is a reduction in long-term expected win in situations where a progressive jackpot is high enough to provide one.

Making Money

With so many casinos competing for customers and play, profit opportunities arise often. Aside from finding and playing meters that have progressed beyond breakeven, there are three common methods for profiting from video poker (four if you count owning a machine).

New Schedules

There's no telling what will materialize. Arizona Charlie's recently offered a game called Royal Aces. This schedule paid only even money (instead of 2-1) for two pair, but overcompensated by paying $1,000 (instead of $31.25) for four aces. With proper play, these machines returned better than 102%. They lasted about two months before being pulled by the casino.

Promotions

Consistent money can be made playing promotions that casinos run for short periods of time to stimulate action. Here are three examples of promotions that were run in the spring of 1993.

• The Continental paid ladies double when they hit 4-of-a-kind on Tuesday nights. The bonus was worth about $20 per hour.

• The Sahara paid a $1,000 bonus when you hit a royal flush during the first 10 minutes of every hour (one day a week). That meant a $1,200 meter became $2,200, a $2,500 meter became $3,500, and so on during the bonus period. Players drank at the bar, watched the clock, and played like mad with a 3.5% advantage for ten minutes.

• The King 8 paid triple for four-of-a-kind kings or eights on 9/6 machines. The bonus raised the return from 99.5% to 101.3%. Because the bonus applied to dollar machines, the profit potential was better than $35 per hour.

To participate in promotions, you must know about them. The *Las Vegas Advisor* is a good source for this information.

Slot Clubs

Some savvy players do nothing but play a breakeven game of video poker, and accumulate tons of slot-club points that can be redeemed for cash, merchandise, free rooms, meals, and other amenities.

Finding High Meters

This letter comes from an *LVA* reader.

I spent five days in Las Vegas about a month ago mainly to play blackjack and video poker. I must have visited at least forty casinos trying to find a good progressive jackpot on the 8/5, 25¢ video poker machines, but the largest jackpot I could find was $2,400. Is this unusual or are jackpots of $3,000 or more rare? Maybe I was just unlucky in my search. Is there any shortcut to finding high jackpots?

The writer wasn't unlucky; jackpots over $3,000 are indeed rare these days. It's due to a combination of two factors: 1) the number of Las Vegas visitors knowledgeable about video poker is continuously increasing, which means more video poker players who are naturally drawn to the higher jackpots; and 2) professional teams jump on the high meters when they approach the $3,000 level. Both factors result in machines with the highest meters being played and hit more often. The only shortcut is frequenting the casinos and being on the lookout. Within the Las Vegas video-poker-playing community, there's an information conduit by which word of high meters (and good promotions) spreads. Consequently, the casual player can not beat the pros to the big meters on a consistent basis. Don't give up hope and quit looking, however. You will, on occasion, happen onto good situations before the word gets out.

Try These Machines

Here's a good bet that has panned out for the last few years. A bank of machines at the Sahara's Safari Bar consistently reaches the $2,200 breakeven level. I've spotted the meter above $3,000 on several occasions, and it's been as high as $4,000. Why? One reason is the machines have a "back-up meter" with a jackpot that progresses even though it isn't displayed. When a royal is hit, the back-up meter becomes the new jackpot and it is usually well beyond the standard $1,000 starting point. A second reason is the slow speed at which the machines operate. Video poker professionals and other knowledgeable players look for two things in choosing a machine: a positive expected return; and a machine that plays fast. The more hands they are able to play in positive situations, the more money their time is worth. These Sahara machines are older, so they play (and progress) too slowly for the pros to bother with, even at levels above $3,000. The result is the perfect tourist video poker opportunity. Take a look at these machines. The bartenders will offer you a free drink when you buy in for any amount, and you can join the Sahara's slot club to qualify for additional bonuses.

Assuming you find a positive meter at the Sahara (or somewhere else), and are able to play video poker with a jackpot above $2,200, what is your time worth in terms of expected monetary return?

Your expected return is a product of three factors:

- Your skill level.
- Your speed level.
- The machine's pay schedule, including the amount of any progressive jackpots.

Assuming you've taken steps to raise your skill level, the two variables in the equation are the amount of the royal-flush payoff and the number of hands you are able to play per hour. This *Speed Chart* lists expected return per hour based on these two factors. Example: You find a machine with the royal flush meter at $3,000 and you play about 450 hands per hour. Your expected profit is $11.67 per hour (arrow).

DOLLAR AMOUNT OF ROYAL FLUSH JACKPOT (25¢, 8/5)

HANDS PER HOUR	$1700	$2000	$2200	$2500	$3000	$3500	$4000	$5000
100	($1.42)	($0.51)	$0.10	$1.03	$2.59	$4.17	$5.75	$8.94
150	($2.13)	($0.77)	$0.15	$1.54	$3.89	$6.25	$8.63	$13.41
200	($2.85)	($1.02)	$0.21	$2.06	$5.19	$8.34	$11.50	$17.88
250	($3.56)	($1.28)	$0.26	$2.57	$6.48	$10.42	$14.38	$22.35
300	($4.27)	($1.53)	$0.31	$3.09	$7.78	$12.51	$17.25	$26.82
350	($4.98)	($1.79)	$0.36	$3.60	$9.07	$14.59	$20.13	$31.29
400	($5.69)	($2.04)	$0.41	$4.12	$10.37	$16.68	$23.00	$35.76
450	($6.40)	($2.30)	$0.46	$4.63	➡$11.67	$18.76	$25.88	$40.23
500	($7.11)	($2.55)	$0.51	$5.14	$12.96	$20.84	$28.75	$44.70
550	($7.82)	($2.81)	$0.56	$5.66	$14.26	$22.93	$31.63	$49.17
600	($8.54)	($3.06)	$0.62	$6.17	$15.56	$25.01	$34.50	$53.64
650	($9.25)	($3.32)	$0.67	$6.69	$16.85	$27.10	$37.38	$58.11
700	($9.96)	($3.57)	$0.72	$7.20	$18.15	$29.18	$40.25	$62.58
750	($10.67)	($3.83)	$0.77	$7.72	$19.44	$31.27	$43.13	$67.05
1000	($14.23)	($5.10)	$1.03	$10.29	$25.93	$41.69	$57.50	$89.40

You can glean a great deal of information from the chart. Something that jumps out right away is the fact that the magic $2,200 mark is nothing to write home about (boxed column). Even if you play a relatively fast 500 hands per hour, you are making 51¢ for your effort. And that assumes you don't make any mistakes. Good playing opportunities arise in the $3,000-$3,500 range. At that level, even if you aren't perfect, you are still playing with an edge. It's also interesting to note how much you lose on machines with jackpots less than $2,200. You should never play 8/5 machines with less than a $2,000 jackpot. The standard 9/6, 4,000-coin, non-progressive machines are better.

One more important point. This is a table of long-term expectation. The per-hour total is not a "wage" that you can count on collecting after every hour of play. It is an average that includes the royal-flush jackpot. Since it will take you an average of 65-80 hours of play to hit the royal, you will lose money during most playing sessions despite having an advantage. As you can see, video poker is a tough racket.

Video Poker Notes

Poor Players Hit More Royals

Are you tired of hearing your friends tell you about all the royals that they've hit? Can they really be that lucky? Yes and no. They probably hit more royals than you, but they also lose more money. Poor players tend to make more draws that have a chance to result in a royal flush. By doing this they may increase their frequency of hitting by as much as 30%, but it costs them dearly in terms of money lost between royals. This is a common scenario with casino workers who play a lot after work, on weekends, etc. They play for the big win, lose money consistently, but get enough positive reinforcement from the increased royal-flush frequency to keep them

L.V. VP #1

This letter from a Las Vegas Advisor subscriber describes the state of the video poker world outside of Las Vegas.

Just thought you guys might be interested in an evaluation of the three gambling ships now docked off Biloxi, Mississippi. The President is physically the nicest, but for video poker players, the toughest to beat: 7/5 and 6/5 machines right next to one another, alternately. The Isle of Capri has machines with entirely different pay schedules: no payoff for any pairs, and two pair pays 2-1. The Biloxi Belle has regular 8/5 machines throughout. It's the only ship I'd return to.

The two-pair machines are the worst of all, returning only 93.45% with perfect play. They're virtually extinct in Las Vegas, though you'll find plenty of them in Atlantic City and upstart areas like the riverboats. Another interesting observation is that 7/5 and 6/5 machines were arranged side by side. It's amazing, but people will actually play the lower-paying machines, oblivious to the better option only an arm's length away.

coming back. Selectivity of memory is the powerful force that makes them believe they are winning overall. Meanwhile, paychecks continue to disappear. Diligent record-keeping is an effective cure for this malady.

Cards Line Up Behind

Don't agonize over situations like this: You hold (7♠, J♥, Q♥, K♥, 7♣). You discard (7♠, 7♣) and draw (7♥, 7♦). Did you cost yourself four sevens? No. When the machine deals your initial five cards it also deals five cards behind the originals. If you had kept the pair of sevens, the two other sevens would not have shown.

Not Your Jackpot

Here's another tidbit that will help preserve your sanity. If someone sits down at the machine you were about to play (or have just left) and proceeds to hit the royal faster than you can say "you rotten son-of-a...," you have no cause to be angry. It's highly unlikely that you would have hit that royal flush had you been playing instead of them. Video poker machines contain a random number generator (RNG) that runs continuously at a very high rate of speed. The RNG "stops" (to choose the cards you are dealt) when you perform a specific function, i.e., inserting the fifth coin. You would have had to stop the RNG at precisely the same moment that it was stopped by the other player to get that same royal-flush result.

Joker Poker and Deuces Wild

Players love wild-card machines because there are more exotic ways

FULL PAY MACHINES
(PAYOFFS PER COIN PLAYED)

Joker Poker (101%)		Deuces Wild (101.1%)	
Royal no Joker	940	Royal no Deuces	940
5 of a Kind	200	4 Deuces	200
Royal with Joker	100	Royal with Deuces	25
Straight Flush	50	5 of a Kind	15
4 of a Kind	20	Straight Flush	9
Full House	7	4 of a Kind	5
Flush	5	Full House	3
Straight	3	Flush	2
3 of a Kind	2	Straight	2
2 Pair	1	3 of a Kind	1
Kings or better	1		

Per coin payoff corresponding to five coins played and 4,700-coin royal.

to win. Casinos love wild-card machines because proper play is not intuitively obvious and players make a lot of mistakes. Joker Poker and Deuces Wild are video poker versions that are very different from Jacks or Better. Attempting to play them based on the information presented in this chapter is unwise. The idea of beginning with the best pay schedule still applies, however. "Full pay" is a term made popular by video-poker expert, Lenny Frome. It refers to the best pay schedules for each popular version of video poker. The chart displays the Las Vegas full-pay schedules for Jokers and Deuces.

As you can see from the return percentages, there's a case for learning to play these games. Here, more than ever, the *Stanford Wong Video Poker* software is the most efficient route to proficiency. Casinos that have a reputation for offering the best wild-card pay schedules (especially for Jokers) are: Palace Station, Four Queens, Las Vegas Club, Golden Gate, and El Cortez.

5

BLACKJACK

Which game is best for the player? Ask anyone with even a mild interest in gambling and they will probably tell you, "Blackjack." After all, everyone knows that "playing the basics" will get you even with the casino. But what exactly are the basics? Ask 100 players and you'll probably get 100 different answers, which suggests that a lot of people are playing blackjack in a less than optimal manner. You see, for a given set of rules and number of decks, there is one and only one correct way to play any hand versus each of the 13 possible dealer up cards. These plays are delineated in a set of rules known as *basic strategy*. How important is basic strategy? It provides the means to reduce, and in some cases eliminate, the casino's advantage at blackjack.

The level to which basic strategy reduces the house edge depends on the rules and number of decks being used in the game. In the following list of popular Las Vegas blackjack games, the figure in parentheses is the casino advantage versus a basic-strategy player: single deck Strip (0%), single deck downtown (.2%), 2 decks Strip (.3%), 2 decks downtown (.5%), 4 and 6 decks Strip (.5%), 4 decks downtown (.7%), 6 decks downtown (.8%). The difference betweenStrip and downtown games dealing the same number of decks is that most Strip casinos stand on soft 17 (i.e., A,6) while the majority of downtown casinos hit this total. Hitting soft 17 adds an additional .2% to the casino's edge.

While the casino's advantage for slots and other table games runs anywhere from 1.5%-25%, you can get it down to below 1% with blackjack basic strategy. In the best games (single deck, dealer stands on soft 17), you can actually play even with the house. Only a few casinos—Circus Circus, Jerry's Nugget, and Frontier among them—still deal this game.

You must play basic strategy perfectly. An approximation won't do, as you'll see.

The Play of the Public

In 1987, Peter Griffin, author of *The Theory of Blackjack* (Huntington Press, 1988), presented the paper *Mathematical Expectation for the Public's Play in Casino Blackjack* at the Seventh National Conference On Gambling and Risk Taking. [This study was republished in Griffin's *Extra Stuff* (Huntington Press, 1991).] In his study, Griffin observed the play of 11,000 hands of blackjack in Las Vegas, northern Nevada, and Atlantic City. He recorded each departure from basic strategy, calculated the cost of each mistake, and determined that the average player plays at a losing rate that is about 1.4% higher than the basic strategy figures cited above. This means that many blackjack players who believe they are getting the best gamble possible playing their own approximation of basic strategy would actually lose less playing baccarat (1.25% casino advantage) or craps (1.41% on pass or don't pass).

Basic Strategy

If the prospect of breaking even does not offer you sufficient monetary inducement to take the time to learn basic strategy, then I will appeal to your ego. I would conservatively estimate that less than one in every 100 players plays basic strategy perfectly. By learning to do so, you will place yourself in the 99th percentile among all of the world's players.

Though the complete basic strategy should eventually be mastered, you can get by with an abbreviated version. The recommendations in this short version are presented in the order that you will be confronted with the decisions, not in the order of their importance. Rules #3 and #4 are by far the most important. A *soft* 17 is a total containing an ace, i.e., (A,6) or (A,2,4).

Abbreviated Basic Strategy

1) Always split eights and aces.
2) Double 10 & 11 against dealer's 2-9.
3) You hold 12-16; dealer shows 2-6—STAND
4) You hold 12-16; dealer shows 7,8,9,T,A—HIT
5) Stand on 17-21, except always hit on soft 17.
6) Never take insurance.

By adhering to the six rules in this simple strategy, a player can cut the casino's advantage at 21 to between 1% and 2%. To reduce that advantage even further, you must learn the entire basic strategy. Study the tables on the next page. They address every possible situation you will face in a

COMPLETE BASIC STRATEGY FOR SINGLE AND MULTIPLE DECK BLACKJACK

HIT-STAND

	2	3	4	5	6	7	8	9	T	A
12	H	H	S	S	S	H	H	H	H	H
13	S	S	S	S	S	H	H	H	H	H
14	S	S	S	S	S	H	H	H	H	H
15	S	S	S	S	S	H	H	H	H	H
16	S	S	S	S	S	H	H	H	H	H
17	S	S	S	S	S	S	S	S	S	S

HARD DOUBLE

	2	3	4	5	6	7	8	9	T	A
11	D	D	D	D	D	D	D	D	D	D/H
10	D	D	D	D	D	D	D	D	H	H
9	D/H	D	D	D	D	H	H	H	H	H
8	H	H	H	D/H	D/H	H	H	H	H	H

SOFT DOUBLE

	2	3	4	5	6	7	8	9	T	A
A9	ALWAYS STAND									
A8		STAND			D/S		STAND			
A7	S	D	D	D	D	S	S	H	H	S*/H
A6	D/H	D	D	D	D	H	H	H	H	H
A5	H	H	D	D	D	H	H	H	H	H
A4	H	H	D	D	D	H	H	H	H	H
A3	H	H	D/H	D	D	H	H	H	H	H
A2	H	H	D/H	D	D	H	H	H	H	H

SPLIT PAIRS

	2	3	4	5	6	7	8	9	T	A
22	H	P/H	P	P	P	P	H	H	H	H
33	H	H	P	P	P	P	H	H	H	H
44	NEVER SPLIT									
55	NEVER SPLIT									
66	P/H	P	P	P	P	H	H	H	H	H
77	P	P	P	P	P	P	H	H	S/H	H
88	ALWAYS SPLIT									
99	P	P	P	P	P	S	P	P	S	S
TT	NEVER SPLIT									
AA	ALWAYS SPLIT									

NEVER TAKE INSURANCE

* Hit (A,7) vs. ace if dealer hits soft 17.

KEY: H= Hit S=Stand P=Split Pair D=Double Down

blackjack game. When you've learned to play basic strategy perfectly, you will possess the tools necessary to play even with the casino in the single deck games on the Las Vegas Strip, and at only about a .5% disadvantage in most multiple-deck games (about six times lower than your disadvantage on the "loosest" $1 slot machines).

Keep in mind that basic strategy is not someone's subjective impression of how each hand should be played, but rather a mathematically optimal, computer-derived strategy for playing 21. It is completely accurate and must be followed to the letter. Every time you deviate from basic strategy, you cost yourself money.

It will take between four and eight hours of study to learn the complete basic strategy. The combinations down the left hand side of the chart represent your hand. The numbers across the top represent the dealer's up card. Example: You hold (A,4) and the dealer shows a 6, your play is to double down. Where there is a slash (i.e., D/H), the first play is versus a single deck and the second is versus multiple decks. The most important tables are Hit-Stand and Hard Double. They are also easiest to learn.

Learning Basic Strategy

Most players will never learn to play basic strategy perfectly because they can't (or won't) spend the 6-8 hours of serious study that is necessary to memorize this chart. It *can* be tedious. A better alternative is computer learning. A computer lets you practice by actually playing. As you play against computer-generated hands, the program alerts you to errors as you make them. Since it's more like playing a game than doing a chore, you learn faster and more completely. Stanford Wong's *Blackjack Analyzer* is the best software on the market for this purpose, and it can be purchased for less than $30.

Considerations for Beginners

Following are some comments relative to general play and some tips for beginners.

Fewer Decks are Preferable

Try to play in games employing the least number of decks. The casino advantage lessens slightly as the number of decks drops. But more importantly, fewer decks usually means more shuffling. This is an important plus for beginners. Most novices do not play basic strategy perfectly, and Strip single deck games are rare. This means you will usually be playing at a disadvantage. More shuffling means fewer hands played and less exposure to the house edge.

Play Crowded Tables

Crowded tables mean fewer hands per person per hour. Play with friends or squeeze onto crowded tables. It's more fun and less costly.

Which Seat

This is unimportant. Some players think that you can better "control" the game by playing *third base* (the last seat to act). How? You're not psychic. You don't know which card will be next out of the deck. Playing third base will not allow you to exert any special control over the outcome of the hand. If anything, it's best to avoid the last seat. Other players often blame the third-base player when things don't go right. Who needs the aggravation?

The Other Players

Many blackjack players worry about the skill of other players at their table. This is also unimportant. Bad players who make bad plays will help you as often as they hurt you. Your hand is independent of theirs and, in the long run, unaffected by their mistakes.

Improving Your Chances

There are a few tricky methods that you can use to improve overall results; this one has to do with cutting the deck. When the dealer offers the deck for a cut, it is often possible to catch a glimpse of the bottom card. The value of this card is important to you, especially if you are playing a single-deck game. Without getting into lengthy explanations, I can tell you that it is to the player's advantage to have a high ratio of high cards (9s, 10s and aces) in the deck. If you spot a high card on the bottom, cut the deck low to ensure that the card will be dealt some time during the round. Cutting an ace into play is particularly advantageous. Conversely, it is to the casino's advantage to have more low cards in the deck (2-7). If you see a low card on the bottom, cut the deck high so the low card will not be dealt. You have effectively removed a low card from play. Remember: high card, cut low. Low card, cut high. High-Low. Low-High. Easy.

You can take this even further by watching for the bottom card after the cut and the *burn* card (the card placed in the discard tray prior to the dealing of the first round). These cards are also gone from that round. The effect of removing one low card from a single deck game is enough to give you a minute advantage on the ensuing hand. If you are fortunate enough to see two low cards prior to the deal of a single deck, you have a nice opportunity to raise your bet. Two low cards seen in a double deck will usually provide you with about an even gamble. In four decks or more, this approach will not produce an edge. Don't get too excited; this strategy will not make you a casino killer. But every little bit helps.

Places to Begin

Beginners are understandably reluctant to sit down the first time. Your best bet is to play with a friend, and choose a low-limit game where you are less likely to run into players gambling for high stakes.

Low Limits

Blackjack games that allow minimum bets of less than $5 are everywhere. Even though recent years have seen a drastic drop in the number of casinos dealing $1 blackjack, you can still find this minimum at a table or two in about 15 casinos, and downtown casinos are most likely to deal the dollar game. Two- and three- dollar minimums are always easy to find, even on the Strip. The Reel Deal Casino was the last to deal 50¢ blackjack during its brief tenure in 1992.

Fun Pits

Bally's was the first to create a "Fun Pit," a separate area in the casino where blackjack games have low limits and the attitude of dealers and pit bosses is less serious. Harrah's followed with their "Party Pit." The concept is great, and these places are perfect for beginners, except for one drawback—poor rules. Dealers hit soft 17 (in the Fun Pit only) in both casinos, and there are doubling restrictions at Bally's. This means that players give up more to play here. Still, since the jovial atmosphere makes for a slower game, it turns out to be a fair trade.

Beginner's Tables

A few casinos are finally installing beginner's tables where you play real money for small stakes ($2-$5 limits) and are assisted by a patient dealer whose job it is to help you learn the game. The Las Vegas Hilton ("Learning Center") and the Tropicana both have beginner's tables.

Games and Conditions

Single Decks

Since fewer decks are better, single decks are obviously best. Single-deck blackjack is still very common in Las Vegas. Depending on the competitive climate, you'll find between 15 and 30 casinos dealing the game. Casinos that have a long history of dealing at least one single-deck game at all times are: Circus Circus, Frontier, Slots A Fun, Vegas World, El Cortez, Fitzgerald's, Four Queens, Golden Gate, Golden Nugget, Horseshoe, and Jerry's Nugget. As already mentioned, single decks on the Strip are best.

The Best Game

Occasionally, casinos offer blackjack games that are beatable with a knowledge of basic strategy alone. The most common combination of rules that provide a player edge is: single deck, dealer stands on soft 17, and double down allowed after splitting. With these rules, the player has a .1% advantage. This edge is very small. A $5 bettor has an expected return of about 30¢ an hour with perfect play. This game usually surfaces at one or two casinos at a time. For the past two years it's been dealt at the Frontier.

PAIR SPLITTING VS. SINGLE AND MULTIPLE DECKS (DOUBLE AFTER SPLIT ALLOWED)

		Single	Multiple
2,2	split vs. dealer's	2-7	2-7
3,3	split vs. dealer's	2-8	2-7
4,4	split vs. dealers	4-6	5&6
5,5	Never Split		
6,6	split vs. dealer's	2-7	2-6
7,7	split vs. dealer's	2-8	2-7
8,8	Always Split		
9,9	split vs. dealer's	2-9 (except 7)	
T,T	Never Split		
A,A	Always Split		

Double Exposure

In this game, both of the dealers cards are dealt face up. In exchange for being allowed to see the dealer's hole card, you must make other concessions, the most damaging of which is losing ties (ties neither win nor lose normally). The playing strategy for Double Exposure is vastly different from that employed in a standard blackjack game. This game should be avoided.

Las Vegas Club

The Las Vegas Club advertises "the most liberal blackjack rules in the world": double down any time, including after splits; double down even after taking one or more hit cards; unlimited splits, including aces; late surrender; six cards without going over 21 is an automatic winner. Should you rush to play this game? Not really. One reason is the compensating unfavorable rules in this game. The Las Vegas Club uses six decks and dealers hit soft 17, which works out to a casino advantage of .1% when the player employs perfect basic strategy for all of the exotic options. Since few players have the expertise to do this, the casino's advantage is greater still.

Multiple Action Blackjack

Multiple Action Blackjack (developed by the Four Queens) is one of the most interesting blackjack variations to come around in years. The game is played in the same way as traditional 21, except players can wager on up to three spots that are arranged vertically in front of each betting position. Once the wagers are set, play commences as follows. The player gets two cards. The dealer takes an up card, but not a hole card. The player plays his hand (making decisions based on the card the dealer is showing). The dealer then deals himself a hole card and plays his hand according to the usual dealer hit/stand rules. The difference in this game is that the dealer's final result affects only the player's first wager. After winning, losing, or tying that hand, the dealer discards all but his original up card. He then takes a new hole card, and plays the hand again with the new result affecting the second wager. He then takes a third hole card to play vs. the third wager. This game represents a brilliant innovation on the part of the casinos for two reasons. First, it speeds up the game, allowing the house to book more action. Second, it entices players to misplay hands. If the player goes over 21, he loses all three bets automatically. Players afraid of this "triple bust" are tempted to stand with stiff totals (12-16) vs. dealer high cards (7-ace), which is a costly error. The fact that you are playing against three separate hole cards does not alter the proper strategy. Basic strategy is the same whether you encounter decisions one at a time, or three at a time as you do in Multiple Action.

Techno Gadgetry

Technology is beginning to creep into the blackjack picture. Here are two recent developments.

Arizona Charlie's was the first to experiment with a prism device built into the table to check beneath tens for dealer naturals. The device is called MAXTime. When the dealer gets a ten up, he simply slides the cards over MAXTime, and through a small window is able to view the corner of the hole card. Aces are marked with the letter "A" in all four corners. If there's an ace in the hole, the viewing window displays the A. If no ace, the window displays plain white space. Dealers know immediately if they have a natural, but have no additional information concerning hole cards that are not aces. This method of checking the hole card is now being used in several casinos.

Shuffle Master is the name of a shuffling machine that deals a single deck out of a shoe. The system uses two separate decks, which are dealt one at a time and never intermingled. After mechanically shuffling one deck of cards, the machine loads the deck into a mini-shoe for dealing. While the dealer deals the first deck (from the shoe), the second is reshuffled by the machine. It's a fast and efficient process that does not alter the game's odds in any way. Shuffle Master is already being used to speed up pai gow poker, and it may soon impact on the Atlantic City blackjack scene. Most people don't realize that the primary reason there are no single decks in Atlantic City is because "hand held" games are prohibited. The Shuffle Master-dealt single deck is not hand held. This may be what Atlantic City casinos and blackjack players have been waiting for.

Advanced Play

Learning to play blackjack is like learning to lift weights. Athletes who take up weight training find that their early progress is rapid. That is, the amount of weight they can lift increases significantly right away. However, they later find that more and more work is required to make smaller and smaller gains. Such is the case with blackjack play. The gains from learning basic strategy are substantial, but progressing beyond this stage into the world of card counting and professional-level play requires much more study in return for improvements that come much slower and in proportionately smaller doses. The information presented in this chapter is all you need to realize that first stage of significant improvement. For those who are interested in learning more, there are many good (and bad) books, newsletters, and software programs on the market. See the Appendix for a directory of the best products.

6

SLOT MACHINES

Every time the papers announce another million-dollar slot jackpot, it lights the fires of slot players everywhere. Characteristically similar to the lottery (unintimidating, easily accessible, possibility of large payoffs), slot machines are the number-one revenue producers in Las Vegas casinos, earning more than 60% of the win. How? Simple. Slots beat players regularly. Still, casino data and surveys show that gamblers love slots. They love the clanking of the coins, the trance-like state that play induces, and the brilliantly conceived Pavlovian reinforcement that the machines are programmed to dispense.

Hints

If you must play slot machines, here are a few tips to assist you.

• The casino edge is lower when you play the larger-denomination-coin machines, but you also have a greater expected loss. This is a difficult concept to grasp. Extrapolating from Nevada's most recent monthly revenue statistics, we find that 1¢ slots win about 12% of the money played through them, 5¢ slots win 9%, 25¢ slots win 7.5%, and $1 slots win 4.5%. If maximizing your chances of leaving a winner is your top priority, then higher denomination machines are your best bet. But again, you stand to lose more money at the higher limits.

Denom.	Hold %	Per Coin Win	Per Hour Loss
1¢	12.0%	.12¢	$ 1.08
5¢	9.0%	.45¢	$ 4.05
25¢	7.5%	1.87¢	$16.87
$1	4.5%	4.50¢	$40.50

• The casino edge is (usually) lower when you play maximum coins, but to what degree is not as easily definable as it is in video poker. The only advice I feel comfortable giving here is for you to let your personality and bankroll objectives guide you. If you're prepared to lose your whole gambling allotment for a shot at the big money, then you should certainly do all you can to lower the casino advantage, which means play maximum coins.

• Machines do not become "due." Don't waste hours staking out a machine so you can pounce when you feel it's ready to pay.

• Machines with very large jackpots have a greater *drain*, which is the expected loss when you don't hit the top prize.

• Machines with lower jackpots pay back small amounts more frequently. Though the long-term return equals that of the large jackpot machines, you usually get more play for your money when the top jackpot is smaller.

• If you play dollars or quarters, join casino slot clubs when available. A portion of the money you lose can be recouped through club benefits.

Playing Strategy

A winning slot-playing strategy doesn't exist. Regardless of what you read or are told, and with the obscure exception of being able to identify and finance an attack on a positive progressive slot meter, there simply is no way to win playing the one-armed *bandits*.

Penny Slots

You can still find them at Little Caesars and Silver City on the Strip, and the Plaza, Western, and Gold Spike downtown. Penny slots are set to win between 10% and 15% of your money. Not too good; but at only 3-5¢ a pull, it will take about eight hours to lose a $25 stake. Can you win? It's unlikely, although one person hit for a world-record $95,172.50 on the penny progressives at the Western in 1986.

Other Slot Records

Nickels—$864,554, hit at the Stardust, 1/93, on a Nevada Nickels progressive slot.

Quarters—$2,472,819.04, hit at Bally's, 6/93, on a Quartermania progressive slot.

Dollars—$9,346,876.45, hit at Harrah's Reno, 7/92, on Megabucks.

Linked Systems

Except for the pennies, every record for slot jackpots was set on linked progressives. Several years ago, a slot manufacturer (IGT) created the Megabucks system, which linked slot machines across the state of Nevada to create large jackpots. While these jackpots are the highest around, you'll pay dearly to play for them. The casino hold on Megabucks is 10.2%, and Megabucks jackpots are paid in installments over 20 years. No wonder several casino companies with multiple properties have followed suit and introduced their own linked systems.

Where to Play

These two letters address the great mystery of where to play, and where not to.

There are some places you should tell your readers to avoid. We crossed the street in front of this place as we were going for ice cream. They announced "Double Jackpot Time!" so we went in. All the workers kept yelling at me, "Play this machine!" I gave the girl a $50 bill and asked for $20 in tokens. She gave me the whole $50 in tokens. She kept saying, "Play this one! Play this one!" It was ridiculous. I think these places are ripping off the public and giving downtown a bad name.

Slot-machine-only casinos like a few of the little clubs downtown must work hard to get customers in the door. They have to work even harder to make them stay. Change girls who tout machines are often hoping you will get lucky, hit a jackpot, and tip them. Have you heard the story about the boy outside the racetrack who touted each horse in a seven horse race to seven different people? One of the horses had to win.

Is there an "official" or "unofficial" best-slots place in Las Vegas?

There are neither official nor unofficial best-slot places. Nevada does not publish slot statistics by individual casino, so there is no way to know exactly who's paying back what. But even if the stats were available, there

---

What's That Smell?

They've done it with neon and flashing lights, with bells and sirens, with jangling coins, cocktail-waitress uniforms, even oxygen. Now they're doing it with smell. A year-long study at the Las Vegas Hilton conducted by the Smell and Taste Research Foundation in Chicago concludes that ventilating a certain mild aroma, which is vaguely noticeable, near slot machines increased player spending by up to 45%.

---

would be little difference in return from place to place *of similar size.* As a group, larger casinos pay better than smaller ones because they work on greater volume. A uniformity in payout percentage among casinos of like size can be verified in Atlantic City because individual casino statistics are published there. In Nevada, you should choose the large casino with the best slot club. Another indicator is a casino's video poker machines. If these machines, whose return percentages *can* be calculated, are good, it's reasonable to assume that their slots will also be "liberal." Again, bigger is definitely better here. Don't fall for the myth that the smaller Mom & Pop joints are looser. It's economically impossible.

7

TOURNAMENTS

Tournament play is a very specialized area of gambling in which your primary adversary is not the casino, but rather the other tournament players. The major blackjack and crap tournaments with large entry fees and huge top prizes are contested by a group of "tournament junkies" who have honed their skills over several years of participation. Though anyone can get lucky and win a major tournament (especially a blackjack tournament), novices are ill-advised to risk large sums of money in these skill-oriented situations where they are likely to be outgunned. Slot tournaments, on the other hand, are suitable for anyone who can afford the price of entry.

Slot Tournaments

When they first became popular in the mid- to late-'80s, the majority of casino slot tournaments could only be described as horrible rip-offs. The public tolerated this condition because they had not yet learned how to assess a tournament's value. Most players placed significance on the wrong aspects of the tournaments' prize structure; specifically, they were concerned with what percentage of the field would win a prize or how many ways there were to win. Casinos recognized this and structured tournaments that paid small prizes to as many as four out of five contestants. Tiny prizes were given for session winners, daily winners, last place finishers, closest to the average, etc. Lost in all of this was the most important consideration: *the percentage of the total amount collected in entry fees that is returned in the form of prize money.* This entry fee/prize-money relationship is often referred to as *tournament equity.* Today, the situation has improved dramatically. Competition has forced casinos to return larger portions of the entry fees. Many pay back everything. You can use equity comparisons to identify value in slot tournaments. Here's how.

The Concept of Equity

What makes the equity consideration so important? Mainly, it's the fact that everything else is equal. All tournament competitors play the same number of rounds, they have the same number of handle pulls or credits, and machines are assigned randomly. Unless there is a time consideration, where some will get more spins, everyone has an equal chance of winning. This is the nice thing about slot tournaments. They're fair—unless the casino raids the prize pool.

Let's reduce the situation to its simplest terms.

Imagine there are only two competitors, you and I. We each pay a $10 entry fee, then play a one-round tournament. From the $20 in the prize pool, the winner will be paid $15 and the loser will be paid $5. If we play two tournaments, each of us should win once ($15 prize) and lose once ($5 prize). After two tournaments, we each expect to have won $20 in total prize money ($15 + $5), which is the same amount we've spent in entry fees (2 x $10). This is an even-equity tournament.

Now let's say a third person enters the tournament. At the same $10 per-person entry fee, we now have $30 in the prize pool. It will be paid as follows: 1st place—$15; 2nd place—$10; 3rd place—$5. What should happen? After three tournaments, each of us will have won once (+$15), taken second once (+$10), and taken third once (+$5). That's $30 total per player, the amount of three $10 entry fees.

Are you beginning to get it? It works the same for a tournament with 200 competitors that pays 100 places. After 200 games, each player expects to land one time in each of the 200 possible finishing positions, and ultimately break even. Of course, in an example this large it is unlikely that it will work out exactly this way. Still, this is the proper way to analyze the gamble.

Now let's go back to our two-player tournament. What if the casino decides to keep some of the money we've put up in entry fees? Perhaps they take out $5 for "costs." Obviously, the prize pool has been reduced. It now contains only $15, and no matter how they decide to award the money, after two tournaments we each expect to win a total of $15. But remember, we've paid $20 each in entry fees. This is a negative-equity tournament (15/20 = a 75% return). The bottom line is: both you and I will lose money over the long run. What's more, we will lose at a rate equal to the percentage taken out by the casino multiplied by how much we spend in entry fees. In this example, that's 25% of our $20 in total entry fees, or $5. If we were to play this game 100 times, we would end up losing 100 x $10 x 25%, which is $250.

Negative equity is what makes state lotteries such a horrible gamble. Approximately 50% of the entry fees (the total paid by consumers for lottery tickets) is taken out for administration, advertising, and whatever's left over for funding the cause for which the lottery has been created. Your expected loss when playing most state lotteries is 50% multiplied by the amount you spend on tickets.

By the way, "prizes" means *prize money*. Casino tournament directors often argue that the value of prizes that are distributed to all entrants (T-shirts, radios, etc.) should be included in the calculation of total money returned. I don't agree. Give me the money and I'll buy my own merchandise. John Ascuaga's Nugget in Sparks (Reno area) has done this in the past. Rather than buy a gift for you, they rebate $25 of your entry fee in casino chips. Players who want a souvenir Nugget T-shirt can purchase it in the gift shop and still have money left over.

Now that you understand the impact of equity on participants in a slot tournament, you can see how the percentage returned becomes progressively more important as entry fees get higher. If you pay a $1,000 entry fee to play a 75% equity tournament, you can only expect a $750 return. You must now decide if you can recoup that $250 expected loss via savings on rooms, meals, shows, and other amenities you receive for entering the tournament.

Do It Yourself

To determine a tournament's return percentage, you need to know three things: the sum of all the prize money, the number of players the prize structure is based on, and the entry fee. All this information is readily available on the flyers with which casinos advertise their tournaments. The following schedule is a real example from a tournament at the Sahara:

Entry Fee: $99

1st	$10,000	
2nd	5,000	
3rd	1,600	
4th	625	
5th	400	
6th-25th	125	($2,500)
26th-60th	100	($3,500)

Based on 253 entrants

Follow this method to calculate the return percentage.

1) Add the total of all prizes: $23,625.

2) Multiply the entry fee by the number of entrants the prize structure is based on: $99 X 253 = $25,047.

3) Divide the amount returned by the amount taken in to get the return percentage: 23,625/25,047 = 94%.

Now follow this method to calculate your expected loss.
1) Find the return percentage by the method shown above.
2) Multiply the entry fee by the return percentage. The result is the amount you can expect to "win."
3) Subtract that figure from the entry fee. This will be your expected loss for playing the tournament.

Let's put it all together. We see that the entry fee is $99 and that the return percentage is 94%. The equation as specified in step two is: $99 x .94 = $93.06. $93 is our expected win, or more accurately, the expected return on our investment. Step three tells us to subtract this amount from the entry fee: $99 - $93 = $6. We've now determined that it will cost us an average of $6 to participate in this slot tournament.

Tournament analysis can get very complicated, as pay schedules are usually not as straightforward as this example (there are often session prizes and other prize distributions that must be factored in), but the method outlined here will work after all the variables are defined.

Twice as Nice

On rare occasions, a tournament will return more than 100%. In 1991, Harrah's held a mini-slot tournament that returned 200% of the money they collected in entry fees. The expected return to each contestant was $50, twice the $25 they paid to enter.

Vacation Value

When evaluating a slot tournament, there is one more factor to consider. I call it "vacation value." If the value of rooms, parties, gifts, and other freebies that come with the tournament exceeds your expected monetary loss, then the tournament is worth playing. In the Sahara example, the entry-fee included a tournament cocktail party and brunch, a gift, free cocktails at casino bars, and the casino rate on a room. The extras were worth much more than the $6 expected loss.

Along these lines, some tournament directors (usually those from casinos that return the lowest percentages) argue that the "experience" provided by their tournament and the opportunity for old friends to get together is more important than a sterile cost/return analysis. No argument from me. If you enjoy an event because you're treated well at a specific sponsoring casino, then stick with it.

One more thing. To promote excitement, casinos program tournament slot machines to pay back well over 100%. Be aware of this and don't expect the frequent payoffs to continue when you play the machines on the casino floor.

Strategy Tips For Timed Tournaments

Some tournaments give you a set period of time to play (rather than a set number of credits). The following strategy enhancements will help you in these tournaments. Equity is even more important here. Once you've identified a timed slot tournament with even or positive equity, even the slightest improvement in play will yield an advantage over the field. These suggestions may seem obvious, but they are routinely ignored by slot tournament players.

Play Fast—In tournaments where rounds are timed, you can obtain a slight edge if you can get more spins than the average player. This is accomplished by staying focused and concentrating on your own play. I've seen players stop in the middle of their round to cheer for an opponent who has hit a jackpot. This practice will reduce your spin total. I once played in a press slot tournament at the Tropicana. After 15 minutes, I was in third place. During the final five minutes the two players who were ahead of me tired. One began tapping the machine's spin button with her elbow. I managed several extra spins in the last five minutes and pulled away to win.

Conserve Energy—I've noticed that many players frantically pound the spin button. This causes them to tire and lose spins. Tapping the button lightly is a more efficient method.

Prepare—Before playing, familiarize yourself with the combinations that produce large payoffs and rest when you hit one. Take care, however, to resume play as soon as the meter stops registering credits. I've seen players sit for close to a minute without realizing that their machine was ready to be played.

Mini Tournaments

Competing successfully in the major non-slot tournaments will require some study and practice. You can learn about tournament strategy from Stanford Wong's excellent book, *Casino Tournament Strategy*. The best way to gain experience is by playing mini tournaments. A mini tournament is a one day (or evening) event where participants enter for $10 to $25 and compete for a top prize of around $1,000. They're just like the big tournaments, except the stakes are lower. Several casinos run daily minis for slots, video poker, blackjack and craps.

8

SPORTS BETTING

In 1991 I wrote a guest column for *USA Today*. The subject was sports betting. The premise of my article was that gambling is a form of entertainment, and that nowhere is this more apparent than in sports betting. I wrote:

Even the smallest bet can turn an otherwise dull sporting contest into a riveting, energy-charged experience that's guaranteed to get your adrenaline pumping. Has your spouse been complaining about your game-day preoccupation? Try going partners on a $10 bet and see if you perceive a change in attitude.

Your expected loss on a typical $11 sports wager is about 50¢. Divide that by the three hours it takes to play a game and you wind up with a 17¢ per hour expected loss. You'll pay 25 times that rate just to go to a movie (50 times if there are two of you). Sports betting is one of the greatest entertainment values in the world.

Placing a sports bet is not difficult. There are two methods of betting: *pointspreads* (for football and basketball) and *money lines* (for baseball).

Football Betting (Pointspreads)

Approximately 40% of all sports wagers are made on football. The following quick primer will allow you to participate.

Wagers are made in increments of $11 (to win $10), and most casinos will accept $5.50 bets (to win $5). Look at the example below.

1003	Chicago Bears -5	
		41-1/2
1004	L.A. Rams	

This *line* provides all the information you need to place a wager. The team listed second is the home team. An easy way to remember this is to think, top city "at" bottom city. In this case, Chicago at L.A.

Chicago is the favorite, listed at minus 5 points. This means that you give up (*lay*) 5 points when you bet on the Bears. For you to win this bet, the Bears must not only beat the Rams; they must beat them by more than 5 points.

There will be no number after the underdog, but the relationship is symmetrical. When you bet the Rams, you get (*take*) 5 points. You win your bet when the Rams win the game, or if they lose by less than five. With a final score of Bears 30 - Rams 28, a wager on the Rams would win because the Bears did not *cover* the 5-point *spread*.

The *total* is the number on the right (41-1/2). It is a separate bet on whether the combined points scored by both teams will go over or under the posted number. In the case of a 30-28 score, a bet that the total would be over 41-1/2 points would win.

The numbers preceding the team names should be used to make your bet. Tell the ticket writer the number of the team you want to bet, and the amount you are betting. Example: "Number 1004 for $11," means you are betting $11 on Los Angeles +5 (getting five points). If you bet a total, give him the number of either team and specify either "over" or "under" the total. Pay the writer the amount of your wager and he'll give you a ticket with your bet printed on it. Check the ticket for accuracy, then put it in a safe place; it is your receipt to collect if your bet wins. If you lose, you can throw the ticket away, or add it to your collection (there are players who've wallpapered their bedrooms with losing tickets).

Notes

- If the score were to end Bears 33 - Rams 28, the bet would be a tie (*push*). A tie is a tie; all money is refunded.
- Points scored in overtime always apply to the final outcome.
- If you see the designation PK instead of a number (-5 in our example), there is no favorite. The game is called a *pick*. If your team wins, you win your bet regardless of the margin of victory. You still bet $11 to win $10 on the team of your choice.
- The minus symbol is sometimes dropped. If you see a line posted with a number and no minus sign, mentally insert the minus symbol in front of the number. The team with the number beside it is always the favorite.
- Whether you bet teams (*sides*) or totals, remember to bet in units of $11. Casinos will accept any wager from $5.50 to the casino maximum, but they may round the payoffs down on odd amounts (this is called *losing breakage*).
- The information above is also applicable for basketball betting.

The Casino Edge

The standard bet-$11-to-win-$10 football-betting proposition gives the casino a 4.5% advantage. Casino sports books sometimes run promotions that allow you to bet less than this standard -110 price (Sands, Hilton, and Las Vegas Club in the '92 season). Possible variations are "lay prices" of -108 and -105. The -108 reduces your expected loss to 3.7%; the -105 reduces your expected loss to -2.4%.

Football Betting

Lay Price	Casino Advantage	Loss Per Hour *(per $11 wagered)*
-110	4.5%	19.8¢
-108	3.7%	16.3¢
-105	2.4%	10.6¢

Football Contests

Season-long football contests are very popular. In addition to being a fair gamble (often positive-equity tournaments used as loss leaders), football contests provide a lot of bang for your gambling buck. Entry fees of $25-$50 provide four months worth of action, especially if you are picking well and remain in the hunt for one of the top prizes. Most tournaments are structured to pay winners for best overall (season) and weekly records. That means that even if you're out of contention for the overall championship, you can still win a large weekly prize right up to the end of the contest. Unfortunately, you must submit picks every week, which eliminates everyone except locals, and those who travel to Las Vegas several times a month (and perhaps those who have relatives in town). Sports books usually begin taking tournament entries in August. Casinos that can be counted on to sponsor tournaments with entry fees of $50 or less include: Barbary/Gold Coasts, Palace Station, and Imperial Palace.

Free Contests

Once the season is underway, you can't (or wouldn't want to) enter most Las Vegas football contests because you're out of the running for the overall season prize. However, casinos sometimes sponsor free weekly contests. Prizes are smaller, but it's a free shot just for submitting your picks. Last year, free tournaments were run all season long at Fremont, Sam's Town, Boardwalk, and Harrah's.

Super Bowl Shopping

It's a bettor's bonanza during the week leading up to the Super Bowl. You can bet on anything from who wins the coin toss to which quarterback throws more touchdowns. These out-of-the-ordinary bets are known as *propositions.* If action is what you seek, $50 will buy you enough props to ensure a betting interest on virtually every play of the game.

One of the best parts of the whole Las Vegas Super Bowl scene is "line-shopping" on Super Bowl morning. It's fun to roam the casinos looking for a line that's better than the one your buddy just bet a few minutes earlier. With so many sports books handling so many wagers, lines can change quickly, and with a little creativity, combinations of bets can (possibly) offer a positive expected return. Here are two examples from 1992's Super Bowl between the Washington Redskins and Buffalo Bills.

Combining Props

LVA contributor Blair Rodman and I bet the following: Buffalo Bills +3 points and +165 (bet $100 to win $165 if Buffalo wins outright or loses by less than 3 points); and, Washington Redskins -230 (bet $230 to win $100 if Washington wins the game outright). The total wager was $330 and there were four possible outcomes that would affect the result.

- Buffalo wins outright: win $165 on Buffalo, but lose $230 on Redskins for a $65 loss.
- Washington wins by more than 3: lose $100 on Buffalo and win $100 on Washington to break even.
- Washington wins by 1 or 2: win both bets for a $265 win.
- Washington wins by exactly 3: win the Washington bet for $100 and push the Buffalo bet (money returned) for a $100 win.

Basing our probability estimates on available records of past outcomes, we analyzed our chances via the method in the chart below.

Outcome	Result	(Est.) Probability	Expected Win/Loss
Buffalo wins outright	-$65	.33	-$21.45
Wash. wins by more than 3	break even	.495	0
Wash. wins by 1 or 2	+$265	.075	+$19.88
Wash. wins by 3	+$100	.1	+$10
Expected Result			+$8.43

Expected Return: $8.43 per $330 wagered for 2.55% advantage.

Arbitrage Good

Blair and I do this every year for fun. Since neither of us believe that our opinions are good enough to overcome the bookie's vigorish, we concentrate on the variation in betting lines and try to construct a wager that approaches a perfect arbitrage, which is a combination of bets that locks in a profit regardless of the game's result. While we may not have had the 2.5% advantage we thought we had on this wager, our combination bet was certainly better than any straight bet on sides or totals that we could have made, and our risk was only 1/5 of what it would have been had we wagered the $330 on a single proposition. So, how did we do? It depends. If the combination of our two bets really did have a positive expected return, then one of the bets was almost certainly better than the other—Buffalo, if our post-bet analysis is accurate. Thus, adding the Washington bet reduced our expected profit. We opted for the *hedge* (combination of bets) for three reasons. First, as I've explained, we wanted to reduce or eliminate risk. Second, we had absolutely no idea which bet was the good one at the time that we made it. And third, we were doing it for entertainment, and enjoyed searching out the best line for each part of the bet (Washington had been -260 and higher right up until the last half-hour). In the end, we broke even.

Anyone interested in playing this game should plan on being at the four corners of Flamingo and the Strip on Super Bowl morning. Caesars Palace, The Mirage, Bally's, Barbary Coast, Flamingo, Harrah's, and Imperial Palace will be your hunting grounds.

Gaughan's Gamble

The 1992 Super Bowl will be long remembered for producing one of the most interesting betting propositions ever. The Barbary Coast and Gold Coast (operated by Michael Gaughan) allowed bettors to take Buffalo plus 7- 1/2 points and/or lay Washington minus 6-1/2 points at the usual $11 to make $10. Most Las Vegas casinos had settled on Washington as a 7-point favorite, so bettors backing either team could get an extra half point at the Coasts. Gaughan's gamble was in leaving the Barbary and Gold Coasts vulnerable to be *middled* (losing to bettors on both sides) if the game ended with Washington winning by exactly 7 points. Casinos have offered this type of split line in the past, but never with a key number like 7, which is the second-most-common final-point differential in the NFL (3 is the first). The two casinos stood to lose about $10 million, a huge amount considering the total Super Bowl wager throughout all of Nevada was about $50 million.

Knowledgeable sports bettors were divided as to whether it was a good idea to bet both sides, accepting the high probability of losing the *juice* on one of the bets for a shot at the middle. One who did think it was a good bet was Bob Stupak. He made a highly publicized $1.1 million dollar wager ($550,000 each side). When Washington won by 13 points, 37-24, Stupak lost $50,000. He stood to win $1 million had the middle come in, and Mr. Gaughan admits to some anxiety when Washington led by 14 and Buffalo possessed the ball late in the third quarter.

It's unlikely that a split line will be offered around the number 7 again, and no other number except 3 offers the possibility of a positive play (by simultaneously betting both ways). It's worth noting, however, that if you bet both sides of a one-point middle around any number that may be offered between 1 and 18, an assessment of final point-spread differentials indicates that you will at least marginally reduce the casino edge from the 4.5% you face on a straight bet on sides or totals.

How About a Tout?

Handicapping, or tout, services have grown up around the American sports-betting craze. You see their advertisements everywhere. Salesmen will call you from boiler rooms to tell you about the "five-star lock," the "major mismatch," and the "Monday-night bailout." This may be the ultimate application of "Those who can, do; those who can't, teach." Most services don't have any special expertise that will help you win. Their major talent is selling. A November 1991 issue of *Sports Illustrated* contained one of the best articles ever published on sports-betting tout-services titled "1-900-RIPOFFS." If you've ever been tempted to "invest" in one of these services, locate this issue at your local library and read it first. *SI* took a two-month test drive through the world of sports-advisory services and found "misleading ads, bait-and-switches, repeated claims of fixes coming down, misrepresentation of records, unforgivably high pressured sales techniques, phone harassment, phone threats, phony guarantees, mail fraud, wire fraud and some perfectly dreadful manners."

Even if you do find a reputable service, there's another important financial consideration. Due to the bet $11 to win $10 arrangement, football bettors must win at a rate of 52.38% to break even (veteran sports bettor, Lem Banker, says you need about 56% to make a living). When you pay for advice, even good advice, the win percentage necessary to break even increases. For example, if you pay $20 per pick, and wager $200 per game, you now need to win at a rate of 57.15%. The more you pay, the higher the necessary win percentage rises. Your best strategy is to pick your own.

Baseball Betting (Money Lines)

Baseball is bet differently than football and basketball.

- The team listed second (Red Sox) is the home team.
- Navarro and Darwin are the scheduled starting pitchers.
- The Brewers are the underdog, denoted by the "+". You wager $100

to win $120 or some multiple thereof, i.e., $10 to win $12.

• The Red Sox are the favorite, denoted by the "-". You wager $130 to win $100 ($13 to win $10).

• The numbers preceding the team names should be used to make your bet.

• There will probably be an over/under line posted here also.

• Unless you specify otherwise, you will have "team action," meaning that your bet stands even if one or both starting pitchers is changed before game time.

409	Brewers	Navarro	+120
410	Red Sox	Darwin	-130

The Casino Edge

Notice that the difference between the *prices* (-130 and +120) is 10. This difference is referred to as 10¢ or a *dime*; thus, this is called a *dime line*. The casino (bookie) advantage with this dime line hovers around 2%. Some sports books post wider spreads like -130/+115 (15¢ line) or -130/+110 (20¢ line). Do not bet into these lines; the casino edge goes up as the difference widens. One casino, Barbary Coast, has dealt a nickel (5¢) line, i.e., -120/+115, for the last two years. The casino's edge here is only about 1%. This is one of the best gambles you will find anywhere. A $10 wager buys you three hours of action for a total expected loss of about 10¢.

Best Books

Watching the game you've bet in a Las Vegas sports book enhances the overall experience. Sports books run promotions, sell hot dogs and beer, and generally do whatever it takes to make their venue as exciting as possible. It's the next best thing to being at the stadium. Three casinos boast facilities referred to as "super books." They are The Mirage, Caesars Palace, and the Las Vegas Hilton. These are the places that attract the biggest action and offer the most amenities (multiple viewing screens, plenty of seats, speedy cocktail service). Several casinos offer "big books" (a step below super). They include: Imperial Palace (the IP even has a drive-up betting window), Stardust, Circus Circus, Excalibur, Frontier, Aladdin, Golden Nugget, Horseshoe, Bally's, Rio, Gold Coast, and Palace Station. The latter three have a distinctly local flavor. Everything considered, The Mirage is probably the best place to enjoy the action. The book is beautiful, there's plenty of action and excitement, and hustling cocktail waitresses are not stingy about bringing free drinks to patrons sitting in the viewing area.

Big Payoffs

There's No Such Thing as a Sure Thing

The old adage was proven true once again when Buster Douglas upset Mike Tyson for boxing's Heavyweight Championship in 1990. The Mirage was the only sports book to offer a betting line on the fight; the city's other books considered it too great a mismatch to book action on it. The opening line made Tyson a 35-1 favorite; someone reportedly wagered $70,000 to win $2,000. This forced the line upward until it settled at 42-1. There were reports that someone bet $100,000 somewhere between 35 and 42 to 1, hoping for a return of less than $3,000. The largest bet on Douglas was reported to be $1,500 at 38-1 odds which, when Douglas won, returned a tidy $57,000 profit. The Mirage was rewarded with a big win for their willingness to post the line. The biggest winner, though, was Buster Douglas, who signed a two-fight deal with The Mirage for $60 million.

Texas-sized Parlay

The NFL football playoffs often produce interesting stories of betting bravado. One in 1991 involved the largest payoff ever made on a legal sports wager. A Texan used a series of parlays at Little Caesars sports book to turn an initial bet of $40,000 into $2.4 million. It was reported that the man then bet $700,000 of his winnings on a two-team parlay involving the two League Championship games. Unfortunately for the bettor, he bet Los Angeles and San Francisco, both of whom were defeated.

Man Bites Dog

A sports *future bet* is an advance wager on the winner of a major professional sports championship like football's Super Bowl or hockey's Stanley Cup. These bets typically carry a very high house edge (25% or more) and require that you leave your money with the casino for many months while waiting for the bet to be resolved. Still, future betting is very popular. If you wager on a team that becomes a contender, your small future bet will provide an entire season of excitement—and on occasion, man (the bettors) bites dog (the casino). 1991's baseball World Series was a classic example. The World Series matched two "worst to first" teams, the Twins and the Braves. At the beginning of the 1991 baseball season, future odds on 1990's last-place Twins winning this year's title were 100-1. The odds against the Braves were a whopping 250-1 in many places. Both teams were bet heavily by the public. Since a winning $10 wager on the Twins would pay $1,000 and a winning $10 wager on the Braves would pay $2,500, Las Vegas sports books faced the pospect of losing big no matter who won the series. The Twins won, keeping damage to a minimum at most books. When the 1992 baseball World Series future odds were released, there were no teams listed at odds longer than 100-1.

Score One for the Little Guys—Almost

In late 1991, a group of eight baccarat dealers from the Las Vegas Hilton turned an initial $80 stake ($10 per person) into $103,000 by betting one football game per week, parlaying their winnings, and winning eleven consecutive bets. The dealers' goal was to continue their parlay until they lost, or reached 15 straight wins. Had they been successful, the group would have cashed a $1.3 million profit. The odds against winning 15 straight are about 33,000-1. The odds against winning the remaining four games were only 15-1. Alas, they lost in week 12. The two dealers who made all the winning picks were female.

All-Star Bizzare

The 1993 NBA All-Star game resulted in some major confusion for sports books and bettors. Closing lines at several casinos had the West All-Stars favored +3, and the total score on 267. The nationally televised game appeared to end with the West winning by a score of 135-130 (the network concluded its telecast, and the Associated Press announced the score as a final). The West covered the spread, and the total fell two points under 267. This is where it got weird. Scottie Pippen of the East squad, who'd been fouled as the game time expired, was called out of the locker room to shoot, and make, two free throws, raising the official final score to 135-132. Both propositions should have ended in ties, and all money returned. But the sports books had already paid many tickets based on the earlier score. Some bettors got away with a win which should have pushed, while others threw away tickets that should have been refunded.

RACE BETTING

Most sports books also allow betting on horses (and sometimes dogs) in an area called the race book. If you enjoy betting the horses, fine; but it's not one of the gambling games that rates high on my list for two reasons:

- If you are an unknowledgeable player, you face a high casino edge.
- If you are a knowledgeable player (good handicapper, have access to good information), the casinos won't take your action.

One group of bookmakers tried to buck policy #2. They opened the Sport of Kings race book (located at the corner of Convention Center Dr. and Paradise Rd.) in 1992, and announced that they would accept wagers of almost any size without discriminating against certain "known" horse bettors. Experts predicted that the race book was "going to get their brains beat out." They were right. The losses were early and heavy, and Sport of Kings went pari-mutuel (a system that reduced the handle but eliminated risk) in less than one month.

Sahara Round-up Time

Some race books offer promotions like win bonuses to bring in business, but the bonuses are usually limited to certain days and/or tracks. The Sahara runs a great daily promotion called "Round-up Time." Stanford Wong described it in an *LVA* article reprinted here:

The Sahara offers a valuable concession they call Round-Up Time. If you bet any thoroughbred race with a win payoff of less than $6, the Sahara will round up your winning payoff to the next full dollar amount. For example, if your winning horse pays $5.20, your payoff will be rounded up to $6. Payoffs of exact dollar amounts are not adjusted.

Before a race, you can never be certain that a given horse will win, nor can you be sure that your horse will go off at odds that can be rounded. But for the average horse that wins at odds of less than 2:1, this Sahara promotion adds about 8% or 9% to the payoff. The bonus is more valuable the lower the odds are on the horse. Here's why.

In general, low-odds horses are better bets than long shots. This phenomenon has long been identified in the literature; it is called the favorite long-shot bias. My own work has confirmed this. The bias combined with the Sahara bonus makes almost every horse that goes off at less than even money worth betting. The only big favorites that are not worth a bet are those that are too good to believe. I address this in Chapter 3 of my book, Betting Cheap Claimers.

I'd also recommend betting any claimer going off at less than 2:1, providing it faced cheaper horses in its last race than it faces today, or it faced the same priced horses it is facing today and did not win. Again, see Chapter 3 of Betting Cheap Claimers.

Signs at the Sahara say a $20 max bet is allowed, but the race book will sometimes take a bet larger than $20.

Mini Handicapping Tournaments

Mini handicapping tournaments are another good deal for horse bettors. Excalibur, Circus Circus, and Riviera run tournaments during the week that cost $10 and $15 to enter, and return all the entry fees plus extras like a free *Daily Racing Form* or a buffet. Handicapping tournaments are interesting because most are structured to favor the player who doesn't handicap and picks long shots at random over the handicapping expert who picks low-odds horses.

594-RACE

Call 594-RACE while in Las Vegas for free racing results. The Racing Hotline relays updates from Belmont, Golden Gate and Hollywood Park. You can also get a list of overnight scratches.

9

OTHER GAMES

Keno

Keno has the distinction of being the casino game with the highest house edge. But it is also the slowest game, so the player's per-hour expected loss is in line with the other games. To find out who offers Las Vegas' best keno odds, Robert H. Stauffer, Jr. contributed an article to the *Las Vegas Advisor* in which he compared eight-spot tickets from 46 casinos (the eight spot is probably the ticket played most often because it pays the casino's highest jackpot for the least number of correct selections). The range of payouts for the eight spots he looked at is listed below.

$1 EIGHT-SPOT TICKET

	Low Payout	High Payout
4 numbers	$0	$1
5 numbers	4	10
6 numbers	50	100
7 numbers	1200	2000
8 numbers	18,000	50,000

Due to the differences in payouts, the return percentages vary greatly among casinos. The chart on the following page rates them from best to worst.

The chart provides a representative guide to each casino's overall keno return, and shows what a tough game keno really is. The best return on a standard eight spot affords the casino a whopping expected win of more than 21¢ per dollar wagered. Luckily, keno is quite promotion-intensive. You can often reduce the house edge by taking advantage of bonuses (the Excalibur once conducted a drawing from a drum of losing tickets for a car). Keno coupons that reduce the play price by at least 50% and games that pay

KENO HOLD (IN %)—STANDARD EIGHT-SPOT TICKET

The figures in this chart represent the casino advantage.

Casino	Hold	Casino	Hold
Gold Coast	21.37	Excalibur	29.46
Hacienda	21.49	Tropicana	29.46
Las Vegas Club	23.90	Westward Ho	29.46
Nevada Palace	23.90	California	29.55
Frontier	25.49	Bally's	29.56
Sam's Town	25.89	Continental	29.65
Gold Spike	25.90	Harrah's	29.65
Barbary Coast	26.05	Caesars Palace	29.69
Rio	26.05	Palace Station	29.87
Lady Luck	26.14	Horseshoe	29.98
Santa Fe	26.14	Fitzgeralds	29.98
San Remo	27.02	Aladdin	30.18
Mirage	27.29	Hilton	30.18
Golden Gate	27.76	Maxim	30.18
Bourbon Street	28.52	Desert Inn	30.33
Vegas World	28.58	Four Queens	30.41
Stardust	28.98	King 8	30.90
Western	29.11	Riviera	31.51
Imperial Palace	29.15	Flamingo Hilton	31.72
Golden Nugget	29.45	Fremont	31.81
Plaza	29.45	Showboat	32.15
Circus Circus	29.46	Sahara	32.96
El Cortez	29.46	Sands	33.14

progressive jackpots also offer opportunities to eliminate, or at least reduce, the huge casino advantage.

Special Tickets

Playing "special" tickets is usually not a viable method for reducing the house edge. Here's an example. A press release from the Sahara read:

The Sahara is offering a giant $100,000 keno payoff. The Sahara "Super Eight" ticket is a $1 bet on an eight-spot ticket. To win the $100,000 payoff, the player must catch all eight. No other payoffs are made on the "Super Eight" tickets.

"This is a really healthy payoff for a one dollar bet," said the Sahara keno manager. "We're seeing a lot of action on the 'Super Eight' tickets, and we're looking forward to having the opportunity to pay one."

The ticket has a casino edge of 56.5%. If "a lot of action" means ten tickets per hour 24 hours per day, the Sahara can expect to have the "opportunity to pay one" in about 2-1/2 years.

Pantomime Keno

Because keno has such a high house edge, your best strategy is to not play...or you could try pantomime keno. In pantomime keno, you don't win or lose financially, only psychologically.

The game is easy to play. Fill out a keno ticket but don't pay for it. Then check the results.

Using a standard eight spot as an example, nine out of ten times you will find that your ticket would have paid less than you paid for it, and you are a winner by virtue of your non-participation. After winning game after game of pantomime keno, you'll begin to see the folly in wasting money on the real thing. Of course, if that 1-in-200,000 shot comes in, and you hold a worthless eight spot, well...

Video Keno

Fortune smiled on a lucky woman at the Palace Station when she hit 10 out of 10 on a 5¢ progressive video keno machine for $57,000. A $57,000 win for a 20¢ investment. Smart play, right? Not really. The casino edge with the jackpot standing at $57,000 was 10.2%. The woman's expected result was a loss of about $6 per hour.

Nickel progressives can really fool you. The chart here depicts a standard 5¢ machine that takes 1-4 coins. By subtracting the return percentages (bottom line) from 100, you can see that the house advantage

# SPOTS HIT	# SPOTS MARKED								
	2	3	4	5	6	7	8	9	10
2	14	2	2						
3		40	3	2	2	1			
4			100	14	4	2	1	1	
5				800	92	15	12	3	3
6					1500	348	112	47	28
7						7760	1500	352	140
8							8000	4700	1000
9								9000	4800
10									$57,000
% RETURNED	84.18	83.25	86.14	85.31	85.24	86.31	84.17	84.87	89.80

holds steady around 15% no matter what you play (except for the progressive 10-spot). Like all video machines, it's the speed at which you play that really kills you.

At the next level up, quarter video poker machines usually return about 92%. A fast player's expected loss on quarter machines can easily run $20 per hour. You are far better off playing regular keno in a keno lounge for $1 per game.

By the way, that Palace Station nickel jackpot has to reach nearly $250,000 before it's a breakeven gamble.

Bingo

Playing bingo is a leisurely way to stay busy indoors and beat the heat. The game can be played for low stakes—minimum session buy-ins range from $3-$11—and sessions last about an hour, so your expected loss is lower than if you played blackjack for the same amount of time.

You might think that bingo has a high house edge because of the bad reputation it has earned in charity halls around the country. But bingo as it's played in Las Vegas differs significantly from bingo at your local church bazaar. In recent years, the game has taken on the role of loss leader in Las Vegas casinos. Bingo brings players into the casino, and staggered (bi-hourly) sessions leave them with waiting time that they often spend playing the other games like slots and video poker. Competition for bingo patrons has become fierce and casinos sometimes offer guaranteed prize money that must be paid even if the anticipated number of players do not attend the session. As a result, bingo players may unwittingly encounter situations where they are playing with an advantage, especially in sessions with guaranteed prizes.

Las Vegas' two largest bingo halls are located at the Showboat and at the Triple J Bingo Hall and Casino. Each can accommodate 1,500 players. The Triple J features high-stakes "Indian-style" bingo, which is characterized by longer sessions and higher jackpots, including a big progressive. Other casinos that run big bingo games are: Aladdin, Arizona Charlie's, Continental, Frontier, Gold Coast, Harrah's, Horseshoe, Jerry's Nugget, Palace Station, and Santa Fe.

Free Bingo

Watch the local newspapers for giveaways and coupons for discounted buy-ins and free games. From time to time, casinos offer free-bingo promotions. Don't get too excited; these free sessions are typically packed with players, and prizes are low. The following letter from an LVA subscriber describes a free session at the Hacienda:

A total of $450 is given away every session. I estimate there were 300-400 players, so the expected win per player is less than $1.50. A drill sergeant runs the games, and promises that anyone found with more than six cards will be barred forever. They play funny bingo—picture frames, postage stamps, whatever—and just when I started to understand the formations, someone hollered bingo. This was the most boring hour I ever spent. I love coupons, and I cherish free things even more. However, I think I'll pass on free bingo and watch test patterns on TV!

Notes

The Triple J Bingo Hall in Henderson (just off Boulder Highway next to K-Mart) has a large non-smoking section separated from the smokers by a floor-to-ceiling glass wall.

A publication called the *Bingo Bugle* is available in Las Vegas supermarkets and bingo halls. It includes schedules, announcements of bingo promotions, and most importantly, coupons for many of the major bingo rooms.

Baccarat

The casino's advantage at baccarat is slight, but insurmountable. The edge on the bank bet is 1.06%, the edge on the player bet is 1.23%, and the edge on a tie is a whopping 14%. The 1.06% for bank results from the casino charging a 5% commission on winning bank wagers. Casinos sometimes deal baccarat with bank commissions other than 5%. The Horseshoe has dealt 4% for several years, and other casinos have experimented with commissions of 4%, and even 3%. The effect of these commission reductions is to lower the edge to a point where an opportunity to play for comps arises. In a 3%-commission game, betting $25-$50 at a rate of 100 hands per hour results in an expected loss of less than $10 per hour. Consult this chart for player expectation when baccarat is dealt with commissions ranging from 0-6%.

Player Advantage on Bank Bet at Varying Commissions

Commission	Player Advantage
6%	-1.52%
5%	-1.06%
4%	-.60%
3%	-.15%
2%	.31%
1%	.77%
0%	1.23%

Sahara

The Sahara is a casino that has played with their commission rate in past years. They currently deal 4%, and as recently as December 1992 dealt a 3% commission.

In December 1989, the Sahara dealt baccarat with no commission on winning bank bets up to $100. Players had a 1.23% advantage, for an expected win of more than $100 per hour. After five days of play, the Sahara brought in a detective agency to identify knowledgeable players who were participating in the promotion. Some participants were professional blackjack and poker players. Others just happened to recognize a good proposition. The Sahara began barring players as they were pointed out by the detectives. Those not known continued to play with the same 1.23% edge that had been enjoyed by the expelled players. Stanford Wong summed it up best, "It looks like the Sahara is giving away money, but I guess they're particular about who they give it to."

Craps

The casino edge is a low 1.4% for the line bets—pass, don't pass, come, and don't come. Place bets on the six and eight carry a 1.5% casino edge. All other bets on the layout take such a large bite out of your gambling allotment, you should ignore them. Crap layouts are fairly standard (only slight differences in the unfavorable proposition bets), so shopping for good games is not a concern. Shopping for low limits is viable, and a few 25¢ tables still survive, especially downtown. Players who seek maximum dice action at the lowest disadvantage can water down the edge on their total line action by taking (or laying) full odds. Most Las Vegas casinos deal at least 2X odds. The Horseshoe and the Frontier deal 10X odds ($5 minimum line bet). *Crapless craps*, the Vegas World craps mutant (which also inhabits Little Caesars), has a casino edge on the pass line bet of 5.4%, nearly four times the advantage enjoyed by operators of the standard game.

Roulette

Roulette is an undesirable game because the casino edge is high, 5.26%, and the game plays fast. The casino advantage comes from the green "0" and "00" slots on the wheel. Only one casino in Las Vegas consistently deals a roulette game with a single zero: Sam's Town, on a game located on the second floor. The single-zero game cuts the casino advantage to 2.7%.

On occasion, large casinos (Caesars Palace, Hilton, Mirage, Desert Inn) will deal single-zero roulette—often in special private casinos—to their biggest gambling customers.

The Four Queens went the single-zero clubs one better in September 1991. Winning wagers on single number bets (e.g., 9, 16, 22, etc.) paid 36-1 (the standard payoff is 35-1). This cut the casino edge to 2.63%.

Tropicana Penny Roulette

The Tropicana deals penny roulette on one of its wheels, Monday through Friday from noon to 8 pm. Chips are worth 1¢ apiece. Even if you spread chips all over the layout, your hourly expected loss almost can't exceed 50¢. Get one free drink from the cocktail waitress and you win. There is a one-hour limit per player.

2 not 4

Understanding the difference between the words "for" and "to" is important when comparing casino pay schedules. **For** *means the payoff includes the original bet.* **To** *means the payoff is in addition to the original bet.*

2 for 1 returns the original bet plus $1 in winnings—a total of $2
2 to 1 returns the original bet plus $2 in winnings—a total of $3

As you can see, **to** *is preferable to* **for**. *Most casinos display odds as* **to** *(2-1, 5-1, 20-1, etc.), but some use the word* **for** *to make the payoffs look more attractive. Here are some common examples:*

Roulette (single number bet)	*36 for 1*	=	*35-1*
Craps Big Red (bet on seven)	*5 for 1*	=	*4-1*
Craps (bet on 2 or 12)	*31 for 1*	=	*30-1*
Blackjack machines (natural)	*2 for 1*	=	*1-1*

The last example represents the most effective application of this tactic. Players mistakenly believe the 2 for 1 is superior to the 1.5 to 1 paid on a live blackjack game. In reality, the video version's 2 for 1 is simply an even money return, which costs the player significantly. When you see the word **for**, *beware. It is necessary to subtract one from the payoff number to make valid comparisons*

Poker

Most casinos house a small poker room somewhere on the premises. The two most popular games are seven-card stud and Texas hold 'em. Low-stakes players should visit a few casinos before playing, to compare rakes (commission taken from each pot) in different rooms. High-stakes players, $10-$20 limit and above, have only two choices, Binion's Horseshoe or The Mirage. The Horseshoe's rake is lower, there's easier access to the poker room, and they are very generous with meal comps for poker players. The Mirage is flashier and deals a greater variety of games.

Pai Gow Poker

It's the new (successful) game on the block. Pai gow poker tables are now found in most big casinos. The casino edge varies, but averages about 2.8%. What's good about this game is that it results in lots of ties where no money changes hands. Consequently, your per-hour expected loss is probably less than it is on a crap table where the casino edge is only half as high. It's likely that casinos will soon install automatic shuffling machines on pai gow tables to speed the action and keep the game viable for them. Stanford Wong's *Optimal Strategy for Pai Gow Poker* is a must read if you want to learn the intricacies of this game.

And Finally. . .

Red Dog

The casino advantage is about 2.4%. It doesn't sound bad, but it is. The game is played at a deadly fast pace. Your expected loss at a modest $2 bet level exceeds $10 per hour.

Fast Action Hold 'Em

The casino edge in this new game that's gaining in popularity is 2.5%.

Caribbean Stud Poker

The casino edge is a healthy 4.4% on the basic game. Caribbean Stud also offers a progressive jackpot that you may qualify to win on any hand by adding one additional dollar to your original wager. The top prize is paid when a player is dealt a royal flush. The progressive on the game at Bally's was hit last year for $73,000, reportedly by the road manager for headline performer Barbara Mandrell. With the jackpot at this level, the player's expected loss is about 55¢ per dollar wagered. The meter must exceed $250,000 before betting to win the progressive jackpot is justified.

10

A DOZEN PROMOTIONS

The best way to make money gambling is to exploit a promotion. Money-making opportunities pop up all the time, and they're not always for penny stakes. The following 12 promotions yielded profit opportunities ranging from 8¢ a game to $1,200 an hour.

Free Keno (1/91)

The Silver City allowed players to mark a five-spot ticket and play it free for 24 hours. Hit all five and win $25. It was worth 1.6¢ per game mathematically, but at least 100 times that in entertainment value.

Craps (9/91)

In a Four Queens promotion, when a hard number [(22), (33), (44), (55)] was thrown on the comeout roll, players betting at least $1 on the pass line were given a free $1 bet on that hardway. A $1 bettor had a 7.5% edge. Result: Get paid $2.25 per hour to make $1 pass line bets and order free cocktails.

Football Free Shot (11/91)

The first 100 people to show up at the Aladdin to watch Monday Night Football received a free square in a pool for that night's game. The expected win for playing was about $2.50. There were also free roast beef sandwiches and a drawing for an NFL football during the game.

Blackjack Premium (6/92)

Play blackjack for three hours with $15 minimum bets at Bourbon Street and receive a 10% chip bonus on your next buy-in, maximum of a $50 bonus. A basic-strategy blackjack player had an expected win of about $7.50 per hour.

Slot Rebate #1 (6/92)

The Hacienda offered $5 in free slot play to anyone who was not already a member of their slot club. Sign up for the club, play $5 through any slot or video poker machine, get reimbursed $5 at the club booth regardless of the result.

Slot Rebate #2 (3/91)

The Las Vegas Hilton made the same offer for a $20 rebate. Players had an expected win of $19.

Big Spin (1/93)

The Las Vegas Hilton ran a 100%-equity video poker mini tournament with a powerful bonus thrown in. Between tournament rounds, participants who played 25¢ video poker machines in the casino earned coupons for spins on a free-money wheel. Every time they hit four-of-a-kind playing video poker, they received one spin ticket. The pay slots on the wheel ranged from $20 to $250, and the average return was $33 per spin. This gave the player a 5.69% edge playing video poker. Best of all, players who accrued more than one free-spin ticket were allowed to take their turns consecutively with the wheel being returned to the same starting position each time. By adjusting subsequent spins according to previous results, multiple-ticket holders were able to increase their probability of hitting the $250 slot.

As a friend walked up to take his turn, he quipped: "I know it's worth $33 now. What do you think it's worth on my next two spins?" He hit the $250 mark on his second try.

Big Ace (1/93)

Downtown's little Nevada Casino didn't know what they were doing when they gave out funbooks (to guests of the hotel) that included a "first card is an ace" coupon that could be used with blackjack bets up to the $200 table limit. The coupon gave the player a $74 expected return on a max bet. Players were checking out, then back into the hotel (at $20 every night) to get the $74 coupon.

Video Keno (3/93)

One day a week, the Sahara paid players double when they hit four out of four on 25¢ video-keno machines during the first ten minutes of every hour—a 24% player advantage. The expected win was $13 per ten minutes, or $264 per day.

Blackjack Bonus (11/92)

The Continental dealt what was probably the most player-profitable $5 blackjack game in gambling history. Five-dollar bettors were paid a $500 bonus when dealt two naturals in a row. This occurs about once every eight hours (on a double-deck game). The expected loss playing basic strategy while you waited was $7, making the average net win $493, or more than $61 per hour. That's $310 a day for risking $5 a hand! The Continental had no chance. This no-brain bonus could have been exploited by any novice.

50/50 (4/93)

The Las Vegas Hilton tested a game called 50/50, a blackjack variation with a side bet that allowed you to "freeze" an initial holding of 12-16 and begin a new hand for equal stakes against the existing dealer up card. With proper basic strategy (no card counting necessary), the player had nearly a 2% advantage, and the maximum bet was $1,000. The game lasted three days. The Hilton is rumored to have lost more than a quarter-million dollars.

Vouchers in Barstow (Now)

California commuters can stop at the ABC Reservations booth next to McDonald's and pick up the fabulous Four Queens free-slot-play vouchers. Originally, they were good for $10. They're now down to $5. These vouchers are mighty.

III

Beating

11

COUPONOMY

Coupons are the only way to go. Minimize variance! Find money on the floor. Don't gamble with them.

—Peter Griffin, *The Theory of Blackjack*

I call the systematic and efficient use of casino coupons "Couponomy" (the suffix "omy" usually indicates removal, so this art/science represents the "extraction of wealth via coupon"). For years, Couponomy has been the province of a small group of informed consumers (Couponomists), but the simple concept of analyzing and using valuable coupons can be applied by anyone.

In reality, the practice of Couponomy is not limited to playing coupons. You could call it a state of mind. It means staying alert for opportunities for taking advantage of Las Vegas in all areas—dining, entertainment, and anywhere else that competition creates value for consumers.

Funbooks

A funbook is a marketing tool used by casinos to attract customers. A typical funbook contains a combination of the following:

- Gambling coupons for 21, craps, roulette, keno, and big 6.
- Discounts for drinks/meals/shows.
- Souvenirs.
- Other discounts (beauty shop, car rental, etc.).

The non-gambling coupons are easy to analyze. If the coupon says "free" or two-for-one, you have a money saver. If the offer applies to something you want, use it. Most funbooks contain coupons for free cocktails in the lounge or two-for-one buffets. A husband and wife can save up to $20 per day eating on the coupon circuit. The souvenirs are usually cheap trinkets or a deck of cards, but you'll find that virtually anything bearing a casino logo makes for a potential gift back home. Discounts for beauty shops, health clubs, car rentals, and the like are usually insignificant and can be ignored.

Casinos usually hype their books with claims like "$80 value" and "$170 value." That's nonsense. A good funbook might be worth $10-20 in potential profit and saving. The current Lady Luck funbook is one of the best ever and is only worth about $50.

The real value in most funbooks comes from the gambling coupons.

Gambling Coupons

If someone handed you real U.S. currency, even if only a couple of dollars, you wouldn't throw it in the garbage, would you? Of course not. Why then do so many people ignore the gambling coupons in casino funbooks (sometimes called *lucky bucks*)? Though not exactly cash, most lucky bucks represent the next best thing—a highly effective vehicle for obtaining cash. Gambling becomes a prudent investment when wagers are accompanied by a coupon because *the player has an advantage on every bet!*

Lucky bucks for blackjack, craps, roulette, baccarat, and big 6 pay a bonus, usually $1, on winning wagers. For example: 2-1's pay $2 for a winning $1 wager. There are also 3-2's, 7-5's, and a few other variations.

It may surprise you, but the ratio of wins to losses in most casino games is relatively close. In craps, for example, after 100 bets (on the pass line), you expect to win about 49 times and lose the other 51. The casino edge generated by this 49/51 ratio, multiplied by thousands of decisions, guarantees their profits. But add the bonus payoff from a 2-1 coupon, and the situation is reversed. The win/loss ratio remains the same; however, your 49 winning bets are now paid two dollars instead of one. The result after 100 decisions is $98 in winnings (49 X $2), and $51 in losses. The difference is a net profit of $47 for the player. The value of the coupon bonus is far too great for the casino advantage to overcome.

Limits

The discussion above illustrates why coupons have betting limits assigned to them. If players were allowed to bet any amount of money with advantages approaching 50%, the casinos couldn't survive. Case in point: the Marina (now part of MGM Grand) issued a funbook in late 1989. For some reason, no limit was placed on the amount that could be bet with three key coupons. One allowed you to push (tie) a pass line bet if the shooter rolled 12, a second pushed a field bet if the shooter rolled 5, and the third pushed a blackjack bet when you busted with exactly 22. Used with bets of $500 (the casino limit), the three coupons had a combined value of just under $1,000! Since the rules provided that books could be played at the rate of one per person per day, someone with a bankroll large enough to withstand the fluctuations (risk) inherent in betting $500 per hand of blackjack or craps had an expected win of $1,000 per day. Mega-couponomists descended on the Marina armed with coupons and lots of $100 bills. In less than two days, the Marina ran up the white flag and distribution of the funbook was suspended.

Most casinos limit coupon play to bets of $1, $2, $3, or $5. However, a typical funbook has two or more lucky bucks, and combining them from five or six casinos can add up.

Obtaining Coupons

Before you can use them you have to get them. Ask at casino cages and Welcome Centers. A valid form of out-of-state identification is essential, as funbooks are meant for tourists. A hotel room key can also come in handy. Some casinos require that you present their advertising solicitation—either a voucher or a print ad. Find vouchers at one of Las Vegas' coupon re-loading stations, located in non-casino motels around town, that distribute coupons from racks. The El Morocco (across from Stardust) is probably the city's best stocked and most convenient. Page through all the freebie magazines you see for coupon advertisements. You can often find great coupon vouchers on the road into town. A company that distributes them says that fast food restaurants and service stations in Barstow and Kingman are prime locations for collecting vouchers. Always ask your travel or package tour agent for anything that they may be able to give you.

The Coupon Run

The late-'70s were the glory days of Couponomy. Casinos were very liberal with regard to coupon distribution, and prehistoric Couponomists (mostly under-capitalized, would-be-professional blackjack and poker players) roamed Las Vegas on *coupon runs*. A coupon run was a highly organized foray into 5-15 casinos with the sole objective of generating riskless profits by playing coupons. The coupon runs became very sophisticated, as participants combined hit-and-run card-counting techniques (known as Wonging) with coupon play. On occasion, the run would be conducted at a more leisurely pace—speed being sacrificed for the pleasure of consuming several cocktails, all free with coupons, of course. A run could be completed in less than two hours and would net an average of $50-$75. That was living expenses plus a small gambling stake. Because of casino shift changes, it was often possible to repeat the same run later the same day.

Unfortunately, crazed Couponomists began abusing this low-risk form of funding. When counterfeit coupons began surfacing, casinos were forced to tighten controls and earning a living via the coupon run was no longer as viable an option.

A Fabulous Las Vegas Coupon Tour

Las Vegas visitors can construct their own version of a coupon run; call it a tour. It's the closest thing to a sure thing you'll ever find in Las Vegas! A coupon tour is guaranteed to produce profits over time because the player has an advantage on every bet he makes. Peter Griffin calls it "gambling without fear." "If you play enough coupons," says Griffin, "you will win!" Granted, coupons are not the stuff of which giant scores are made, but you can easily make enough to cover dinner and a show (even *Siegfried & Roy*), and have a little left over for some couponless gambling afterward.

Following is a true account of a coupon run I made in 1989. Many of the funbooks mentioned, and even some of the casinos, are either gone or changed. However, the concept is applicable today. Next to each casino's name is a dollar amount in parentheses. This was the approximate mathematical value of that casino's gambling coupons that I played.

Vegas World ($15.50, $2 registration fee)—This is the logical starting point because it is a timed program. You must return three times in 45 minute intervals to extract the full value of the funbook. Most timed programs are not worth the effort. This one is. Vegas World distributes *funny chips* (non-negotiable slot tokens and chips that can be played but not cashed in). These chips are great because you have a chance to win a lot of money, but your maximum loss is limited to the $2 registration fee. Things went well right off the bat. My first free slot pull produced an $18 winner. Better yet, the machine malfunctioned and paid $19. The remainder of my play netted an additional $17 profit. Great start! I also got a free photo and found two show tickets on the floor. When running coupons, it pays to be observant. After subtracting the $2 registration, I was up $34.

Sahara ($1.88)—I was lucky here too, netting a $12 profit. As I sipped a Molson beer (purchased for 25¢ with a coupon) an elderly lady gave me a complimentary pass for two to *Boy-lesque, the* Sahara's show. I was up $46.

Paddlewheel ($1.62)—Won $3.25 and drank a free Heineken. Up $49.25.

Slots A Fun ($1.71)—There are 2-1 coupons all over the casino. You're limited only by how many you can play without being told to stop. I played four, won three, ate free popcorn and was given a souvenir dice keychain. Up $54.25.

Riviera (33¢)—This was a terrible funbook. They advertise a $75 value but it's made up of $2 off photo processing and the like. I lost $1 and had a free draft beer. Still up $53.25 and slightly tipsy.

Silver City ($2.76)—This was another case of play what you can get away with. The attendant told me to help myself to coupons and a free pen. I played six coupons and won $9. Up $62.25.

Peppermill (44¢)—$2 profit, 25¢ daiquiri and 25¢ ice cream cone. Up $64.25

Sands ($9.89)—This is Vegas' best funbook. Again I did better than expected and won $21 and a free coffee mug. Up $85.25.

Nob Hill ($6.90)—Coupon power carried me through the Nob Hill as I managed to eke out a $1.50 profit despite winning only four of ten plays. Up $86.75.

Holiday ($3.49)—Disaster! I lost all five coupons including a big 15-10 in pai gow poker. A $17 loss, but still up $69.75.

Marina ($2.76)—Free deck of cards and $8 profit. Up $77.75.

Tropicana ($3.39)—The Trop had a blackjack coupon which could be used as either a 3-2 (46¢) or 8-5 ($1.40). I took the extra risk for the extra gain in expectation. I won the bet, the dealer paid me $8 and forgot to pick up my coupon. I placed another $5 on the coupon and extracted an additional $8 with another win; a classic coupon play. After losing two smaller coupons my profit was $12 and a free Tropicana mug. Up $89.75 with one casino to go. I wanted to break the $100 mark badly.

Hacienda ($1.25)—Unfortunately, my last casino had only three coupons. Winning all three would still land me $2.75 short of my goal. I won two and lost one. Up $94.75. Time for another classic coupon gambit. I noticed that a bingo session was about to start. A woman at the door was passing out a pack of six lucky bucks ($2.60) to the bingo players as they entered. I walked in, collected my package, circled the room, and effected my escape unnoticed. Success! I went five for six and had one more free drink. Up $108.75.

Granted, this was a monster coupon run. My expected win (the sum of the numbers in parentheses) was $54.52. A husband and wife team playing a funbook apiece would expect to win about the amount that I did. Wouldn't it be great to start your vacation with a $110 gambling stake, not to mention drinks, souvenirs, shows, and free popcorn? The entire Fabulous Las Vegas Coupon Tour consisted of only 12 casinos and they're all on the Strip.

A year later I conducted another coupon tour, this one involving 19 casinos. After a total of 80 bets, my record was 35 wins and 45 losses. Still, because of the bonuses paid on the winners, I made a $50 profit. This is a great illustration of the power of coupons. Despite losing more wagers than I won, I still made money.

Mini Tour

You don't have to visit 19 casinos. You can pick two or three casinos, collect souvenirs, partake of a free cocktail or two, and make a $10-20 per couple profit. A 1993 comparison of eight easily obtained funbooks—Lady Luck, Fitzgeralds, Fremont, Riviera, Sands, Harrah's, Stardust, and Sahara—revealed a combined value of $28.50. A husband and wife team playing a funbook each had a combined expected return of $57.

Take this strategy down to its lowest terms simply by playing any lucky bucks you happen across during your vacation. Keep tabs on your results and you'll find that you will usually come out ahead.

Do-It-Yourself Analysis

Want to know how much a coupon or funbook is worth? Consult the chart below, then add the value of all coupons for other benefits like drinks, discounts, etc. to get an overall value. Coupons for the big 6 wheel are worth 33¢ for 2-1s and 22¢ for 3-2s. Coupons that make your first card an ace on a hand of blackjack are worth 52% of the amount you are allowed to bet. For example, an ace coupon with a $5 bet is worth $2.60. As a rule, don't play keno tickets unless they are free, or discounted at least 50% (get a $2 ticket for $1).

COUPON	GAME	EXP WIN
3-2	craps	46¢
	blackjack	46¢
	roulette	37¢
2-1	craps	48¢
	blackjack	47¢
	roulette	42¢
7-5	craps	92¢
	blackjack	92¢
	roulette	68¢

Slot Clubs

Slot players have become the bread and butter of the casino industry, generating a greater share of the casino win than the players of all the other games combined. To accommodate this very important sector of the gambling market, casino marketing experts developed an innovation called the slot club. The purpose of a slot club is to reward players for their 25¢ and

Remember Your Couponomy

Here's a great letter from a travel writer—"I assumed that the coupon tour would make good story material, but I didn't expect to net $139 from seven of those silly little books."

$1 slot action with restaurant and room discounts, gifts, special parties, and cash. It's a concept borrowed from airline frequent-flyer programs—give the customers incentive to return, and they will. It was a great idea that caught on. Today you can join slot clubs in almost every major casino.

Clubs vary significantly in terms of value and format, but most award cash and complimentaries based on accumulated points that correspond to your level of play. Points are tabulated via membership cards that are inserted into machines as you play them. Total coins played, rather than money won, is usually the gauge by which points are awarded. Membership is open to anyone who takes the time to register.

There isn't a great deal to consider when deciding whether or not to join a slot club. If you play slots, you should join. It's as simple as that. During the course of your vacation, your play will earn points that can be redeemed for something of value, and the rebate has the effect of reducing the casino's overall advantage.

It's fairly obvious that it is in your best interest to take anything a casino is willing to give back, but you should join slot clubs even if you don't play slot machines. Just by joining—even if you never gamble a single coin—your name will probably be added to the casino's customer data base, which may result in "surprise" offers of discounted rooms or free meals in the future. There's no guarantee that you will receive these, but it's happened before and it'll happen again.

Due to the increased sophistication of computers that track member play, simply signing up may not be enough to qualify you for special offers. It will probably be necessary to *activate* your membership by playing until you accumulate a specified number of points. This point total is usually low enough to be reached in one to two hours of play. Investigate when you sign up. Ask an employee what point total you must reach to attain active status.

Once your membership is activated, you will be entitled to a variety of special privileges. You may receive line passes for shows and buffets or invitations to members-only parties. More importantly, you may qualify for significant lodging discounts on a future trip, and you'll get priority consideration when reserving a room. Most clubs have their own reservations service that sets aside blocks of rooms to accommodate club members during busy periods and holidays. It makes sense to activate a slot membership at a casino where you are likely to stay. As I've already mentioned, the greatest benefits may come later via those surprise offers courtesy of the casino marketing department. Just sit back and see what develops.

Some clubs allow you to collect points on table games by presenting your card to pit personnel prior to beginning play. The concepts outlined above apply when playing table games as well. Remember to present your card. Your normal blackjack or crap play may result in a free dinner or room discount.

Of course, it's possible to earn all sorts of additional complimentaries for extended slot-machine play, but remember, casinos are able to extend rewards because of profits generated by player efforts to earn them. Securing the basic membership benefits for the smallest initial investment should be your primary objective.

Casinos are committed to the slot club concept. As each casino tries to outdo the next, new opportunities will become available.

> ***Warning***
>
> *Take special care that your card has been inserted properly in machines that you play. If it doesn't register, you earn nothing. And don't forget to retrieve your card before you leave.*

How About No Slot Club?

A few years ago, Palace Station made an all-out effort to convince customers that slot clubs are subsidized by "tighter" machines. This is the same angle used by some supermarket advertisers who charge that competitors offering money-saving coupons compensate by marking up other items throughout the store. An analysis of video poker schedules at Palace Station vs. casinos with slot clubs did not support the claim.

Become An Expert

Each slot club is different, with unique twists that distinguish it from the others. You can maximize your gains by familiarizing yourself with every nuance of the best clubs. Learn the key point plateaus necessary for membership activation, and the minimum maintenance requirements needed to keep you in good standing. Play special promotions that earn points at double and triple the normal rates. Make friends in the system.

Make a hobby out of researching different clubs. Slot-club-comp disbursement is still an inexact science, which means there are loopholes just waiting to be exploited. When you know the rules better than the people who made them, you have a big advantage.

Matchplay, Bean Jars, and Hip Packs

Matchplay

Some promotions, especially room packages, include matchplay chips. Matchplay chips must be accompanied by an equal amount of real money when played, and they have an expected value of approximately half their face value. Example: $50 in matchplay chips can be evaluated as being worth about $25.

Drawings and Giveaways

Every May, Palace Station runs a giant slot promotion in which they give away cars and cash. Winners are chosen in a daily drawing. You get tickets into the drawing by hitting small slot jackpots or redeeming promotional pieces Palace Station sends through the mail. If you are good at counting beans in a jar, then you might be able to make a good estimation of the number of tickets in the drum, and you can figure out the value of returning to the casino to check out the drawing. The total value of the giveaway is about $25,000 per day. Divide $25,000 by the total number of tickets in the drum, and multiply by the number of tickets that are yours. Example: You have three tickets in a drum that you estimate has a total of 50,000 tickets. $25,000/50,000 = 50¢, and 50¢ X 3 = $1.50. Decide if your time is worth $1.50.

Souvenirs

Casinos don't dent their bottom line too badly in the free-souvenir department. Pens, keychains, magnets, and semi-worthless trinkets are about all you can expect to find in your coupon-tour goodie bag, unless you target a few specific casinos.

Fitzgeralds gives away baseball hats and sports watches to anyone who presents an ad that runs in the freebie mags. Also look for an ad for a Circus Circus hip pack—perfect for carrying slot coins. The Sands gives away a porcelain coffee mug emblazoned with the Sands logo. It's one of the all-time great Las Vegas giveaways; the Sands recently handed out their five-millionth. Check funbooks for good T-shirt discounts (Lady Luck and Sands have them). Don't forget the great free picture in front of a million bucks at the Horseshoe. And here's one of the best kept souvenir secrets in town: you can get a deck of Caesars Palace playing cards just by asking at the casino cashier's cage in the Olympic section. No cost. No questions.

Betty Bishop Mailing

Is it worth your time to mail a letter of inquiry to the casinos that you plan to visit during your vacation? In a 1990 study designed to answer this question we sent this letter to 137 casinos in the five major U.S. casino areas: Las Vegas, Atlantic City, Reno, Lake Tahoe, and Laughlin. We signed the letters with the fictitious name Betty Bishop and rented a post office box in Southern California. The letters were mailed from California so they would bear a non-Nevada postmark.

August 27, 1990

Dear Customer Relations Manager,

My husband and I plan to make our first visit to [Las Vegas, Atlantic City, etc.] area soon. We will be arriving October 7. Our travel agent suggested we write to the casinos we plan to visit to inquire about special discounts you offer on rooms. Also, any funbooks or coupons you could send would be very helpful. Please find enclosed a self-addressed-stamped envelope for your response. Thank you for your help.

Warmest Wishes,
Betty Bishop

We received some form of response from 94 casinos, better than two-thirds of the 137 total. By area, response percentages were as follows: Lake Tahoe 82%; Laughlin 80%; Atlantic City 75%; Las Vegas 71%; Reno 53%. Return letters arrived promptly. In most cases, the response was an advertisement in the form of a slick three-color brochure detailing the casino's best features. Room rate/package information was also a popular enclosure. The casinos were courteous; many letters were hand written or personalized in some way. A few sent packages that contained show schedules and maps.

Las Vegas

Fifty out of 70 casinos responded. Twenty-four sent coupon books or coupon vouchers; however, many were easily obtainable without sending for them. The Union Plaza sent an excellent coupon book that is usually distributed only by travel agents. The book contains a free breakfast of bacon and eggs, a free lunch, and other valuable coupons. The Rio sent a coupon for a two-for-one breakfast buffet and another for a two-for-one lunch buffet. The Klondike, a small casino at the south end of the Strip, sent a VIP card good for a $10 per night discount on rooms. The Desert Inn put together a great package. No discounts, but everything else you could ask for: a gaming guide; a Las Vegas fact sheet; a show guide; a list of casinos offering funbooks (reasonably accurate); buffet prices; maps of Las Vegas, the Strip and the airport. Someone spent a lot of time putting this one together. Silver City sent a premier package: two free drink coupons and a comp ticket for breakfast or lunch for two in the coffee shop. This is the sort of perk you usually have to earn by gambling a few hours at the table games. The complimentary tickets were accompanied by a full-page letter thanking Betty for her patronage. Outstanding. Best of all was the Imperial Palace. Betty received a "Valued Guest Certificate" good for a free room (Sun.-Thurs.) between the dates of Nov. 25 and December 26. The offer included a free breakfast or lunch buffet for two on both days and a two-for-one pass to the *Legends in Concert* show.

Other Areas

Lake Tahoe—Nine of eleven properties responded. But they were the smaller casinos on the lake that apparently saw an opportunity to woo one more visitor away from the giants. South Shore's Lakeside Inn offered a $10 discount on rooms for showing the return letter they sent back. North Shore's Hyatt sent coupons, maps, and information. The Crystal Bay Club, also on the North Shore, sent a dinner comp for two, plus a voucher for $4 in slot change.

Laughlin—Nothing special. Several casinos sent funbook vouchers and information about the city.

Atlantic City—Eight out of twelve properties responded, but letters contained only brochures and room rates. We expected Betty Bishop to benefit from Atlantic City's unique marketing strategy of mailing free slot-coin vouchers to prospective customers. She did not. It's attributable to Betty's California address. Atlantic City casinos live or die by their ability to attract repeat customers. To accomplish this, marketing departments make fabulous offers to potential customers in major East Coast markets. Customers west of the Rockies are not considered good return-visit prospects.

Reno—The 53% response was the lowest, but that figure is deceiving because Reno is home to many small casinos that did not answer.

Conclusion

Don't waste your time writing to every casino in Las Vegas unless you're a collector of three-color brochures or you want to compare room package deals. If you've already made reservations, it's worth a 29¢ stamp to contact the casino at which you'll be staying. You never know who will handle your request and what they may decide to send. As evidenced by our results, the possibility exists for almost anything, all the way up to a free room.

12

COMPS

Several hundred thousand dollars worth of complimentaries (also known as freebies or comps) are given away *every day* on the Las Vegas Strip. During city-wide events, comps climb into the millions. They're the lifeblood of Las Vegas gambling.

But for a phenomenon that's so prevalent, comps inhabit a shadowy realm defined by casino credit and front deposit money, markers and rating cards, stone-faced floor bosses and pit clerks, and marketing equivalency percentages. To most of us, it's a rarefied world that only high rollers—players who sit all night in a baccarat pit or at a $100 minimum blackjack table—know anything about.

However, the fact is that anybody who comes to Las Vegas can get comped, and everybody does, whether they know it or not. Free parking is a bona fide comp, especially in downtown lots where all you have to do is validate your stub at the cage. Free cocktails for players is an excellent guaranteed comp, even if you're only feeding nickels into a slot machine. Most pit bosses still have the discretion to distribute line passes to the showrooms, as well as drink, coffee shop, and buffet tickets, usually available to table players for the asking.

Still, very little information has ever been disseminated on the subject. It's a book in itself, and it will be. We're extremely fortunate to have landed one of the worlds great experts on all aspects of casino comps from both sides of the pit, Max Rubin. The following are excerpts from his upcoming book, *Comp City*, which will be published in February 1994 by Huntington Press. *Comp City,* written in Max's wry style, not only spotlights, once and for all, the whole enshrouded world of comps, but also details an effective system that enables *anyone* to enjoy a comp status worth a lifetime of free Las Vegas vacations—with much less risk than you might expect.

Ratings

All comps are based on ratings. All ratings are based on a formula that predicts the casino's potential to win a gambler's money. All casinos follow the same formula: the average bet times the hours played times the house advantage. The house then gives you back about 40% of what they expect to win.

To rate your play, the casino gives you a plastic ID card. You hand it to the pit boss when you sit down. He writes down your name, how much you buy in for, and how much you're betting per hand. When you leave, he logs your playing time. This information goes to marketing, then they decide what kind of goodies you get. It works like this:

HANDS	HOUSE	EXPECTED			
BET	PLAYED	ADVANTAGE	WIN	%	COMPS
$100	100 (1hr)	2%	$200	40	$80

In this example, the gambler receives about $80 in hotel comps for each hour he plays because he's rated for a $200-per-hour expected loss. But this is where we can beat 'em. If you play a perfect game of blackjack, you'll lose only about one-tenth of what the house expects you to. So, instead of $200, you lose $20, and still get your $80 worth of stuff.

This, of course, is a simplified example. Qualifying standards for the more valuable comps are very precise. A gambler who bets $25 a hand and plays for four hours gets a room ("R") on the house. If the same player steps up to $50 a hand, the casino picks up his food, too ("R&F"). When he starts betting $100 a hand, he'll be entitled to unlimited room, food, and beverage ("RFB"). Now he gets to ride around town in a limo and slurp champagne like he's some kind of sheik or something.

What does all this mean? In the first place, many of you scrimp and chisel and wring every drop out of every dollar you spend in Las Vegas. And you've still been paying too much! Now you're going to get twice as much for half the money. The only catch is you've gotta play. Still, your vacations will cost you a dime on the dollar, and *you'll* be the sheik. Would you spend $50 to ride in a limo, stay in a suite, eat gourmet meals, see a show, and gamble for two days? Of course you would. Impossible? Hardly. It happens every day.

For Example

We received this letter from LB, a subscriber.

At the Four Queens, I played $5 Multiple Action Blackjack for about two hours and received a comp good for two in the coffee shop and we managed to eat $40 worth of food!

Did you see what LB got for playing $5 blackjack at the Four Queens? A coffee shop comp for two. Big deal, you say? Well, it was a big deal, considering she heroically ran up a $40 tab, which ain't easy in a coffee shop. And would you believe me if I told you that LB's $40 food fest actually cost her less than $2? It's true.

LB played Multiple Action Blackjack at $5 a bet. In this game, you place three bets for every hand played. The house gets out about 30 hands an hour, so LB got in about $900 in action. Due to the 2-to-1 bonus for red naturals, the house edge is barely more than one-tenth of one percent (.0013) assuming she played perfect basic strategy. That means that LB's expected loss was a little more than a buck. Here's the math:

Each bet	$5
Total bets	180
Total wagered	$900
House Edge	.0013
LB's *expected* loss	$1.17
LB's Comps	$40.00
LB's Net Comp Gain	$39.83

Without even knowing it, LB entered the realm of comp wizardry and stumbled onto the best-kept secret in Las Vegas, one that even the most astute casino executives aren't aware of. (I hope you're sitting down, because this one's gonna stun you.)

Max Fact #1: *A world-class card counter can win one bet an hour, at best. An amateur comp wizard can win one bet an hour standing on his or her head.*

The only difference is that the card counter wins money and the comp wizard wins comps. And while the counter is trying to stay invisible, can't drink, has to concentrate on every card, and winds up paying for his room and food, the comp wizard parties the weekend away and gets everything handed to him on a platter.

Think about it. The *LVA* lists the greatest deals in town, but have you ever seen anything published about unlimited food for two in a first-class coffee shop for $1.17? No, and you never will. Why? Because the casinos don't even know they're offering it! Casino marketing departments assume that blackjack players don't use perfect strategy and base their comp policies on a house edge of 2-3%. In fact, the expected loss for a basic strategy player is about 15% of the casino's assumption; *also,* most people don't have the guts to run up a tab as high as our comp wizard, LB.

Of course, once the casino bosses read *Comp City*, they'll realize what they're doing. But we'll still have them, because if they tighten their comp policies, they'll run off the poor players who pay all the bills. So even though they know we're out there, they won't be able to do a damn thing about it. Heh, heh, heh.

High-Level Comps

So far, all I've talked about are some measly little meal comps. Once you've mastered comp wizardry, here's what you can expect to get, what it takes you to qualify, and what it'll cost you when the smoke clears. (The costs listed here are for *expected* losses and apply only to blackjack players capable of perfect basic-strategy play. Actual wins and losses will vary, but over time, these are the true costs you will incur while playing.)

At the high end of the comp spectrum, the sky is literally the limit. In

COMP	WHO QUALIFIES	COMP COST
free parking validation	Anyone with a car (must go to cage)	$0
2 cocktails	Five-cent slot players (5 mins.)	0.02
2 cocktails and tobacco	$2 table-game players (5 mins.)	0.10
2 buffets	$5 table or $1 slot (1 hr.)	1.00
2 coffee shop	$10 table or $1 slot (1 hr.)	2.00
2 nights, casino rate	$15 table or $1 slot (8 hrs.)	12.00
2 nights, free	$25 table or $1 slot (8 hrs.)	19.00
2 nights free, food	$50 table or $5 slot (8 hrs.)	38.00
2 nights, F&B, show	$100 table or $25 slot (8 hrs.)	77.00
2 nights RFB, airfare	$200 table or $25+ slot (8 hrs.)	154.00
suite, golf, airfare	$200 table or $25+ slot (8 hrs.)	154.00
RFB for four	$200 table or $50+ slot (8 hrs.)	154.00
penthouse with works	$500 table or $100+ slot (8 hrs.)	384.00*
private jet/lanai suites	$5,000 table or $500 slot (8 hrs.)	3,840.00*
suites for 30, chartered overseas 727, private chef, private gaming salon, etc.	$100,000 table or $500 slot (8 hrs.)**	

* *Comp Wizardry at this level is impossible to disguise, but comps still run about 30 cents on the dollar.*

** *Lilly livers need not apply. Anybody rich enough to play 100 grand a hand isn't going to read the LVA anyway, but I thought you might like to know.*

January 1993, two friends of mine, high rollers from Amarillo (their *apparent* average bet is $400), took advantage of a full RFB weekend at a top casino, a chartered jet to the Super Bowl, VIP parties at the Rose Bowl, and seats on the 30-yard-line. They got a $5,000+ value for less than $250. Adds a whole new dimension to playing blackjack, doesn't it?

Katie's Komp

At any level of play, it often comes down to knowing how to ask. Huntington Press' mild-mannered, Texas-raised receptionist, Katie was playing pai gow poker at the Gold Coast at $10 per hand. After about an hour, she called the pit boss over and said, "I heard something about comps if you gamble enough. How does it work?"

"When you get done playing, come talk to me," the boss replied.

After another 45 minutes of play, she cashed out (about even for the day). The dealer called the boss and he wrote her a ticket for two for dinner.

The issuance of comps is based on the casino's perception of a player's expected loss. Katie's two-hour, low-limit pai gow poker play represented an expected loss of only $7, yet she was able to obtain a comp worth $30-40. Why? Because the situation was right. She played in a casino that caters to the $5-25 bettor (no chance had it been The Mirage), she played long enough to be seen and remembered, and she asked in the right way. Red-chip bettors can pursue comps with a high chance of success and low exposure to potential embarrassment by using a similar strategy. Also, it's easier for women, so when possible, let the woman do the asking.

13

ENTERTAINMENT

CHANGING SCENE

Like the city itself, the Las Vegas entertainment scene is changing rapidly. Wayne Newton is out. Theme complexes, water parks, high-tech arcades, FX adventures, special-events centers, interactivity, and virtual reality are in. Even the brand of entertainment inside the big showrooms—traditional home to "Las Vegas-style entertainment"—is changing. Headliner shows are giving way to production shows. Traditional showroom performers are being replaced by rock bands. Concerts, both in the casinos and in venues like the Thomas & Mack Center and the Silver Bowl, have become commonplace, sanctioned by the casinos that use big events like a Paul McCartney concert to bring in the baby-boomer gamblers. This chapter first gives you a glimpse into the sci-fi future of Las Vegas, but primarily looks at the Las Vegas entertainment options that exist right now.

The New Wave

We all know about the rivalry between Pepsi and Coke, MCI and AT&T, IBM and Apple, Levis and Wranglers, and *Newsweek* and *Time*. To these giant competitors, you can now add Disneyworld and Las Vegas. As Las Vegas caters more and more to the family market, the Strip will undoubtedly come to resemble the Magic Kingdom. After all, Disneyworld, with its 30 million annual visitors, is the number-one vacation destination in the country, and Las Vegas, with its 23 million, is number two. The more like Tomorrowland and EPCOT Las Vegas becomes, the less the discrepancy in the demographics will be. Especially since Disneyworld will never, in the most fundamental sense, emulate Las Vegas. You can bank on that.

Thus the new places—MGM Grand, Treasure Island, Luxor, Grand Slam Canyon, the Stratosphere Tower, the Fremont Street Experience, the rainbow and roller coaster at Stateline, the interactive theater at the Rio, and the new megaresorts at the Dunes and the Desert Inn—will shape the trends of Las Vegas entertainment into the 21st century.

Brief Preview

MGM Grand—The total property is larger than Disneyland. To put its size into perspective, the swimming complex is nearly 150,000 square feet, which is 25,000 square feet bigger than the Riviera casino, largest in the world. The video arcade is 30,000 square feet, about as big as 15 three-bedroom houses. The amusement park features 12 major attractions, including Grand Canyon Rapids, Deep Earth Exploration, Lightning Bolt, and You're in the Movies. And at $25 admission, it's *way* less expensive than the mouse's joint.

Grand Slam Canyon—The main attraction under the 300,000-square-foot pink glass dome is the world's largest indoor roller coaster. This harrowing ride packs a wallop, with a force of 2-1/2 G's. There is also a nearly vertical flume ride, laser tag in hidden passageways and canyons, eight life-size animated dinosaurs, a magic motion machine, and more. The dome is completely climate controlled.

Luxor—The stunning pyramid contains 29 *million* cubic feet of open space, large enough to feature a scale model of the Manhattan skyline. Sega will operate the video-game amusement center, which will eventually feature large video screens, wraparound sound, and hydraulic seats.

Stratosphere Tower—The elevator ride to the top of the 1,012-foot tower should be a thrill, but probably nothing compared to the open-air amusement ride at the top of Las Vegas' tallest structure.

Fremont Street Experience—If all goes according to plan, the garden of neon will be transformed into the laser amazer: a multimedia sound and light show projected onto a four-block-long, 100-foot-high awning.

Stateline—There's already a merry-go-round and ferris wheel at the Primadonna on I-15; soon to come are a laser rainbow across the interstate and the world's tallest and fastest roller coaster.

Rio interactive theater—Scheduled for completion in April 1994, this high-tech experience allows the audience to have a collective hand in the way a movie develops and eventually ends.

ITT-Sheraton theme park—The ink isn't even dry yet on the prelimi-

---

Sammy Davis Tribute

In what may have been the greatest tribute ever staged by the city, Las Vegas mourned the passing of Sammy Davis, Jr. (in 1990) by dimming the lights of the great marquees on the Strip for ten minutes. Thousands lined the Strip to witness the unprecedented salute.

---

nary deal between the Sheraton and the Desert Inn, but ITT's influence is almost certain to have far-reaching high-tech implications on a new Sheraton megajoint.

The Headliners

In the '80s, you might have gotten whiplash trying to take in all the big names on the casino marquees while driving up and down the Strip. No longer. When Gladys Knight stepped off the Las Vegas Hilton stage on June 23 1993, it marked the end of that casino's quarter century of headliner policy, and left only Caesars Palace, Bally's, Desert Inn, and The Mirage (one week a month when Siegfried & Roy are on vacation) to accommodate headliner talent in Las Vegas. Of these, the Desert Inn is worthy of special mention. In 1992, the DI made a decision to buck the entertainment trend and institute a "return-to-the-stars" policy. The official name of the casino was changed to "The Stars' Desert Inn" to reflect the move. The DI's stable of performers includes: Frank Sinatra, Paul Anka, Liza Minnelli, Shirley MacLaine, the Smothers Brothers, Don Rickles, Barry Manilow, Steve Lawrence & Eydie Gorme, Smokey Robinson, and Willie Nelson.

Other headliners who still play Las Vegas regularly include: Tom Jones, Rodney Dangerfield, George Carlin, Engelbert Humperdinck, Ann-Margret, Jerry Seinfeld, David Copperfield, Johnny Mathis, Julio Iglesias, George Burns, Howie Mandell, and Dolly Parton.

Accurate show schedules are not difficult to find. But obtaining advance price information is only slightly more difficult than hitting a royal flush on a video poker machine (the *Las Vegas Advisor* lists prices three months in advance). Figure on paying a base price of $30 to $75 per person for a headliner show. The average price is about $45.

Hilton Obit
(1969-1993)

Barbra Streisand opened the showroom in July 1969 when it was the International Hotel. The showroom became renowned as the venue for Elvis' mid-1970s comeback, in which he played to 144 straight sold-out audiences. Bill Cosby holds the record for the number of engagements (64), followed by Wayne Newton (38) and Liberace (34). The Andrew Lloyd Webber musical Starlight Express takes over as the Las Vegas Hilton's entertainment staple.

PRODUCTION SHOWS

The production show is a fast-paced, cost-effective, versatile, entertainment hybrid that, in the finest Darwinian fashion, has emerged as the dominant show genre of the new Las Vegas. Don't mistake production shows for extravaganzas; it's all changed. Six-foot-tall showgirls who parade in headpieces and feathers have devolved into 5' 6" dancers in leotards who can execute all the latest street moves. There's more comedy than juggling. Gaucho acts are, once again, a novelty. This is the direction in which Las Vegas showroom entertainment is going, and all things considered, it's a good development for the consumer. There's more now in the way of variety and price options than ever before.

Exercising Your Options

When The Mirage upped the cost of the already outrageously priced *Siegfried & Roy* show by $5 in 1990, the local press quoted Mirage Chairman Steve Wynn as saying, "If they'll pay [what they're paying now], they'll pay $5 more." Ain't it the truth! If you've decided to see a specific show (or entertainer) during your vacation, you're going to pay what it takes. On the other hand, today's market affords you a lot more latitude in your decision-making. Here's an example:

The tab for *Siegfried & Roy* is $72.85 per person, a $145.70 expenditure for two. What if, instead, you buy two tickets to the Stardust's *Enter the Night* at $24.90 per ticket ($49.80 total), and use the $95.90 savings for a great steak dinner at the Rio's All-American Bar & Grille ($40), drinks ($15), and a $40 head start on your gambling stake? Sure, *S & R* is great, but *Enter* is no slouch , and look at how much farther your money can go.

Yes, there really are discernible differences in the quality of the shows, and the differences are fairly well reflected in their respective prices. But for many, a show is a show is a show, and the bottom line takes precedence.

Mini-Reviews

Entertainment tastes are too subjective to devote a lot of space to show reviews. However, a "mini-review" approach (bare-bones considerations only) does provide some useful information and a little direction. The following are arranged by price, least to most expensive, based on least expensive price possible (i.e., late-night, cocktail-only show). The range of potential prices is listed in parentheses.

Viva Las Vegas, Sands ($0-$10)

There's a comedian, a singing impersonator, an Elvis satirist, a little dynamo of a lead singer, and six dancers. Production numbers are a bit tame, and individual performances could be shortened to add snap. At 75 minutes, the show is overlong. But *Viva Las Vegas* must be judged in context: it's in the intimate and historic Copa Room at the Sands, it's an early-afternoon show that easily outpaces the city's few other daytime options, and it's very inexpensive (discounts with funbook).

Allen & Rossi, Vegas World ($6)

Not really a production format, but a very good show and bargain. The showroom is big, crowds are large, and music is live. It's a true night out.

Crazy Girls, La Cage, and *The Improv,* Riviera ($9-$20)

The price includes a dinner buffet worth $7, so the real range of prices is $8-$13. Choose one of three shows: *Crazy Girls* (topless revue), *La Cage* (female impersonators), or *Improv* (comedy club). One of the city's best values.

Country Tonite, Aladdin ($19-$23)

The genie dons a Stetson and Tony Lamas for 90 minutes as cloggers, fiddlers, and yodelers perform at the Aladdin, in the only C&W revue in Las Vegas. Singers croon well-known tunes from Patsy Cline to Garth Brooks, and dancers two-step, waltz, and square dance on a stage that extends into the audience. The music comes from a nine-piece ensemble, instead of the usual taped accompaniment. The audience is encouraged to join in, and it does. The fun is hard to resist. *Country Tonite* offers mostly good, down-home, family entertainment (there's a little adult humor). The showroom is intimate, and the spectacle is large enough to be enjoyed from any seat in the house.

Boy-lesque, Sahara ($19)

Long-running, campy, female-impersonation show. *Boy-lesque* was the rage during its heyday in the '80s, serving up a risque, no-holds-barred act (for $5.95) that was the embodiment of the anything-goes-in-Las Vegas mystique. The current version has suffered from "new and improved," however, and offers little beyond a glimpse back at a Las Vegas classic. Better value for female impersonation at the Riviera's *La Cage.*

Les Folies Bergere, Tropicana ($19-$39)

The longest running revue in Las Vegas (34 years, with a few years off here and there) combines a few of the old extravaganza features with some contemporary updating. A good solid show that will not disappoint, especially if you catch it for the bargain cocktail-show price. This is one of only three revues that still offer a dinner show. The *Las Vegas Advisor* has had a long-standing promotion with the Tropicana for 2-for-1 admission (cocktail show) for our subscribers. At $9.50 per ticket, this is probably the best show value in town.

Lance Burton—A Magical Journey, Hacienda ($22)

After nine years as a featured performer in the Tropicana's *Folies Bergere,* Lance Burton moved to the Hacienda. This is a classic case of good news, bad news. The good news is Lance Burton is an awesome magician. He's won a million magician's awards and he deserves them all. Also, the show is clever and unique. The bad news is Lance Burton talks. In his act at the Tropicana, Burton rarely spoke. He let his attitude do the talking and it worked. In this show, he speaks throughout and destroys the aura of non-approachability that is so important to his act. Also, the show costs $20 and doesn't include drinks or gratuity. A little expensive.

If you love magic, see this show. If you don't, there are better show options for the money.

Splash, Riviera ($32)

The elder statesman of the new-style production shows, *Splash* debuted way back in 1988. It's a great show—very fast and contemporary—and a good deal late-night. Players Club members still get 50% off with their membership card, a deal that rivals the *LVA*'s *Folies Bergere* arrangement for value.

Legends In Concert, Imperial Palace ($23.50)

Legends in Concert has been a fixture at the Imperial Palace since 1983. The secret to the show's longevity has been its producer's ability to find cast members that really look, act, and sound like the legendary performers they portray. No easy feat since everything in the show is live, including the music. The line-up changes but usually features impressions of personalities like Bobby Darin, Roy Orbison, Marilyn Monroe, the Blues Brothers, Neil Diamond, Liberace, Madonna, and Elvis.

Because there is no nudity, *Legends* is considered one of the better shows for children, even though most kids will not recognize all the performers. For adults, it's an entertaining 90 minutes.

Enter the Night, Stardust ($25)

Enter the Night has something that will appeal to almost everyone—traditional parading showgirls; contemporary dance; a great laser light segment; live music; and spectacular costuming, lighting, and sets. The main act, Vladimir, was named by *People Magazine* one of the "50 Most Beautiful People in the World" in 1991. He "flies" around the showroom, soaring and dive-bombing with the aid of two straps attached to an unseen hydraulic lift. It's fascinating. The show contains nudity, and children are not permitted. The Stardust leaves 7-5 & 3-2 gambling coupons on the showroom tables. They're worth 92¢ and 46¢, respectively.

***King Arthur's Tournament,* Excalibur ($25)**

The second of the three remaining dinner shows, this is the only show where everyone gets dinner. The dinner is good: Cornish game hen, potatoes, vegetable, roll, soup, dessert, and choice of beer, sangria, or soft drink. The meal is served without utensils. *King Arthur's Tournament* provides a great opportunity for parents to treat their children to a showroom experience. Knights compete in a jousting match and engage in extremely well-choreographed bouts of hand-to-hand combat. The audience is encouraged to cheer for the knight that represents their particular seating section.

***Spellbound,* Harrah's ($26.50)**

If you like magic, you'll like *Spellbound.* It has a male magician, a female magician, a combination male/female team of magicians, even a comedian magician. By the time the show's over, you may be magicianed out. Fortunately, they're good magicians. *Spellbound* is a fair alternative for

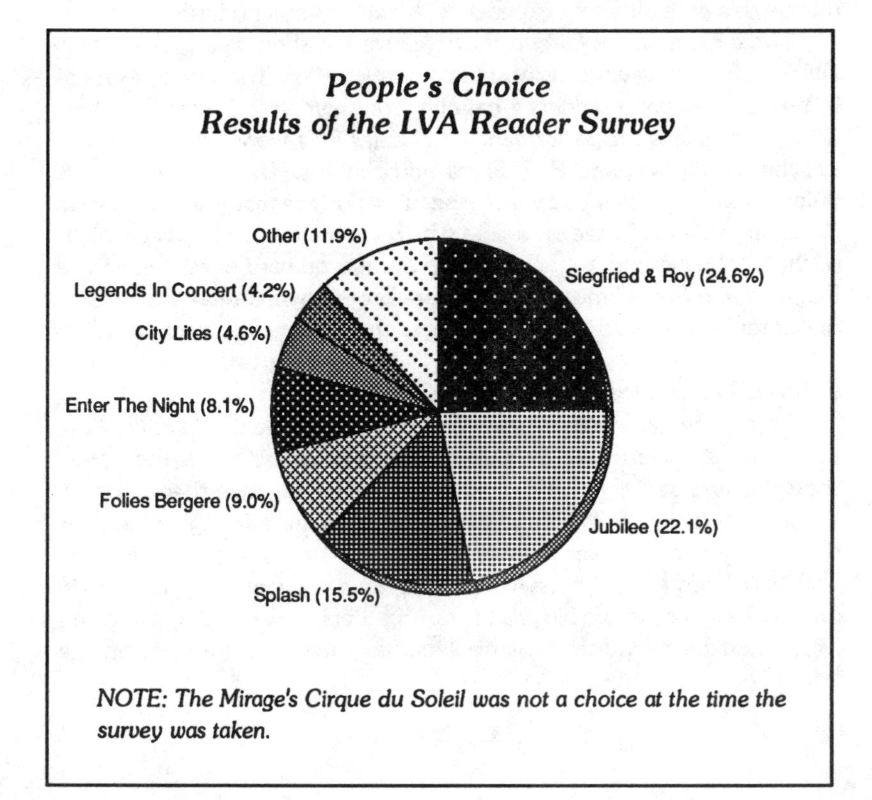

NOTE: The Mirage's Cirque du Soleil was not a choice at the time the survey was taken.

children (especially kids who like magicians), as there's no nudity and very little off-color humor. The show is slightly pricey, but you can knock $5 off by using a coupon from the Harrah's funbook.

City Lites, Flamingo Hilton ($28-49)

Good show, old show, dinner show. Like *Folies Bergere* and *Jubilee, City Lites* features showgirls, larger-than-life production numbers, and variety acts (ice skating, in particular). Dinner is typical banquet food, with seating at 6 pm assigned by the maitre d'.

Cirque du Soleil, The Mirage ($38.50)

Moving to Treasure Island December 1993

It's a clear case of culture versus cost. On one hand, *Cirque du Soleil* is an entertainment happening: a combination of theater, dance, music, comedy, acrobatics, and new-age elan that the creators term "Nouvelle Experience." On the other hand, it's one of the highest priced shows in town, a fact that some will begrudge regardless of its entertainment value, simply because a dozen Las Vegas show options are available at half the price. If cost-consciousness is your criterion, look elsewhere. If you seek a memorable entertainment experience, however, look no further.

Three elements of *Cirque du Soleil* set the show apart. The first is intimacy. This is the ultimate in audience participation. The second element is music. A live band renders a haunting/rousing/mystical score that stays with you long after the performance concludes. The score's composer says that his influences were Pink Floyd and Brahms. The third element is uniqueness. The closer you watch, the more you see that's different—one circus ring instead of three, no animals, no communication via speech (high-pitched babbling and a cracking whip are the primary cues). Much like *Siegfried and Roy, Cirque* is really more Broadway than Las Vegas. One of our reviewers called it "the greatest, strangest show I've ever seen."

Jubilee, Bally's ($40)

Last of the Las Vegas extravaganzas. All the elements of the old-time production shows are here: the glitzy costumes and massive sets, the topless showgirls and scantily clad dancers, and the outrageous specialty acts. *Jubilee* is frozen in time, a throwback to a couple decades ago, when this type of stage spectacle was synonymous with Las Vegas entertainment. The $10 million production, most expensive in town, continues to pack 'em in on the strength of its two big production numbers, the saga of Samson and Delilah and the sinking of the Titanic. Since the showgirls are topless, no one under 18 is admitted.

***Siegfried & Roy*, The Mirage ($72.85)**
See Siegfried & Roy Saga (page 160).

Seating

How to get a good seat in the showroom is one of the great lingering Las Vegas mysteries. If you haven't been through it before, the anxiety grows as you get closer and closer to the front of the line. How do you avoid getting marooned in the nosebleed section? Well, there's a lot of good news and a little bad with regard to this dilemma.

The Good News

Reserved seating is taking over. With the opening of The Mirage came a reserved-seat policy, similar to the method used at concerts and sporting events. Under a reserved system, tickets and gratuities are prepaid, and purchasing tickets early (rather than digging into your pockets for tip money) should secure the better seats. The new policy was bad news for the high rollers who were used to flipping out a $100 bill for preferential seating. It was even worse news for the show captains and maitre d's who had made big livings accepting those hundreds. But despite employee resistance, other showrooms are now switching, one by one, to reserved seating. It currently runs about 50/50: reserved vs. the old maitre d'/seating-chart system. More importantly, all the headliner showrooms (except Desert Inn), where seat location is apt to be a bigger concern, are now reserved seating.

And what about that old system? More good news. The concern over good seats is way overblown. Most showrooms are fairly intimate, so seats throughout are adequate, especially for viewing the production shows. And if the showroom isn't overflowing, you'll often be taken down toward the front even without a tip. Chutzpah helps. If you don't like where you are being seated, and don't mind speaking up, you'll almost always improve, if only slightly, by asking.*

The Bad News

If it's really important that you be close to the front, you probably won't want to risk not tipping—and it's still not a certainty that you'll get exactly what you want. Circumstances vary widely, but the consensus is that you are better off tipping the maitre d' (man at the entrance with the seating chart) than the captain who seats you; $10-$20 for a couple should do it in

---

**An upgrade usually entails moving closer to the stage. The private booths are very difficult to get, as they are often saved for the casino's high rollers or the biggest walk-in tippers.*

even the biggest rooms. The problem with this is, sometimes it doesn't.

I've always favored this approach: look confident, smile, be friendly, look the seating people in the eye, and take your chances. Just looking like you know the ropes and are a potential tipper often yields good results. If you like your seats, you can tip the captain if you want to. If not satisfied, either ask the captain for something better, or wait until the maitre d' has a lull and approach him about upgrading. If you go back to the maitre d', you'll need to accompany your request with some monetary inducement. The showroom worst-case scenario is that you tip someone and *still* get poor seats. With this approach, that can't happen. Remember that you are never obligated to tip, especially if you're not satisfied.

The Waltz

The practice of taking a party to a bad seat, then switching to a better location after a tip, used to be known as the Waltz. The move toward reserved seating in the major showrooms is eliminating the need for customers to learn the latest step.

A Tale of Two Tokes

Toke is Las Vegas vernacular for a tip. Here are two interesting (and true) showroom tipping stories that shed a little more light on the subject.

Toke #1 — Upon entering the showroom, an usher looked at our tickets and said: "Maybe we can upgrade these seats for you." A member of our party took the bait and handed him a $10 bill for the extra consideration. It was near showtime, and he assumed there might be a prime booth available. The usher proceeded to seat us in the same seats indicated on the ticket.

This was a reserved-seat show, which means you're stuck with the seats you're issued at the box office. Seating personnel are not supposed to have the power to change that, and tipping in this situation is of no value. Where reserved seating is in effect, your best work is done dickering at the counter when you buy your tickets.

Line Passes

A major showroom drawback is standing in line. If you play the table games, you may be able to avoid lines by requesting a line pass from someone in the pit. Next to parking validations, line passes are the easiest casino complimentaries to obtain. If you normally bet from $5 to $25 dollars on table games, or play the dollar slots, you should have no trouble securing a line pass.

Toke #2—My party of four was seated near the back of the showroom (okay by me but my guests wanted to move up). I approached the maitre d' and asked that we be moved closer. He was less than enthusiastic so I handed him a $5 bill. We were moved into a booth in the center of the showroom.

The move was right, but the result was far better than you could have expected. A booth for $5 is almost unheard of; however, it illustrates that none of the rules pertaining to showroom-seating-success are written in stone.

The Tax Facts

Unfortunately, most show price listings don't convey the bottom line with regard to the cost of an evening's entertainment. Prices are almost always listed by the base admission. But showgoers are also hit with a hefty 17% tax (10% entertainment and 7% state). Then there's the matter of the gratuity where it is not included in the price (about 50% of the shows). It's your option, but it could mean an additional 10-20% tacked on. Result: a show listed at $40 will cost at least $46.80 and as much as $55.

Finding Discounts

The ultimate discount is a casino comp. The biggest gamblers receive comps (free passes) to any show they want. If you're not a high roller, though, your chances of paying less than full price for the premier shows are slim (room/show packages sometimes provide discounts). You'll have to look to the less prestigious shows to secure significant savings. With a little investigation, you'll be able to see many shows for less than full price.

There are several places to look for show discounts. Casino coupon books often include discounts and 2-for-1 offers. Thumb through every freebie magazine that you see. The editorial information in these magazines is generally unreliable because reviews are based on casino advertising, but they are a great source for finding show discounts. The local newspapers, especially Friday and Sunday editions, are another valuable source. Examine any printed material that you come across in hotel check-in packages or in flyers placed in your room. Car-rental agencies sometimes distribute fun packages that include discounts for shows. Inquire about senior or children's discounts. Investigate slot clubs. And don't rule out requesting a comp from pit personnel if you've been playing one of the table games for a couple hours with average bets in the $15 to $30 range. Once again, the key is in looking for the bargain.

Serendipity

Certain shows just don't get discounted. *Siegfried & Roy* and *Cirque du Soleil* at The Mirage are two of them. For a long time, it seemed that *King Arthur's Tournament* at Excalibur was another. Then an advertisement appeared in the newspapers for 2-for-1 tickets to the show. "Crowd counts were down and we wanted to stimulate some action," was the explanation from Excalibur's public relations department. Casinos sometimes spring these offers without warning via ads in the local newspapers. Take a few minutes daily to peruse the *Review-Journal* or *Sun* newspapers when you are in town. You may happen upon an unexpected bargain.

THE SIEGFRIED AND ROY SAGA

This article appeared in the *Las Vegas Advisor* in May 1990. It appears here unchanged (key updates are bracketed) and in its entirety because it addresses the reserved seating situation so well. It also provides the in-depth review that Las Vegas' best show deserves, and, at the end of the article, identifies a fantastic ploy for obtaining great seats.

"Lines and tigers and dares, oh my!"

It's been the talk of the town all year. The new *Siegfried & Roy* show at The Mirage was heavily promoted, then delayed, and finally staged under a previously unsuccessful reserved seating system—and a revolutionary price of $56 plus tax ($61.82 total). [Now $72.85.] What's it all about?

Lines...

The only way to see the show is to purchase tickets at The Mirage, in person, up to three days in advance. You may only make reservations over the phone if you are a guest at The Mirage. Working on the theory that being near the front of the line would secure a good seat, I went to The Mirage at 8 am on a Thursday, one hour prior to the opening of the box office. Surprise! Two long lines were already snaking through the casino. The 75 people in the line for casino guests were nothing compared to the line for non-guests. I took my place behind 178 others ticket buyers. The leaders in line had arrived at 5 am and pitched camp as if they were buying tickets for a rock concert. They told me that others began showing up at about 6 am.

At 9 am the box office opened and the lines began to file toward two separate ticket booths. By this time the guest line tallied 159 people. The non-guest line was far too long to count. Neither line received priority treatment and both moved gruesomely slow. Four hours later, tired and frustrated, I reached the ticket booth where I was clobbered with a $62 charge for a single ticket and two drinks. A couple must pay $124; a family of four, $248—there are no discounts for children. What kind of show could this be? Would Siegfried & Roy perform nude? Would I be allowed to ride a white tiger? What could possibly be worth what I had just experienced?

Tigers...

I had read all the reviews. They were glowing, of course. But reviewers don't spend four hours in line. They don't get to view the situation from the perspective of a tourist who is wasting four precious hours of a once-a-year Las Vegas vacation. Reviewers call in their request for tickets and pick them up at the Will Call booth 15 minutes prior to showtime. They are aware of the $62 price, but they don't pay it. I, on the other hand, experienced all of these wonders and was primed for some big-time Mirage bashing.

But something went wrong. Siegfried & Roy didn't cooperate. I hadn't planned on the show being good, let alone the best I've seen in Las Vegas. The production was more Broadway than the Strip.

The 1,500-seat Theatre Mirage is spectacular, the music is rousing (the show's creator calls it Pink Floyd meets Wagner), the cast is huge and the sets are a product of 1990's technological wizardry. I'm not a big fan of magic, but the illusions were slick. The famous white tigers were awesome and, at one point, there were a dozen of them on stage at once. The audience loved it. I loved it.

Dares...

The Mirage's reserved seating represents a grand experiment with regard to Las Vegas entertainment policy. The system is meant to eliminate additional expenses beyond the ticket price. No tipping the maitre d' for a better seat. No tipping drink servers. No hidden taxes. The $61.82 is all inclusive. It is also supposed to give the little guy (with five hours to blow) the advantage when it comes to seating—$100 tippers be damned. I intended to test these claims.

A friend who works at The Mirage urged me to try to get a seat in the pit. "That's where they put the high rollers," he said. When I got to the ticket booth I asked the ticket attendant how much extra I would have to pay for such a seat. "You want the pit" she asked? "No problem, same price." All I had to do was ask. I opted instead for a seat farther back.

That night when my Heinekens were served, I asked the waiter if the tip was included in the price. "Well, yes," he replied, "but we only make 85¢ per ticket." It was a soft hustle and I decided to explore by giving the waiter a small gratuity. Twenty minutes later he was back asking if I wanted more beer. An encore appearance by a drink server in a big showroom is rare and I thought I might get the response (free drinks) that I was looking for...but no. My two fresh Heinekens were accompanied by one fresh bill for $8.

Fifteen minutes into the show it was time for the real test. I approached a green-jacketed usher. While flipping through a wad of hundred dollar bills,

I made it clear that price was no object in fulfilling my desire for a better seat. It was a blatant set-up, entrapment at its best. "Sir, we're not allowed to take money but I'll see if I can help you," he said. Wow! I'd never heard that response in Las Vegas, but the game wasn't over yet. The young man led me to a woman for whom I repeated the request, complete with flashing hundreds. This time the prey was paying more attention to the bait. Still, she didn't extend her hand for a reward up front. She asked where I was sitting and told me she would investigate. In less than five minutes she found my table and led me to a perfect seat near the front. I offered a ten-dollar bill and this time she took it.

Big deal! I believe the prospect of a large tip prompted her attention, but I honestly feel that my request would have been honored without the money. The show was in progress, the seat was available, and no one was displaced. No way to hang anyone here.

Oh My!

Almost nothing materialized the way I expected. I thought I would be first in line. I wasn't. I thought I would hate the show. I didn't. I thought I could trap The Mirage. I couldn't. Things certainly weren't like this back in Kansas.

My conclusion is that you will not feel you were "taken" for the $62 tab. Everyone I talked to felt the show was worth the money. Unfortunately, the four-hour wait is intolerable. Here are a few suggestions for getting around it:

Pick the off nights. Thursdays, Fridays, and Saturdays are the worst for crowds. Sundays are better and Mondays or Tuesdays are best.

Forget early arrival. Everyone in line is allowed to purchase up to ten tickets. The good seats up front go fast and you'll end up waiting for nothing, as I did.

Don't worry about your seat. I walked to every corner of the showroom. There are no real bad seats. Even those way back and to the side are adequate. If you call 792-7777, you can get the current status on ticket availability and the length of the line.

Attend the late show. The 8 pm show is the most popular. You'll always get better seats at the 11 pm performance.

By pure chance, I may have stumbled across the best strategy of all. As mentioned above, I eventually ended up at one of the showroom's premier tables. I wondered how long those already seated had waited in line to secure their spot. Almost everyone indicated that they had waited less than half an hour.

"What time did you get here," I asked?

"About 10:30."

"That's impossible, I was here from 8 am until noon!"

"Not 10:30 am, 10:30 *pm*"

They had all purchased tickets from the "cancellation line." With approximately 3,000 tickets being sold nightly, a fair number of people have to cancel due to changes in plans and The Mirage puts those tickets up for sale prior to the show. Because so many were at the same table, I suspect that a few good seats are held back to cover last second contingencies, then thrown in with the cancellations when it's apparent they won't be needed.

Go ahead and sleep in, you'll get good seats.

The cancellation ploy continues to be a viable strategy, not just at *S & R*, but at any showroom with reserved seating, especially on slow nights. Arrive late and ask if any of the good seats remain. You might end up with one of those prized booths.

A proviso: After reading this account, a Mirage spokesperson called to warn that cancellations don't always materialize, and following my advice could result in a person being "shut out." That risk does exist. But this is Las Vegas. You can always make reservations at another show so you have something to fall back on.

ENTERTAINMENT ALTERNATIVES

Lounges

The heyday of casino lounges was in the early '60s; big names performed for other big names who would show up at all hours of the night to watch. By the mid-'70s, the lounges were being overrun by slots and keno. Today, the lounges are played by a talented group of contemporary musicians (few comedians). Lounges still rate as a top entertainment value. Most have no cover charge and no minimum drink purchase.

Top Lounges

The Desert Inn's headliner policy spills into the lounge. The 250-seat Starlight Theatre harkens back to the golden age of Strip entertainment. It's nostalgic, like being in a time warp back to the '60s. Performers run along the lines of Buddy Greco, Frank Sinatra, Jr. (and his fabulous band), and the most popular of the Starlight's performers, Sam Butera and Keely Smith.

Four Queens' French Quarter Lounge is another nostalgic room that features lesser-known names from the past: Herman's Hermits, the Platters, the Ink Spots, the Kingston Trio, B.J. Thomas.

One of the most popular and longest-running entertainment events in town is "Monday Night Jazz" at the Four Queens. Charlie Byrd, Jack Sheldon, and Kenny Burrell are among the jazz notables who perform. Lots of people congregate outside the lounge to listen to the show, which is beamed across the continent via Public Radio at 8:00 pm PST.

Cleopatra's Barge at Caesars Palace is a nightclub-like dance spot on a rocking boat. Most other lounges also have space for dancing. Good lounges are found at the Sands, The Mirage, Aladdin, Palace Station, Maxim, and Tropicana.

Top Lounge Performers

You can still see stars in the lounges (especially at the Desert Inn). Tiffany, the pop phenom of a couple years back, recently played the lounge in the Las Vegas Hilton for two weeks. For the most part, however, the lounges are played by a group of bands that move from casino to casino. They have reputations for putting on a good show, and are followed by their faithfuls. It's actually better to follow the performers than the lounges. Expect a hopping lounge whenever these groups are playing.

Older crowd: Freddie Bell; The Checkmates

Younger crowd: Cook E. Jarr; Santa Fe; Jonathan

Both: Sidros Armada

Comedy Clubs

They come and go, but three have been around for several years now: *A Night at the Improv* at the Riviera, the *Comedy Stop* at the Tropicana, and *Catch a Rising Star* at Bally's. All run $13-$15. Of the three, Riviera's Improv has hosted the most recognizable names—Bruce Baum, Kip Addotta, David Frye, Rhonda Shear—of late.

Country & Western

The Palladium, a huge nightclub on Industrial Road behind The Mirage, is Las Vegas' most popular C&W nightclub. This countryfied disco is popular, but you'll face long lines, high drink prices, and a cover charge.

Las Vegas on Film

Las Vegas has become a major site for the filming of movies (Rain Man, Honey I Blew Up the Kid, Honeymoon in Vegas, Indecent Proposal) and television (Crime Story, Hearts Are Wild, Caesars Challenge). Visitors can view filming or get free tickets to audience participation events if they know where things are happening. Get advance information by calling the Nevada Motion Picture Division's Event Hotline at 702-486-7373. The recorded message will also tell you when and where movies are shooting, and even provide casting information. You could wind up in the movies.

A better alternative is the Dance Hall & Saloon at the Gold Coast. You'll get your fill of country here too, without the lines and expenses. Plus, when you want a break, you can walk out into the casino, switch over to either of two lounges with live entertainment, go bowling upstairs or to a movie, grab an ice cream cone, or play bingo.

There also are Western dance halls at Sam's Town and Nevada Palace.

Non-Casino Hotspots

The nightclub scene has been flavor of the month for years. The enduring happy-hour joints are TGI Friday's at East Flamingo and Maryland Pkwy. and the Elephant Bar at Maryland Pkwy. and Karen. The major night spots are the Shark Club on Harmon across from Aladdin, the Metz on the Strip just south of the Aladdin, and Club Rock off the Strip west of I-15.

Holidays & Special Events

Holidays

Contrary to popular opinion, holidays are observed in Las Vegas. Many casinos put on special buffets serving traditional fare for Easter, Thanksgiving, and Christmas.

St. Patrick's Day—Big downtown party (avoid it): food and drink specials at casinos and bars all over town.

Valentines Day—People getting married in droves.

Fourth of July—Firework displays are sponsored by different casinos.

Halloween—A big day in Las Vegas. Frankenstein plays Megabucks, Dracula orders a Bloody Mary at the 21 table, skeletons roll the bones—patrons dress up and visit their favorite casino "haunts."

Christmas—Many would say that the words Christmas and Las Vegas don't belong in the same sentence. Not true. The city really gets into the holiday cheer. Casinos decorate. Cocktail waitresses and dealers actually smile. The two casinos with the most holiday spirit are Excalibur and Rio. Excalibur turns the whole casino into a giant Christmas scene, complete with Santa for the kids. The front lawn of the Rio becomes home to the "largest Christmas tree in the nation," an enormous white fir standing over 100 feet tall. And for lights, check out the Caesars Palace fountain. Keep in mind, though, that December is vacation time for many Las Vegas performers. Most showrooms close for all or part of the month.

New Year's Eve—New Year's Eve is a wild night. Every major casino has some kind of celebration, although many are private parties. All the shows stage special performances, usually with dinner and dancing. Here are a few examples from last year:

- Aladdin—*Country Tonite* $29.95, or dinner and dancing in the Imperial

Ballroom $75.

- Gold Coast—Orchestra in the Grand Ballroom, open bar $37.50.
- Bally's—Doc Severinson and the Fifth Dimension $175, or *Jubilee* $38.
- Flamingo—*City Lites*, dinner $125.

Special Events

Certain events have evolved into traditional big days in Las Vegas. You need to know when they are, so you can decide whether you want to participate in, or avoid, them.

Super Bowl Sunday (end of January)—Just as New Year's Eve is Las Vegas' biggest night, Super Bowl Sunday is its biggest day. Big screens, free drawings for T-shirts, hats, mugs, memorabilia, $1 hot dogs, 50¢ drafts, former NFL players, special gambling propositions, and 150,000 visitors set the scene. Unless you've been invited to one of the high-roller parties, you'll face the seemingly formidable chore of choosing a viewing venue. But don't worry, it's kind of "can't miss." Your only real decision is whether to attend one of the "low-roller" parties or just wing it on your own. Low-roller parties charge a $15 or $20 entry fee for free food, beer, and festivities. They're congenial and comfortable, but you're locked into staying in one place. The alternative is the *free* and loose approach. If you're in town early, monitor the local papers during Super Bowl week for late-breaking casino party plans. Even if at the last minute nothing strikes your fancy, simply arrive early at any of the major sports books. The jostling, camaraderie, and overall hubbub at The Mirage or Caesars Palace during the game are really the essence of the Las Vegas Super Bowl experience.

The NCAA Basketball Tournament (mid-March)—This is an exciting time in Las Vegas. Sports books are packed.

World Series of Poker (late April and early May)—This yearly event at Binion's Horseshoe is your chance to see the world's best poker players in action. First prize for the $10,000 buy-in, no limit, Texas Hold 'em World Championship is $1 million.

Kentucky Derby Day (first Saturday in May)—Race books hop with special parties, mint juleps, and Derby souvenirs.

Cinco De Mayo (May 5)—Major properties feature performers for their Hispanic clientele.

Grateful Dead Weekend (late May)—The Dead play three shows at the Silver Bowl toward the end of the month. They all sell out, which means 120,000 Deadheads are afoot.

Helldorado Days (May)—Month-long celebration that culminates with a rodeo. The town goes Western for a while.

MDA/Jerry Lewis Telethon (September, Labor Day)—Hosted by the Sahara. Many well-known stars show up to perform. There is no charge to attend.

National Finals Rodeo (early December)—The NFR invades town for ten days in December, but the event sells out as early as May. The rodeo has a profound effect on the Las Vegas entertainment scene. Names like George Jones, Randy Travis, Reba McEntire, the Charlie Daniels Band, Ricky VanShelton, Wynonna Judd, and Dolly Parton appear on marquees all over town.

Spectator Sports

Boxing

Las Vegas is the most popular fight venue in the world. Major championship matches are coveted by the large casinos because free tickets are excellent bait for luring the cherished high roller. Paying to see a big fight is expensive, and there are no tricks (other than comp-wizard tactics) that will spare you having to pay full price. The least expensive tickets for a major fight might go as low as $50, but you have to secure them right away; the lowest priced tickets always sell out first and fast. Cards featuring up-and-comers or over-the-hillers are run at some of the smaller casinos, such as the Riviera, Aladdin, and Plaza. Regardless of the competitors, celebrities from both the entertainment and sports worlds are always in attendance.

Baseball

One of Las Vegas' most underrated summertime entertainment values is a day or night at the ballpark rooting for the Las Vegas Stars, the minor league affiliate of the San Diego Padres. General admission tickets are only $4 for adults and $2.50 for children. Call 386-7200 for schedules and information. Free tickets to Monday-night games are often available at area 7-11 stores.

Hockey

Las Vegas will become home to a professional hockey franchise when its new team takes the ice in October 1993. The Las Vegas Thunder will be the 13th member of the International Hockey League. The Thomas & Mack Center will serve as home ice. The Santa Fe Ice Arena will probably serve as a practice rink. The IHL is the level directly below the NHL, so you can expect a good brand of hockey.

The Name Drop

Las Vegas isn't known as the Entertainment Capital of the World for nothing. Here is a partial list of headliners who have appeared here in the past decade, culled from 90 issues of the *Las Vegas Advisor*. Even a quick perusal will amaze and shock you. And the list is by no means complete!

George Burns, Bob Hope, Perry Como, Frank Sinatra, Dean Martin, Jerry Lewis, Paul Anka, Sammy Davis Jr., Sarah Vaughan, Liberace, Victor Borge, Dizzy Gillespie, Steve Lawrence, Eydie Gorme, Jackie Mason, Shecky Greene, Four Freshmen, Billy Eckstein, Ink Spots, Fats Domino, Jerry Lee Lewis, Ray Charles, Everly Brothers, Bill Medley, Ben E. King, The Platters, Vic Damone, Charley Byrd, Mickey Rooney, Donald O'Connor, Debbie Reynolds, Bellamy Brothers, Carol Channing, Tom Jones, Engelbert Humperdinck, Jim Nabors, Bill Cosby, Robert Goulet, Wayne Newton, Shirley MacLaine, Imperials, Coasters, Herman's Hermits, Frankie Valle & the Four Seasons, Frankie Avalon & Annette Funicello, Brenda Lee, Fats Domino, Chubby Checker, Bobby Vinton, Carl Perkins, Aretha Franklin, Jerry VanDyke, Don Rickles, Buddy Hackett, Johnny Mathis, Lainie Kazan, Harry Belafonte, Tony Bennett, Neil Sedaka, Little Richard, Four Preps, Alan King, Doc Severinsen, Rip Taylor, Julio Iglesias, Petula Clark, Connie Francis, Ringo Starr, Paul McCartney, Ann Margret, Rich Little, Jack Jones, Joan Rivers, Rodney Dangerfield, McGuire Sisters, B.B. King, Dion, Buddy Greco, James Brown, Della Reese, Kingston Trio, The Lettermen, Temptations, Paul Revere & The Raiders, Jan & Dean, Beach Boys, Smothers Brothers, Arlo Guthrie, Grateful Dead, Bob Dylan, Johnny Cash, Roy Clark, Glenn Campbell, Diana Ross, Charo, Diahann Carroll, George Benson, Lola Falana, Earth Wind & Fire, Chicago, Manhattan Transfer, Olivia Newton John, Hank Williams Jr., George Carlin, Liza Minelli, Dionne Warwick, Burt Bacharach, Crosby Stills & Nash, Jefferson Starship, Lionel Richie, Smokey Robinson, Commodores, Marilyn McCoo, 5th Dimension, Barry Manilow, Andy Gibb, Toni Tennille, Donna Summer, Al Jarreau, Santana, Keith Richards, Van Halen, Aerosmith, Alice Cooper, Bad Company, Melissa Manchester, Doobie Brothers, Allman Brothers, George Thorogood & the Deleware Destroyers, Blue Oyster Cult, Kansas, Rush, Ozzie Osbourn, Neil Young, Joe Cocker, The Unknown Comic, Tony Orlando & Dawn, Cher, Stephen Stills, David Brenner, Juliet Prowse, Shirley Jones, Joey Heatherton, Leon Russell, The O'Jays, Lou Rawls, Ann Murray ,Kenny Loggins, America, Juice Newton, Buffalo Springfield, Jefferson Starship, Cheap Trick, Dire Straits, Don Henley, Moody Blues, Jose Feliciano, Little Feat, Air Supply, Fleetwood Mac, Stevie Nicks, Lindsay Buckingham, April Wine, Kenny Rogers, Melissa Manchester, Helen Reddy, Harlem Globetrotters, Seals & Crofts, Sha Na Na, Sherman Hemsley, Pointer Sisters, Alabama, T.G. Sheppard, Eddie Rabbitt, Suzanne Sommers, Jim Stafford, Lee Greenwood, Conway Twitty, Merle Haggard, Barbara Mandrell, Tanya Tucker, Mel Tillis, Willie Nelson, Statler Brothers, Oak Ridge Boys, Waylon Jennings, Charlie Daniels, Lacy J. Dalton, Crystal Gayle, Moe Bandy, Mickey Gilley, K.T. Oslin, Janie Fricke, Ronnie Milsap, Reba MacIntyre, Tammy Wynette, Mac Davis, Genesis, Gallagher, Heart, Mary Wilson, Luciano Pavorotti, Gloria Loring, Bolshoi Ballet, Rudolph

Nureyev, Robert Guillaume, Eddie Money, Ann Jillian, Natalie Cole, Ben Vereen, Gladys Knight, Bernadette Peters, Vikki Carr, Nell Carter, Barbara Eden, Kool & The Gang, Roberta Flack, Maynard Ferguson, Jeffrey Osborne, Luther Vandross, Gregory Hines, Robert Palmer, Yakov Smirnoff, David Steinberg, Gary Muledeer, Gloria Estefan & Miami Sound Machine, Hall & Oates, Huey Lewis, Fabulous Thunderbirds, Gary Shandling, Sting, David Copperfield, Howie Mandel, Jay Leno, Louie Anderson, The Judds, Randy Travis, George Strait, Scorpions, David Sanborn, Kenny G, Whoopie Goldberg, Sam Kinison, Sandra Bernhard, Elayne Boosler, Alan Bursky, Phylicia Rashad, Sheena Easton, Lisa Lisa, Cult Jam, INXS, Andrew Dice Clay, Rosanne Barr, Tom Arnold, Bobcat Goldthwait, Damn Yankies, Pia Zadora, Tiffany, New Kids on the Block, Paul Rodriquez, Sinbad, Ivana Trump, Living Color, Oingo Boingo, Bobby Brown, Dennis Miller, Tim Allen, Paula Poundstone, Richard Jeni, Pudgy, Penn & Teller, Jerry Seinfeld, The Highway Men, Garth Brooks, Dwight Yokum, Vince Gill, Billy Ray Cyrus, Branford Marsalis, Winton Marsalis, The Neville Brother, Metallica, Def Leppard, U2, Guns 'n Roses, Harry Connick Jr., The Rippingtons, Rita Rudner, Bon Jovi, Tesla, Warrant, Marky Mark and the Funky Bunch, Quiet Riot, Slaughter, Sass Jordan, Hammer, Bobby Brown, Whitney Houston, Paula Abdul, Latoya Jackson The Whispers, Brad Garrett, Doug Kershaw, Earl Thomas Conley, Maria Conchita Alonso, Keith Washington, Joe Diffie, T. Graham Brown, John McEuen, Gypsy Kings, Vincent Fernandez, Rickey Van Shelton, Lupita D'Alessio, Jack Sheldon, Red Holloway, Sam Most, Carl Fontana, Shorty Rodgers, Bud Shank, Donald Byrd & Al Heath, Herb Ellis, Dave Friesen & Eddie Henderson, Richie Cole, Pete Christlieb, Olga Breeskin, Marlena Shaw, Carl Saunder's Big Band, Gene Redden, Nana Mouskouri, Abbe Lane, Jackie Vernon, Rascals, Dick Berk, Si Zentner's Big Band, Kenny Burrell, F. Beverly & Mays, Peter Allen, Contraband, Ana Gabriel, Yuri, *and* Mijares.

14

50 WAYS TO LEAVE YOUR PIT BOSS

What can you do to keep gambling losses in check during your vacation? The most common advice is: set a daily gambling-loss limit and stick to it! It's prudent, reasonable....and almost impossible to follow. What do you do when you're forced out early? How do you fill your time until the clock strikes midnight and you can dip into the next day's allotted playing stake?

The following list of 50 non-gambling activities may be the answer. The list is not arranged in alphabetical order. Instead, Wet 'n Wild is listed in its rightful position at the top, while the others are placed in logical groupings. Activities connected to casinos are the first group, then activities for kids, museums, tours, etc. Check them out and make your plans.

1 Wet 'n Wild

2601 Las Vegas Blvd. So. (next to Sahara Hotel), 737-7873. Open April-September. Prices: $17.95 adults (10 yrs+); $13.95 children (3-9 yrs); $3.95 senior (55+).

2. Grand Slam Canyon

Industrial Rd. (behind Circus Circus), 734-0410, Open year round. Price: $10 admission (applicable towards rides).

3 Movie Theaters - Gold Coast

367-7111. Prices: $3.75 matinees (before 5:45 pm weekdays & 2:00 pm weekends and holidays); $6.75 adults; $3.75 seniors (64+) & children (13 & under). Children under four not permitted in theater. $1 popcorn & candy.

4 Omnimax - Caesars Palace

731-7901. Daily, 2:00 pm-10:00 pm. Prices: $5 adults; $3 each for groups of 15 or more; $3 seniors (55+), hotel guests, and children (4-12 years).

5 Volcano, White Tigers, Dolphins - The Mirage

791-7111. Volcano and white tigers are free. The dolphin exhibit is open 11am-7pm weekdays; 9:00 am-7:00 pm weekends. Prices: $3, children under three free.

The Volcano

The Mirage volcano is the Strip's #1 lure. The volcano is activated on a strict schedule that is interrupted only by meteorological considerations. Here are some tips for viewing the spewing:

- *The volcano is set off every 15 minutes from 8 pm to 1 am (winter hours, 6 pm to 1 am).*
- *The volcano is only activated when winds are light, which means it's often quiescent. When the red lanterns near the sidewalk are illuminated, the volcano is down until further notice.*
- *An excellent place to take in the spectacle is from a window seat in the second floor coffee shop of the Casino Royale across the street. Have one of their good hamburgers, hot dogs with kraut, shrimp cocktail, or a 50¢ draft beer while you get your fill of the fireworks.*
- *If you want to line up with the throngs on the sidewalk in front of the volcano, a great place to park is the lot to the northwest of the main entrance to Caesars Palace. This former valet lot has been converted to public parking. It can be accessed from the Strip, and is also the perfect secret parking spot for visiting the casinos on the other side of the street—Flamingo, O' Shea's, Imperial Palace, Harrah's, Casino Royale, and Sands. Use the nearby crosswalk.*

6 Magic Motion Machine - Excalibur

597-7777. Daily, 10:00 am-11:45 pm. Prices: $2.50

7 Binion's Photo

382-1600, open 4 p.m. to midnight, free.

8 Golden Nugget's Gold Nuggets

385-7111, 24 hours, world's largest nuggets displayed around from lobby next to California Pizza Kitchen.

9 Arcades (all major casinos)

Circus Circus Midway and Excalibur Fantasy Faire are the most popular.

The video arcade in the basement of the Forum at Caesars is the most high-tech, the one at Bally's is the biggest.

10 Festival Fountain—Forum at Caesars
Four animatronic statues of Greek gods, with dancing waters, lasers, and high-tech sound; every half hour between 10 am and 11 pm, free.

11 Antique & Classic Auto Collection - Imperial Palace
Located on fifth floor parking facility, 731-3311. Daily, 9:30 am-11:30 pm. Prices: $6.95 adults; $3 seniors and children (5-12 yrs); under five years free.

12 Ice Skating - Santa Fe Casino
658-4900. Open all year long. Public skating beginning 11:00 am week-days, 1:00-4:00 pm weekends. Prices: $6 adults (13 yrs+); $5 children (12 & under). Skate rental $1.75.

13 Roller Skating - Crystal Palace
Three locations: East—4680 Boulder Hwy., 458-0177; North—3901 N. Rancho Dr., 645-4892; West—4740 S. Decatur Blvd., 253-9832. Prices: $4-$5.

14 Scandia Family Fun Center
2800 Sirius Ave. (west side of I-15, on Rancho, south of Sahara). 364-0070. Open all year long. Sunday-Thursday, 10:00 am-midnight; Friday & Saturday, 10:00 am-1:00 am. Miniature golf $5, batting cage $1.25, go-carts & bumper boats $4, arcade.

15 Competition Grand Prix Family Fun Center
2980 Sandhill Rd. (off Boulder Hwy.), 431-7223. Weekdays 2:00-10:00 pm; weekends 10:00 am-midnight. Prices: $3.50 for 10 laps in go-cart.

16 Las Vegas Stars (minor league baseball)
Cashman Field, Las Vegas Blvd., north of downtown, 386-7200 (call for schedule). Prices: $4 and up.

17 Health Clubs
The spas at Bally's, Caesars, Desert Inn, Riviera, and Tropicana are open to the general public. The Sporting House and the Las Vegas Athletic Clubs are open to walk-ins.

18 Liberace Museum
1775 E. Tropicana Ave, 798-5595. Monday-Saturday, 10:00 am-5:00

pm; Sunday, 1:00-5:00 pm. Prices: $6.50 adults; $4.50 seniors; $3.50 students; $2 children (6-12 yrs); under six years free.

19 Guiness World of Records Museum
2780 Las Vegas Blvd. So. (1 block north of Circus Circus), 792-0640. Daily, 9:00 am-9:00 pm. Prices: $4.95 adults; $3.95 seniors, students & military; $2.95 children (4-12 years); under four years free.

20 Lied Discovery Childrens Museum
833 N. Las Vegas Blvd., 382-5437. Tuesday, Thursday, Friday & Saturday, 10:00 am-5:00 pm; Wednesday, 10:00 am-7:00 pm; Sunday, noon-5:00 pm. Closed Mondays. Prices: $5 adults; $4 seniors & students; $3 children (2-12 years); under two years free.

21 Las Vegas Museum of Natural History
900 N. Las Vegas Blvd., 388-1399. Those who visit Las Vegas on the heels of "Jurassic Park" dinosaurmania can see three of them in all their mechanical majesty. Daily, 9:00 am-4:00 pm. Prices: $5 adults; $4 students; $2.50 children (4-12 years).

22 Zoological Park
1775 N. Rancho Dr., 648-5955. Children's petting zoo. Daily, 9:00 am-5:00 pm. Prices: $5 adults; $3 seniors & children (2-12 years); under two years free.

23 Ethel M's Chocolate Factory and Cactus Garden
2 Green Valley Business Park, Henderson, 458-8864. Candy factory tour (one free sample). Daily 9:30 am-5:30 pm. Free admission.

24 Kidd Marshmallow
8203 Gibson Rd., Henderson, 564-5400. Marshmallow factory tour. Monday-Friday 9:00 am-4:30 pm. Free admission.

25 Vegas (potato) Chips
2945 N. Martin Luther King Blvd., 647-3800. Potato chip factory tour. Monday-Thursday, 8:30 am-noon. Free admission.

26 Golf

There are about 20 courses in the Las Vegas area. Desert Inn (733-4290) is considered the premier public course. Craig Ranch (642-9700), Los Prados (645-5696), and Las Vegas Municipal (646-3003) are among the least expensive ($10-$20).

A unique course has just opened at the Angel Park Golf Club in

Walking Tour

Have you ever had an urge to walk the Strip? Slow down, you may be letting yourself in for more than you've bargained for. It's only three miles from Excalibur to the Sahara, but that's without factoring in side excursions into any casinos (some set well back from the street) or fighting the elements—sun, heat, wind, crowds, traffic. Especially during the dangerously high temperatures of May through September. You may want to reconsider that afternoon stroll up the Strip.

The accompanying map is easy to use. The numbers represent the distances between major casinos. Using the Tropicana/Excalibur corner as the starting point, you can easily determine distances between casinos. Just subtract the lower number from the higher (unless you are using either of the two southernmost casinos, Hacienda or Vacation Village, in which case you add). For example, if you wish to calculate the distance from The Mirage to the Fashion Show Mall, subtract 1.3 from 1.8. The difference is .5, or half a mile. Walking further than this distance during the summer months may place you at risk of spontaneous combustion. At the very least your feet might get hot.

Caesars Forum

The main entrance to the $100 million Forum at Caesars Palace gives you a good indication of things to come. A 20-foot statue of Athena graces the gargantuan circular lobby. Atop four classical Roman columns, a shrugging Atlas supports the roof. Goddesses peer down on video poker machines. An Italian market street stretches beyond to the central piazza under a changing Mediterranean sky. And the Tasmanian Devil with a spear and Daffy Duck with a shield stand aside Bugs Bunny in a chariot at the entrance to the Warner Bros. Studio shop.

Only in Las Vegas! The contrast is jolting at times, but overall, the Forum is a visual and sensual extravaganza, easily the most important attraction that opened in Las Vegas in 1992. What Caesars is to casinos, the Forum is to malls.

The details of this Roman marketplace are exquisite: the 240,000-square-foot mall is framed by slab stone floors, railing-lined balconies, columns and arches, and a realistic sky that changes from sunrise to sunset colors in three hours. When completed, it will host 70 stores and restaurants. The prices, of course, will raise the eyebrows of even the highbrows. At Vasari, for example, T-shirts go for $100, polo shirts for $300, and silk suits in the low four digits. Davante sells designer sunglasses such as Armanis for $185 and Cazals for $700. Sudachis sells jackets made from burlap coffee sacks for $455. The reason, we're told, that denim jeans at Armani cost $80 is the "relaxed, leisurely crotch." And Louis Vuitton's products are all behind glass, except for the $2000 suitcases.

Shoes at Schooz start at $100; the plaid and check sports jackets at Cuzzens only Bugsy Seigel could afford. Elegant costume jewelry at Landau Hyman runs in the $100-400 range. At Antiquities, a Good Humor two-wheeled pushwagon sells for $6700 and a Cadillac rear-end sofa for $7500. Brookstone features yuppie gadgets like a talking scale ($100). Sungear displays Raybans at $60.

The Thomas Charles and Minotaur galleries spotlight some of the finest art you'll see within 400 miles of Las Vegas. Prices start in the high four digits and soar to the mid fives. The Museum Store, on the other hand, is more affordable, with fine art reproductions as low as $15.

The Forum is kid-friendly. There's Warner Bros. with its Looney Tune souvenirs (cartoon clothes, mugs, magnets, clocks, posters, rubber stamps, cards, aprons, jewelry, books, sound-tracks, videos, and stuffed Taz, Sylvester, Tweety, Speedy Gonzales, and not to forget Foghorn Leghorn), along with the Matonic Tunnel, paint computer, and large-

screen video. Animal Crackers has the toys, Sweet Factory is a little like Willie Wonka's Chocolate Factory (check out the Magic Marble Machine). At Foto-Forum you can get a personalized souvenir video postcard, print, or T-shirt for under $20. Try on a pair of high tops at Just For Feet and step onto their court to shoot some hoops. Cyber Station downstairs is one of the more high-tech video arcades in town.

The main entertainment at the Forum, though, is the Festival Fountain, with shows on the hour. Laser lightning and stereo thunder awaken Bacchus, god of wine and animatronic MC. He introduces Plutus, who infuses the dancing waters with merry-go-round music; Venus, who blots out the sun and conjures laser constellations on the ceiling; and Apollo, who strums his fiber-optic lyre strings (though it's more like he's scratching his stomach). Finally, Bacchus bows out with a burp.

The Forum is open from 10 am to 11 pm daily. The main entrance is at the west end of Caesars casino, and the exit delivers you onto the people mover back into the casino. It's unique, exciting, and endlessly eye-opening—a must-see attraction.

northwest Las Vegas. The course recreates 12 of the most famous par-three holes in the world, including the island green at PGA West, the sixth at the Riviera, the seventh at Pebble Beach, the double green at St. Andrews, and the "Postage Stamp" at Royal Troon. The course is public, and affordable.

Your best source for golf information is the annual Nevada Golf Guide, available from *Nevada Magazine*. The 40-page supplement includes a complete directory of the 60 courses in Nevada and environs, a tournament calendar, maps, tee tips, slope ratings, and feature stories on links etiquette, celebrity designers, and Nevadans on tour. This guide is indispensable for any golfer vacationing in Nevada. Contact *Nevada Magazine* at 1800 Hwy. 50 East #200, Carson City, NV 89710, (702) 687-5416.

27 Bowling

Bowling centers are located at the following casinos: Gold Coast, Sam's Town, Santa Fe, and Showboat.

28 Shooting

American Shooters Supply—3440 S. Arville, 362-1223. The Original Survival Store—3250 Pollux Ave., 871-7795. The Gun Store—2900 E. Tropicana, 454-1110. Shooting ranges prices: $4-$10.

29 Archery Den — Indoor Shooting Range

3900 W. Charleston (at Valley View), 878-1790. Monday-Friday, 11:00

am-8:30 pm; Saturday, 11:30 am-6:00 pm. Price: $5 for two hours. Must have own equipment.

30 D & R Balloons (champagne balloon rides)
4390 W. Tompkins, Suite 3, 645-7609. Balloon rides - $135/person (2 person minimum), children half price ("but not too young"). Flight duration: 1hr to 1hr 15min. Morning & afternoon flights. Special pre-dawn flight $175/person. Open 7 days a week Sept.-April or May, depending on weather. Also fly from St. George, Utah during summer months.)

31 Red Rock Canyon
Follow Charleston Blvd. west for 15 miles, 363-1921. Thirteen mile scenic loop (hiking trails). Spring Mountain Ranch (state park) is at end of loop. Picnic, tours, occasional concerts and plays. Free admission.

32 Old Nevada/Bonnie Springs
Follow Charleston Blvd. west past Red Rock Scenic Loop turn-off, 875-4191. Old West town tours. Daily, 10:30am-6:00 pm. Prices: $6.50 adults, $5.50 seniors, $4 kids (5-11 yrs). Free petting zoo; horseback riding, $15/hour.

33 Spring Mountain State Park
Continue west (right) on Charleston Blvd. two miles, 875-4141, open 8-8, admission $3, Tours, picnicking, summer concerts.

34 Mt. Charleston Stables
Highway 39/Kyle Canyon Rd, 1-872-7009. Horseback riding. Weekdays: $18/one hour, $31/two hours, $41/three hours. Weekends & holidays: $22/one hour, $35/two hours, $45/three hours. Guided tours available.

35 Clark County Heritage Museum
1830 Boulder Hwy., Henderson, 455-7955, admission $2. Interesting exhibits on local history and industry, good break on the way to Hoover Dam and Lake Mead.

36 Black Canyon Raft Tours
1417 Pueblo Dr., Boulder City, 293-3776. Meets at Gold Strike Casino (west entry) at 10:15 am, returns at 4:00 pm. Open daily Feb. - Nov. Prices: $59.95 adults; $35 children (under 11). Lunch included.

37 Grand Canyon Tours
Bus, Helicopter, plane. Several tours in the yellow pages. Price by air runs $70-$140.

38 Hoover Dam

35 miles southeast of Las Vegas, 293-8321. Tours of the electrical generating plant. Daily, 9:00 am-4:15 pm; special summer hours, 8:00 am-6:45 pm. Prices: $2 adults; $1 seniors; children under 12 free.

39 Lake Mead

30 miles southeast of Las Vegas. Beach, recreation, sightseeing. Lake Mead Resort & Marina, 293-3484. Rental of ski, fishing, and patio boats. Jet ski rentals, $85-$110 a day. Numerous boat and equipment rentals in Yellow Pages.

40 Lake Mead Cruises

293-6180, variety of cruises on the *Desert Princess* sternwheeler: breakfast ($16.50 adults, $8 kids), afternoon ($12 adult, $5 kids), early dinner ($23 adults, $10.50 kids), dinner-dance ($32.50).

41 Valley of Fire State Park

Lake Mead Dr. to Northshore Rd. past Lake Mead, turn off on NV 169 into state park. 397-2088. Big red rocks, weird formations, scenic drive.

42 Lost City Museum

In Overton, 50 miles north of Las Vegas, 397-2193; admission $1. Large collection of local Pueblo (Anasazi) artifacts from the 10th-12th centuries.

43 Free Ride to Laughlin

Several companies operate excursions to Laughlin. The fee is usually returned by the sponsoring Laughlin casino. Check freebie magazines.

44 Shopping Malls

There are three main malls: The Fashion Show (on the Strip); The Meadows (Valley View); The Boulevard (Maryland Pkwy.).

45 Shopping - Western Emporium

5111 Boulder Hwy., 454-8017. Huge western wear outlet, knick knacks.

46 Shopping - Gambling Books

Gamblers Book Club, 630 S. 11th, 382-7555. Gamblers General Store, 800 S. Main, 382-9903. Gamblers Bookstore, 4460 W. Reno Ave., 365-1400.

47 Shopping - Odd

The Spy Factory (surveillance gizmos), 2228 Paradise Rd., 893-0779. Bell, Book & Candle ("spiritual specialists"), 1725 E. Charleston, 384-6807.

Don Pablo Cigar Co. (watch 'em roll 'em) 3025 S. Las Vegas Blvd., 369-1818.

48 Night Life (dancing)

Disco/pop: Shark Club, 795-7525; the Metz, 739-8855. Rock: Club Rock 593-2446; Country/Western: Sam's Town, 456-7777; Gold Coast, 367-7111; The Palladium, 733-6366. No dancing: TGI Friday's, 732-9905; Hard Rock Cafe, 733-8400. Call for directions.

49 Concerts/Cultural

Thomas & Mack Arena, 895-3900. Artemus Ham Hall, Judy Bailey Theater, 895-3801. Aladdin Theatre for the Performing Arts, 736-0250. Call box offices for schedules.

50 People Watching—Everywhere! All the Time!

15

DINING

After returning home from Las Vegas, the first few times you dine out will be different, difficult, because the regular prices in normal places will seem so prohibitive. This usually fades after a while, but if it doesn't, don't worry. Just start planning your next pilgrimage to Bargain City.

A look at the most recent *Nevada Gaming Abstract* provides interesting information relative to food values in Las Vegas. The *Abstract* contains departmental income statements for Nevada casinos that gross $1 million or more per year in gaming revenue. All departments (casino, rooms, etc.) show profits, except one—the food department. Casino restaurants lose money over the course of a year due to low prices and liberal complimentary policies. The percentage losses on food are listed here:

Strip	< 8.9%>
Downtown	<36.9%>
Statewide	<13.5%>

If these statistics are a little bland, the values they represent are the exact opposite: great food at low prices. To test the conclusion of the *Gaming Abstract*, simply employ the same method of research that we've used successfully for 15 years—taste and pay.

Dining Tips

Call Ahead

If you've heard or read about a special anywhere other than a current ad in the media, make a quick call to the casino restaurant to make sure the special is still offered. Casinos change offers often. It only takes a minute on the phone to verify that a special is still available.

Arrive a Little Early

If a buffet or meal special begins serving at a specific time, arriving even

15 minutes prior can save you much more than 15 minutes in waiting time.

Make Reservations

For some reason, no one thinks it's necessary to make reservations in Las Vegas. It is. You can't reserve in buffets or coffee shops, but you can in most other restaurants.

Changeovers

Buffets usually close for a half hour to change fare between breakfast and lunch, or lunch and dinner. By arriving toward the end of breakfast or lunch, you can often pay the lower price, munch through the changeover, and sample the food from both sessions.

The Counter Play

If there's a line to dine, counter attack. Many of the best restaurants are coffee shops, most of which have long counters in the back. Check immediately for open seats, especially if you are dining solo. The counter play is a surprisingly powerful strategy that will serve you well at busy joints like the Horseshoe coffeeshop.

Discounts

Low prices get lower yet with 2-for-1's and discounts.

Paper Profits—The entertainment section of the *Las Vegas Review-Journal* is a prime source for obtaining valuable meal discounts. Two-for-ones and dollar-off discounts are common. The Friday edition is best for this.

Freebie Mags—Flip through every one you see.

Airline In-Flight Magazines—Another good source for discounts, especially the perforated center-section in the America West magazine.

Funbooks—They're always changing, but coupons are good for discounts and 2-for-1's on everything from hamburgers (Flamingo) to gourmet dinners (Lady Luck). The king of dining discount coupon books is the Las Vegas *Entertainment* book (see box).

Bad Dining

Not all Las Vegas dining specials are good. Watch out for:

Low-priced seafood buffets—Be wary of a "seafood buffet" (except those recommended here) for less than $10.

Low-priced steak, and lobster deals—Casinos love to advertise these combos at catchy prices like $7.77, $8.88, or $9.99. After the hype, they're usually the same, a tiny dried-out lobster tail accompanied by a tiny dried-out steak.

Marquees—Meal offers always look great on a casino marquee in TEN FOOT LETTERS. Don't be seduced just because it's up in lights.

Coupon Monster

More than 200 two-for-one restaurant discounts for fast food, bars, medium range and gourmet restaurants are jammed into this monster coupon book. Many coupons can be used for 50% off when dining solo. Most restaurants are not in casinos, but the 1993 edition contained coupons for discounts in the amounts listed in the following casino restaurants: Pasta Pirate (California) $20; Redwood Bar & Grill (California) $28; All American Bar & Grille (Rio) $16; Antonio's (Rio) $18; Da Vinci's (Maxim) $26; Cassidy's (Fitzgeralds) $17; House of Lords (Sahara) $26; La Terrazza (Sahara) $10; Charcoal Room (Hacienda) $21; Tony Roma's (Fremont) $12; and La Bella Pasta (Nevada Palace) $19.

Entertainment *is best known as a half-price hotel club. When you purchase the Las Vegas edition, you are automatically eligible for substantial room-rate discounts at participating hotels in the U.S., Canada, Mexico, and overseas. This feature won't necessarily come into play on your Las Vegas visits—even this program can't compete with the best casino room deals—but it can save you a ton when you travel to other destinations. There are also coupons for movies, baseball games, miniature golf, bowling, health spas, and special entertainment events.*

No Las Vegas resident should be without this book. A local can crush the purchase price with savings on fast food, pizzas, and movie theater discounts alone. Visitors should be able to recoup costs in a trip or two, but will have to consider if the effort to recoup (eating at specific restaurants) is worth the purchase price.

The book costs $30 in bookstores, $33 via mail. Order from: Entertainment Publications 3009 Rigel Ave., Las Vegas, NV 89102, 702-871-8444.

Travel writer recommendations—During a three-day visit, travel writers simply don't have the time to comparison shop. They usually wind up touting the most heavily advertised dining specials in town, and they just love what they read on those marquees.

BUFFETS

Las Vegas could easily be called Buffet City; approximately 40 casinos offer a buffet of some kind, and there are major differences in both price and quality. The least expensive buffet in town is $2.29 for breakfast at Circus Circus. The most expensive is $29.95 for Sunday Brunch at Bally's. The average cost of a Las Vegas buffet is $4 for breakfast, $5 for lunch, and $7.25 for dinner. There's a reliable correlation between price and quality, which means you take your chances when you opt for that $4.50 dinner buffet.

Top Two

Buffets at the Rio and the Palace Station are a step above all the others.

Rio Carnival World ($3.25-$7.25)—The Carnival World is to buffets what compact discs are to albums—nothing less than a quantum leap in the Las Vegas buffet culture. Five serving islands specialize in different ethnic fare: Mexican, Chinese, Italian, Brazilian, and American; and a sixth serves only desserts. Each island is a buffet in itself, with several entrees and side dishes. The most popular is Rico's Amazon Grille (which is really a Mongolian barbecue). Selections at the other food islands cover everything from fresh pasta to carved roast beef. The breakfast menu includes pancakes, waffles, French toast, bagels, muffins, fritters, eggs (scrambled, Benedict, and cooked to order), breakfast meats, hot cereal, and fruit.

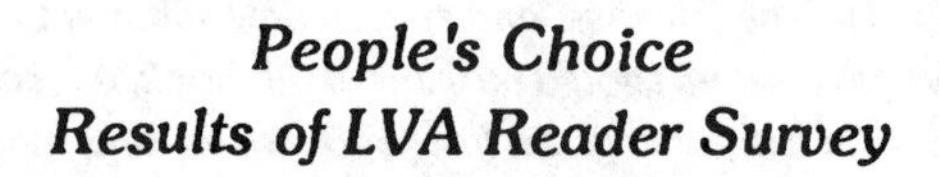

Buffet preference is very subjective. This category garnered 819 votes in our LVA Reader's Poll. Here's how the public chose.

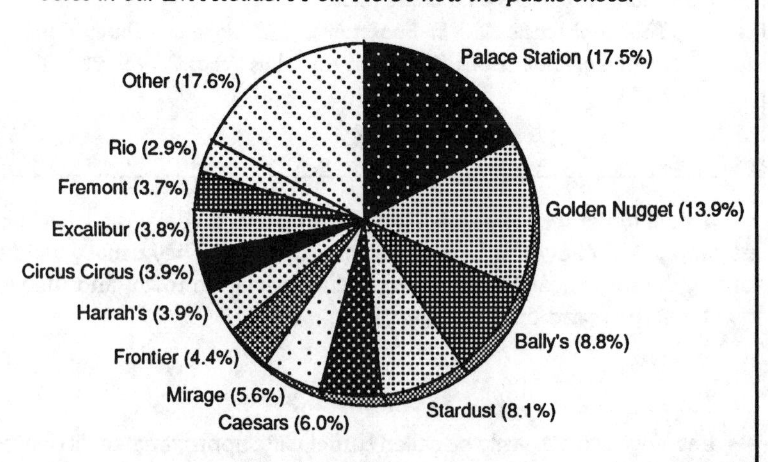

NOTE: The Rio's Carnival World Buffet was not a choice at the time the survey was taken.

Palace Station Feast ($3.95-$7.95)—Palace Station was the first to use an "action" format where as many as three short-order chefs prepare entrees on open grills before your eyes, ensuring freshness and personalized preparation. Excellent quality and variety: London broil, fried calamari, quiche, fajitas, pizza, hamburgers, Osso Buco, and sirloin steaks cooked to order. The menu changes daily. And here's a great feature. By calling 367-2428, you can access a recording that tells you the breakfast, lunch, and dinner menu for any day of the current week, as well as serving schedules and prices.

Next Best

These buffets are very good and have been for some time. They rate just a notch below Rio and Palace Station.

Bally's ($6.45-$11.95)—Good for salads and peel-and-eat shrimp for brunch.

Golden Nugget ($4.75-$9.50)—Famous for their bread pudding. Try to dine Sunday evenings; you get the best of the Sunday brunch plus the fresh dinner entrees.

Las Vegas Hilton ($5.99-$9.99)

The Mirage ($6.50-$10.50)—Excels in salads and desserts. Best peel-and-eat shrimp of any buffet in town.

Frontier ($5.95)—Dinner only.

> ### *Getting in Line*
>
> ***Lines can be a problem at the best buffets. The rule of thumb for avoiding them is: early for breakfast, late for lunch, and early or late for dinner.***

Good

This third group still won't disappoint.

Stardust ($4.95-$7.95)—Coupon discounts are common. Good value with any discount.

Caesars Palace ($6.50-$11.95)—A little overpriced but quality food.

Riviera ($3.95-$6.95)—Vastly improved. Look for $1-off coupons.

Gold Coast ($2.45-$5.45)—Excellent fried chicken. Includes one free frozen cocktail.

Circus Circus ($2.29-$3.99)—Price is right. Uninspired menu but best of the ultra-lows. Lines can be outrageous at dinner. Best for a quick lunch.

Friday Seafood

Seafood buffets come and go. They're usually served Friday nights only. Lines are almost always long.

Fremont ($11.95) —Good cold shellfish.

Frontier ($7.95) —Cold shellfish and salmon.

Gold Coast ($5.95) —About as good as a $5.95 seafood buffet gets. Lines are seldom a problem.

Sunday Brunch

A Sunday champagne brunch is a special (splurge) event for most; price gets thrown out the window in favor of the best experience. That makes the Sunday Brunch choice relatively easy, since two Las Vegas brunches stand far above the competition in terms of quality: the "Sterling" at Bally's and the "Island" at the Tropicana.

Bally's Sterling ($29.95)

Gourmet entrees are supported by a well-stocked sushi bar, omelettes cooked to order with everything from lobster and tomatoes to sturgeon and vodka, an array of gourmet dishes, and goblets of fresh strawberries, raspberries, and blueberries for dessert. About the champagne, this letter came from an *LVA* reader:

I make it a point to check the label on the bottle of champagne being poured. It was a Laurent-Perrier Brut. I'm looking at a flyer from a discount liquor outlet which lists the wine at $17.49 a bottle. No wonder I thought it so good.

The room is beautiful and spacious, and waitpeople are everywhere. Bally's takes their brunch seriously, as the following overheard exchange indicates:

Waiter: "If you want something you don't see, please ask."
Patron: "What if I want a T-bone steak?"
Server: "I'd try to round one up."
Patron: "How about a bowl of Cheerios?"
Server: "That would be tough, but I'd have to try."

Tropicana Island ($20.95)

The room at the Tropicana is not as classy, but the food selection is even better than at Bally's—especially if you're into different and exotic gourmet fare. The following are standard at Tropicana: ceviche, salmon tar tar, three different caviars, three preparations of smoked salmon, a sushi/sashimi bar, a fresh pasta station, and a dessert station preparing crepes Suzette and banana's Foster.

Who's Best?

Since it's *pick 'em* in terms of food quality, it boils down to a price comparison. At Bally's you pay $32.05 before the tip, which could run an additional $3-6. At Tropicana you're out the door for $25.56 (tip is included in price). Bottom line for brunch: a party of two at Bally's pays $70-75, a party of two at Tropicana pays $51. It's a pretty easy choice.

Lower Price

These three lower-priced brunches are also good: Caesars Palace, $13.50; Desert Inn, $10.95, Golden Nugget, $9.95

BREAKFAST

The once-famous Las Vegas 99¢ breakfast is now an endangered species. They show up from time to time in promotions, and there are still a few late-night specials, but most now run closer to $2.

The best breakfast in town, and one of the greatest on-going Las Vegas deals ever, is the Horseshoe's ham, and eggs for $2.50—two eggs, potatoes, toast, coffee, and a slice of ham that covers the entire plate. It's called the "Natural" and is served until 2 pm every day. There are a lot of copycat ham and eggs breakfasts around town, and for the most part they're good too, but the Horeshoe's is the best.

The Rio has held firm for about a year now with a lumberjack breakfast of T-bone steak and eggs and all the panckakes you can eat for $2.99.

The Frontier serves good breakfasts until mid-morning in Michelles: $2 bacon and eggs, $3 steak and eggs.

Big breakfast buffets are the new trend. For about $4, you can get eggs and omelettes cooked to order, fresh fruit, muffins, waffles, fresh orange juice, coffee, and much more. The two best breakfast buffets (by a wide margin) are those at the Rio and Palace Station.

Arizona Charlie's still offers a choice of three 49¢ breakfasts on the graveyard shift.

LUNCH

Lunch is almost always an on-the-go thing in Las Vegas. Buffets, snack bars, finger foods or a sandwich in the coffee shop are the usual choices. Caesars has a good Food Court in the Olympic Casino called La Piazza. Of several options in the $5 range, the best play is the salad bar. Opt for the small plate and heap on pasta salads and fresh vegetables. It costs $2.95 (a similar salad in The Mirage's California Pizza Kitchen next door costs $9). Big savings, no lines, no tip, no hassle. The fast-food joints have somehow wormed their way into the casinos. With so many meal bargains around, it still amazes me to see people lining up for Wienerschnitzel's and Wendy's. O'Sheas, the fast food king of the Strip, now houses a Burger King, Subway, Baskin Robbins, and Dunkin Donuts. The Mardi Gras Food Court at the Riviera has the other centralized fast food on the Strip.

Horseshoe

When in doubt, you'll never go wrong at the Horseshoe, no matter where within the casino you wind up eating.

Snack Bars—There are two, one on each side of the casino (original Horseshoe and old Mint). If one is busy, check the other; menus are the same. These snack bars sell the best turkey sandwiches in town ($2.70). What makes them special? The meat is sliced from fresh turkey roasts that are prepared daily. The sandwich comes loaded, and accompanied by hot peppers.

The "Chef's Special" ($1.40) is a bowl of ham and beans, and a big slice of cornbread. A huge batch of beans is prepared fresh every morning at 11 am, and served around the clock until the supply runs out (sometime the next morning). They use a different bean everyday—navy, lima, pinto, black-eyed peas, sometimes red. Careful if you're salt-sensitive; the cooks overdue it on occasion. There are Las Vegas locals who have eaten this meal every day for years.

From 6 am to noon you can get a complete breakfast of scrambled eggs, sausage, and biscuit for $1.

Finally, there's the Horseshoe's famous chili ($2.40). Some call it greasy; they call it authentic.

Deli—Transplanted New Yorkers swear that this is the best casino deli in town. The bagels & lox plate ($5.95) is so big it easily feeds two. Heaping sandwiches—pastrami, corned beef, brisket ($5.25)—come with pickles and potato salad. Salami, bologna, and soups are also available. There's cheese cake ($2) and bobka ($1.50) for dessert. Hours are 9 am-11 pm daily. The deli is located in the sports book. Peruse the big board and watch the television monitors while you eat.

DINNER

Gourmet Meals and Special Experiences

For many, a Las Vegas vacation wouldn't be complete without one special meal. For some that means the best quality possible (gourmet). For others, it's something a little extra.

Gourmet Rooms

There are probably more gourmet restaurants per mile along the Strip than anywhere else in the world. They're good, they're expensive, and they definitely require reservations. The most acclaimed are Palace Court (Caesars Palace), Le Montrachet (Hilton), Rhapsody (Tropicana), Monte Carlo (Desert Inn), and Stefano's (Golden Nugget). Spago and The Palm have just come on line in the Caesars Palace Forum. Comparatively unknown, but considered the best by many, is Michael's in the Barbary Coast.

For the best combination of food and overall experience, try Hugo's Cellar at the Four Queens. Both food and ambience are superb (Hugo's was voted Las Vegas' Most Romantic Restaurant). Hugo's is big on the little touches—roses for the ladies and complimentary chocolate-covered fruit after dinner. Meals come with the great Hugo's salad cart from which you

Awards

There are no five-star/diamond restaurants in Las Vegas. Mobil four-star status is currently afforded Palace Court at Caesars Palace and the Monte Carlo Room at the Desert Inn. A third restaurant, Pegasus at Alexis Park, was a four-star selection prior to 1993.

build your own perfect salad using any or all of a dozen fresh condiments—shrimp, artichokes, eggs, chunk bleu cheese, even whole anchovies. The cost runs $100-150 per couple (after tip) if you do it right with appetizers and a bottle of wine. Because of the room's popularity, making reservations even weeks in advance of your vacation is a good idea.

Special Experiences

Here are three options for the big night out, and none will set you back as far as the gourmet rooms (although the Bacchanal is close).

Bacchanal, Caesars Palace—There are two reasons to visit the Bacchanal: the food and the experience. Dinner gets underway with a visit from your wine goddess, who displays an impressive long-distance technique of filling silver goblets with your choice of white or red. Don't worry, she'll be back. Wine is unlimited during the meal and it's included in the dinner price.

The six-course meal plays out as follows:

I relish tray — A combination of fresh vegetables, fruit (fresh and dried), and must-try whole-grain breads.

II seafood appetizer—Crab claw, shrimp, and scallops in a ceviche-style marinade.

III pasta appetizer—fettuccini alfredo with an assortment of condiments served in silver bowls.

IV salad— Caesar, of course.

V entree—Several choices: lamb, beef, chicken, duck, fish. The rack of lamb is best.

VI dessert — A cherries Jubilee/bananas Foster combination, raspberry-filled chocolates, and coffee.

During dinner, you'll be entertained by a light show, strolling belly dancers, and a guest appearance by Caesar and Cleopatra themselves. The wine goddess-administered back rub is optional, but keep in mind that a tip for this service is customary. The $80 per person price is all-inclusive, so you know what you're getting into from the start. If you can fit this meal into your trip budget, you're guaranteed to have a great Las Vegas story to tell when you go home.

Lilly Langtry's, Golden Nugget—Lilly Langtry's Cantonese restaurant is a local favorite. But more notable than the food is Mike Skinner, resident magician par excellence. Mike wanders the premises bewildering diners with his even-seeing-is-disbelieving close-up magic. It's the best dinner and show deal in town. Call to confirm he's working.

Wild Bills Saloon and Steakhouse, Excalibur—An equal emphasis is placed on food and fun. The restaurant is actually a big western dance hall where live bands play C&W, and free dance lessons are provided mid-week. Steaks range from an $11.95 top sirloin to a $19.95 NY strip, and you can get away for less by ordering something other than steak; pork chops

Garden of the Gods

The special herbs used by the chefs in Caesars Palace's four-star/diamond Palace Court are not imported. They're not even grown commercially. They're harvested from an herb and flower garden located adjacent to the Caesars Palace swimming pool that's called, appropiately the "Garden of the Gods."

or chicken are less than $10. Wild Bills is especially good for larger groups that want to whoop it up a little during the main course. Reservations are not accepted.

Steaks and Prime Rib

Las Vegas does beef, probably in more sizes and prices than anywhere else. Consult the listings in Chapter 1 to find the best and most consistent steak and prime rib dinners. Following is a similar rundown by price.

Under $5

Both the Horseshoe ($2) and California ($3) steak dinners are late-nighters. The California is a good alternative when lines are long at the Horseshoe.

The Sands serves a good prime rib in the coffee shop for $4.95. Apply the discount from the Sands funbook and you get it for $3.95.

$5-$10

Palace Station's $6.95 T-bone is the best available-at-any-hour steak in town.

The California prime rib ($5.95) comes with vegetable, baked potato, beverage, unlimited salad bar, and cherries Jubilee for dessert.

Prime Play

The Four Queens gives you $5 in free slot play when you buy an $8.95 prime rib dinner in Magnolia's coffee shop. The expected win from the slot play is about $4.95 so the true cost of your dinner is $4. The worst you can do is cash nothing and eat an $8.95 prime rib. The best you can do is hit a royal flush, make $1,000, and eat an $8.95 prime rib.

Michelle's at Frontier and the Skyrise at Circus Circus serve a cut of prime rib for $5.95 and $6.95 respectively that would cost $15 in your local steakhouse. The Frontier's comes with "atomic horseradish"; hold on to your hair.

$10-$20

Quality rises dramatically at this price level.

The California's 18-ounce Porterhouse could be the best complete steak dinner at any price ($12.95). The meal includes seafood chowder or salad topped with shrimp, boiled redskin potatoes and a caramel/apple/ice cream dessert called hot apple dumpling. The special is served from 5:30-11 pm in the beautiful Redwood Bar & Grille, but it's not on the menu, you'll have to ask for it.

Jerry's Nugget serves the King Kong of prime ribs for $17.70, 24 hours a day in the coffee shop.

Three specialty beeferies also reside in this price category:

Binion's Ranch Steakhouse, Horseshoe—The menu isn't extensive, but what's there is prime. Giant steaks and prime rib run $18-$20.

All-American Bar & Grill, Rio—The steaks are better than the prime rib here. The bill for two steak dinners with all the trimmings and two selections from the unique domestic beer bar will run less than $35.

Sir Galahad's Prime Rib House, Excalibur—Prime rib only (no other entree choices) in four different serving sizes. There are virtually no choices to be made here. Meals are served with mashed potatoes, creamed spinach, Yorkshire pudding, and soup or salad.

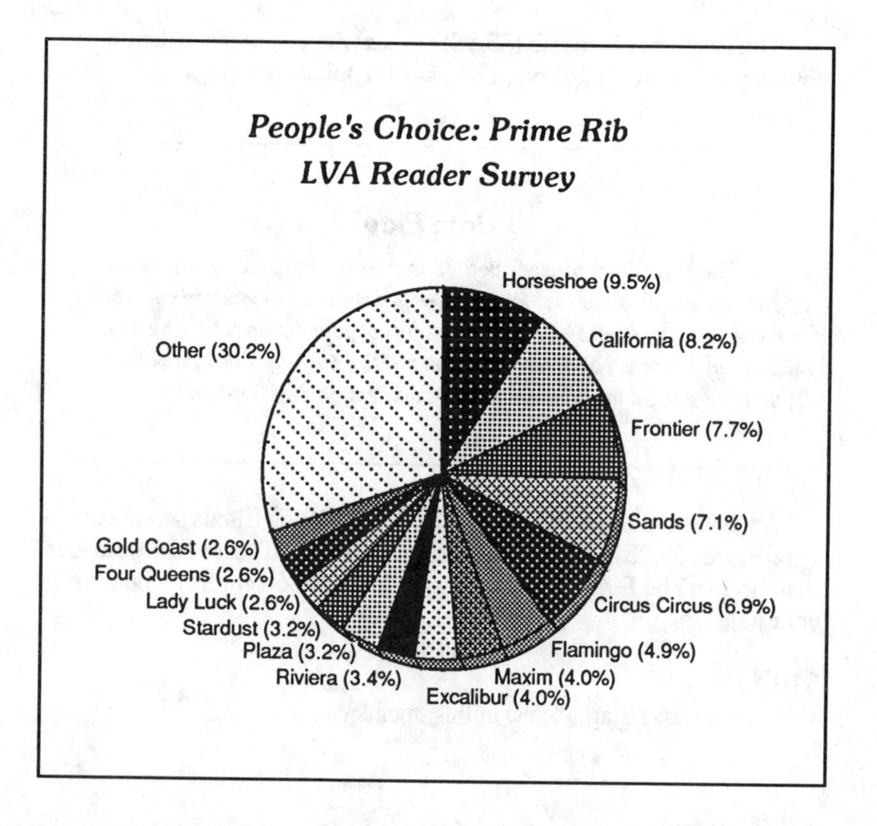

Seafood

Crab Legs

Crab legs are a popular casino special. Here are some tips for assessing quality. *Snow* or *king* is the first distinction you must make. Probably 90% of advertised crab-leg specials are what the casinos call snow crab, which are the smaller legs, the ones that bend your fork when you try to open them. They usually come in one-pound portions with prices ranging from $7-$10 (King 8 recently did a pound for $4.95). These plates are good if you don't mind the fight and the mess. Most steak and crab specials use snow crab legs. Most seafood buffets use snow crab legs. If you see a special that says "crab legs," you can be sure they mean snow crab legs.

King crab legs, on the other hand, are hard to find outside of the gourmet and higher-priced restaurants. They run $20+ in the big rooms, which is still significantly less than they'll cost in any other city in the country. And every three years or so, someone decides to use king crab as a loss leader. Since December1991, that place has been Palace Station. The casino's Fisherman's Broiler serves 16 ounces of king crab legs nightly (sometimes weekends, sometimes not) for $10.95. According to a waiter at the restaurant, Palace Station serves 200-250 pounds of crab legs on an average night, to 60-70% of the diners. Going on two years in existence, this special is entering the rarefied realm of the all-time-great Las Vegas meal deals.

A second casino known for excellent king crab specials in the $10 range is El Cortez.

Lobster

You have to be careful with lobster specials. The little 4- to 6-ounce tails that get paired with a steak for surf and turf are often lacking. The best ongoing low-priced steak and lobster specials are served in the coffee shops at the Stardust ($7.95) and the Rio ($6.99), but even these are no better

---

Top Crab

As good as the Palace Station king crab deal is, it still ranks only second compared with the best-ever crab deal. In the summer of 1985, the Gold Strike Casino near Hoover Dam ran a $3.95 Friday-night seafood buffet with unlimited king crab legs. Not just good crab legs, great crab legs—teenage mutant ninja king crab legs. Those Friday nights produced the most glorious, gluttonous feasts you could ever imagine. Patrons would make five or six trips through the long line, taking nothing else but the enormous legs. The room was understaffed and mountains of shells were piled everywhere by night's end. It was a monster deal, even by Bargain City standards.

---

than adequate. The same with lobster tail and live Maine specials. Proper preparation is crucial, and the typical coffee shop high-volume turnover is not consistent with this objective. Three casinos have earned a reputation for serving good lobster specials most of the time.

Poker Palace Live Maine—The Poker Palace in North Las Vegas has for five years held the line on their live whole Maine lobster special—$9.95, 24 hours a day. The lobsters come fresh from a tank located in the restaurant. After several years of offering this special around the clock, Poker Palace cooks know exactly how long to boil 'em. As if the price weren't low enough, the casino runs specials from time to time. The lowest it's ever been is $5.95 (midnight to 5 am). The out-of-the-way/slightly rough North Las Vegas location detracts from this value. But a security guard is stationed in the parking lot 24 hours a day, and if you aren't concerned with ambience (wine served in a beer glass), this is a first-rate meal value.

El Cortez—Dating back ten years to the days of their famed double lobster tails, the lobster specials in Roberta's (formerly Cafe Cortez, and before that the Gourmet Room) have been reliable.

Continental Lobster Tail—In April 1983, the Continental debuted a complete lobster-tail dinner for $4.49, served 24 hours a day in the coffee shop. Both the lobster and price were amazing, and that original deal still ranks as one of the best Las Vegas food bargains of all time. A decade later, the lobster tail is $9.99 and is still served 24 hours. Not worth going out of your way for, but still a good meal.

Other casinos run live Maine specials occasionally. Each year's lobster harvest has a lot to do with the number of new specials hitting town. The $20+ lobster dinners in the gourmet restaurants are invariably excellent.

Fresh Seafood Bars

Las Vegas is not famous for these. The Sands has a seafood bar in the main casino near the showroom where you can get clams and oysters on the half shell, peel and eat shrimp, and chowders. The new buzz is Buzio's, the oyster and seafood bar at the Rio. The restaurant is fashioned after the great John's Oyster Bar at John Ascuaga's Nugget in Sparks with a row of steam kettles behind the counter for preparing the classic seafood soups like cioppino, gumbo, bouillabaise, and pan roasts. So far, though, Buzio's is not filling the big shoes of big John's in terms of quality, and it's a bit pricey. After the dust settles, your best bet for clams, oysters, and peel-and-eat shrimp is one of the Friday night seafood buffets.

Sushi

You'll have no problem finding sushi houses throughout Las Vegas, but the best sushi play is a Sunday brunch at either Bally's or Tropicana. Tuna, yellowtail, octopus and more, all freshly sliced and served. All you can eat.

Italian

Pasta Palace, Palace Station

Overall best Italian, with fantastic food served in heaping portions. Just reading the menu is an experience. It includes all the standards, plus off-beat dishes like pasta and greens a mixture of linguini, spinach, broccoli, garlic and oil ($8.95). You can also make a meal of designer pizza and a calamari appetizer for less than $15. The Ravioli Fra Diavolo—fried ravioli and linguini with chunks of lobster in a garlic marinara ($9.95)—is a premier recommendation.

Pasta Remo, San Remo

Meals come with all the salad and breadsticks you can eat (similar to the Olive Garden chain), and the salad is exceptional. The room is intimate: checkered tablecloths, wine-bottle candles, the works.

Alta Villa, Flamingo

Best for appetizers. The risotto and scampi ($4.95) and eggplant Florentine-style ($3.60) are superb. The entrees don't quite measure up to the appetizers, but prices are fair and you won't go away hungry.

Lance-A-Lotta Pasta, Excalibur

Prices and the clever name are the two highlights here. At best, this is a quick, inexpensive pasta fix. They also serve lunch.

COMPARING THE PASTA

PRICE*	QUALITY
1. Lance-A-Lotta Pasta ($24)	1. Pasta Palace
2. Pasta Palace ($30)	2. Pasta Remo
3. Pasta Remo ($37)	3. Alta Villa
4. Alta Villa ($38)	4. Lance-A-Lotta Pasta

SELECTION	ATMOSPHERE
1. Pasta Palace	1. Pasta Remo
2. Pasta Remo	2. Alta Villa
3. Alta Villa	3. Pasta Palace
4. Lance-A-Lotta Pasta	4. Lance-A-Lotta Pasta

**Approximate price for two assuming one pasta entree, one meat or fish entree, two appetizers, salad or soup, and two glasses of house burgundy.*

Antonio's, Rio

One of the premier Italian experiences in Las Vegas, Antonio's is the choice for expensive Italian dining (about $50 for two with drinks). Presentation is the key word here. You won't know whether to eat your salad or take a picture of it. Beautiful decor, legions of waiters, good food too.

Mexican

Guadalajara Bar & Grille, Palace Station

The cuisine is described as "Mexican, Southwestern, and TexMex." Sounds a little different, and it is. Guadalajara takes a lively approach to the preparation of tacos, burritos, chile rellenos, and enchiladas. Sauces are spicier and meals are more exotic than at most Mexican restaurants, at least those you'll find in Las Vegas. Portions are huge and prices are very low. Best fajitas in town.

Tres Lobos, Stardust

More traditional. A blue collar Mexican restaurant where the food is good and the portions are large. Tres Lobos is a good alternative to Guadalajara if spicy isn't your bag. Meals are $1-$2 more expensive than Guadalajara, but the atmosphere is a little nicer and you'll rarely encounter long lines

La Salsa, Caesars (in the Forum)

Fresh, healthy, and good food. The black beans are lard-free and organic; meats are lean, charbroiled and tasty; and the chicken is skinless. The salsa bar features three varieties of sauces, along with chopped onion and fresh cilantro. Happy hour is from 4-7 pm with beer, taco, and margarita specials. Also try the *agua fresca*, a refreshing fresh-fruit drink. Best of all, free samples (sometimes food, sometimes drinks) are handed out to the audience outside at the Bacchus extravaganza.

Miscellaneous Values

Shrimp Cocktail

The Golden Gate has been home to the best shrimp cocktail in Las Vegas since 1959. The cost then was 50¢. It remained 50¢ for more than 30 years, until the price was finally raised to the current 99¢ in 1991. Even at twice the price, it's still the best shrimp cocktail deal in town. A few facts:

- The Golden Gate serves nearly two tons of shrimp per week.
- The shrimp are served in an old-fashioned sundae glass, not plastic cups.
- There are no cost-reducing lettuce or celery fillers, just shrimp and the

Golden Gate's "secret" cocktail sauce.

- No limits are imposed. You may order as many as you like.

Gourmet Salad Bar

The Flamingo's gourmet salad bar is not a buffet. It's served in the Flamingo Room, a comfortable, quiet, tri-level restaurant with top-quality food and service. Make a big meal out of marinated chicken breast, lox and smoked whitefish, chopped chicken liver, peel-and-eat shrimp, hearts of artichoke and palm, spinach and tomatoes, crumbled blue cheese, and top it all off with tropical fruit and yogurt. Good option for vegetarians.

Hot Dog

The designation of best hot dog in Las Vegas is predicated on spectacle, not taste. In other words, whose is biggest. The numbers are these:

LAS VEGAS' MONSTER DOGS

	INCHES	*OUNCES*
Lady Luck ($2.75)	11.5	8.0
Boardwalk ($1.06)	10.0	6.6
Westward Ho ($1.02)	10.0	5.8
Slots A Fun ($1.02)	9.5	6.8
Casino Royale ($1.06)	9.0	6.8

The Lady Luck dog is the best quality, too—"all Vienna Beef." Consuming an entire monster dog provides you with another great Las Vegas story to tell your friends back home.

DRINKING

Las Vegas has always been a haven of low-cost libation. Casino operators know that it's in their best interests for their customers to be drinking, and casino operators are always looking out for their best interests. Players drink free; non-players drink cheap (and so become *potential* players). While playing the slots you are generally at the mercy of the wandering cocktail waitresses. At the tables, however, you can request a drink from your dealer or the pit boss, who will call a waitress to take your order. The drink is free, but it is customary to tip the waitress. No need to go overboard. Tip according to service as you would anywhere else. This policy extends outside the casinos to the local bars. Bartenders will always comp you at least one free drink when you buy a roll of quarters to play their video poker machines.

Best Bars

In all but the most posh casinos, you'll pay less for drinks than you do when you're not in Bargain City. The bars listed in the Chapter 1—Horseshoe, Golden Nugget, Vacation Village, Palace Station—are the best or most interesting in town. Here are a few more:

Horseshoe Downstairs—A big selection of imported beer for $1.25 per.

Slots A Fun—Nicknamed *Heineken Headquarters* for holding steady with the un-Strip-like price of 75¢ for Heineken in the bottle.

Rio—The All-American Bar & Grille offers a one-of-a-kind premium domestic beer selection for $2.50 per bottle—Specher Amber Ale from Wisconsin, Alligator Beer from Florida, Pappy Kershenstine's Premium Rattlesnake Beer from Texas.

O'Sheas—Draft Guiness Stout or Harp for $1.25.

Casino Royale—One of the last bastions of half-a-buck brew on the Strip. View the Mirage volcano from a window on the second floor where the bar is located.

Holy Cow!—Las Vegas' first micro-brewery has just opened on the corner of Sahara Avenue and the Strip.

Best Cheap Drunks of the Past Decade

- *5¢ draft—Holiday International, circa 1980; Main Street Station, 1992*
- *10¢ draft—Treasury, circa 1979; Vacation Village, 1992*
- *25¢ draft—Westward Ho, 1983; Dunes, 1983; Slots A Fun, 1984; Opera House, 1984; Vacation Village, now*
- *All drinks 25¢—Bingo Palace, 1983*
- *Free Keg Party—Klondike, 1983*
- *Twelve-pack of Meisterbrau for $2.88—Opera House, 1985*

16

VITAL STATISTICS

HERE COME THE BRIDES

Las Vegas is the Wedding Capital of the Country—77,000 performed in 1992, including a constant parade of celebrities. It's easy—no blood test, no waiting period. It's cheap and fast—as little as $60 and 15 minutes from start to finish. It's an opportunity to combine the ceremony with the honeymoon. And social constraints are nearly nonexistent—bikinis are as acceptable as tuxedos, and you don't even have to get out of your car.

Though dozens of chapels line the Strip and each of the large hotels has one, an elaborate June wedding in Las Vegas, like any elaborate wedding, must be planned months in advance. Quickie nuptials, however, are still a cinch. Simply appear at the Marriage License Bureau, 300 S. 3rd St. downtown, 455-4415, with your money ($35), your ID, and your fiance. It's open from 8 am to midnight Monday.-Thursday., and 24 hours Friday., Saturday. and holidays (very busy on Saturdays). Then, for a no-frills justice-of-the-peace knot-tying, walk a block over to 309 S. 3rd St. to the office of the Commissioner of Civil Marriages, open the same hours as the License Bureau, where a deputy commissioner will unite you in holy matrimony for another $25. No appointments, no sermons, just "I now pronounce you. . ." and it's done.

The renowned wedding chapels of Las Vegas offer a more traditional setting, with flowers, organ music, and a minister. Most are grouped around the courthouse, or on Las Vegas Blvd. South between downtown and Sahara Avenue. The basic chapel fee is $40-60, and $35 is the recommended donation to the minister. Of course you can pay more: silk boutonniere ($5); bouquet ($45); photos ($50 and up); limo ride to the courthouse ($25 toke to the driver). You can really run up a tab by arranging for live organ music, having tapes made of the wedding, renting tuxes and gowns, buying rings, cakes, and garters all right there on the premises. Most chapels book weddings at half-hour intervals, so even without reservations, you might be able to squeeze your ceremony into an available slot.

Chapels Of Interest

Little Church of the West

One of the oldest buildings in Las Vegas, dating back to 1942. It's been moved from its original location at the Last Frontier Hotel to its present grassy and shady location next to the Hacienda.

The Candlelight

Probably the most popular chapel, with a 24-hour conveyor belt of ceremonies.

L'Amour Chapel

Features red velvet love seats in the chapel, a store full of wedding gowns for rent or purchase, and a 36-foot RV, "Weddings on Wheels," for getting married anywhere—outside The Mirage, for example, just as the volcano blows.

The Little White Chapel

Joan Collins and Michael Jordan got married here (not to each other). They've offered a drive-up window for "take-out weddings" since Valentine's Day 1991. A call button summons the minister-on-duty, who leans out the window and shouts the ceremony as "The Wedding March" is broadcast from overhead speakers. "We are gathered here together at the drive-up wedding window. . ."

KIDS

Kids are in in Las Vegas. It's a simple matter of staying ahead of the competition. As gambling proliferates throughout the U.S., Las Vegas must become more than just a place to gamble. It must evolve into a full-service family vacation destination, and by definition, that includes children, too.

Where to Stay

The Circus properties—Circus Circus, Excalibur and Luxor—are generally considered the best places to stay with children. If you like these hotels and can book them, fine. But staying in a hotel that's near one of these is almost as good. Kid-friendly casinos in the Circus Circus area include Riviera, Westward Ho, and Sahara. These provide easy access to Wet n' Wild, Grand Slam Canyon and, of course, the Circus Circus midway. The casinos near Excalibur and Luxor are Tropicana, San Remo, and Hacienda. The big draw here is the MGM Grand and its theme park. A perfect choice is the Tropicana because of its outstanding pool complex.

One other alternative is to stay at either the Las Vegas or Flamingo

Hilton in order to take advantage of the Las Vegas Hilton's "Youth Hotel," which is for Hilton guests only.

Of all areas in Las Vegas, downtown is the least desirable for children.

Attractions

In the summer of '94, MGM Grand (theme park, amphitheater), Treasure Island (live pirate battle), and Luxor (Circus Circus pyramid) will be the main draws, not only for children but adults as well. Many other kids attractions are also available in Las Vegas, especially during the summer.

Outdoors

The Wet 'n Wild water theme park is still Las Vegas' main attraction for kids. The park is open from morning till dark seven days a week all summer long, with scaled back hours in April, May, September, and October. There's enough to do at Wet 'n Wild to occupy an entire day, but it can get expensive, running up to $25 per child (over 10) when you include the price of food and drinks in the park. Two-dollar discount coupons are published everywhere, including the Riviera funbook. The park is located next to the Sahara Hotel.

Grand Slam Canyon is located across the street behind Circus Circus. Okay, it isn't outdoors, but under a vented pink space frame. But that also means it's not merely a summer attraction, remaining open year round. GSC is more an amusement park than a water park, consisting of two big thrill attractions, a roller coaster and flume ride.

The Scandia Family Fun Center is another attraction that can take up the better part of a day. The center offers miniature golf, batting cages, go-carts and bumper boats, and a big arcade. It's open all year long. Kids can also ride go-carts at Competition Grand Prix Family Fun Center located on the east side of town, but Scandia is the biggest and closest to the Strip.

The Las Vegas Stars minor league baseball team plays at Cashman Field throughout the summer. Tickets are $4 for general admission. It's an enjoyable night out. Beginning in late 1993, Las Vegas will also have a minor league hockey team.

Other possibilities (requiring a drive): the small zoological park on N. Rancho Dr. has a children's petting zoo. Old Nevada/Bonnie Springs, about 25 miles west on Charleston, has an old West town, a petting zoo, and horseback riding. Another day trip is Hoover Dam and Lake Mead, about 35 miles out of town (head south on Boulder Hwy.). The dam has $2 tours of the electrical generating plant, and you can swim, ski and fish at the lake.

In the Casinos

Probably the two most commonly asked questions concerning kids in Las Vegas have to do with casino etiquette. Kids are tolerated by casino security if: 1) they're moving through on their way to someplace else, or 2) they're standing in a line that extends into the casino, such as in front of a buffet. You'll attract some heat if you stop to play with kids in tow. A good way for the under-agers to get a glimpse of the action is to park them in a non-casino area where they won't be so obvious. Two good places are the Circus Circus midway and Caesars La Piazza food court where you can buy them a Coke and seat them on the rail.

The Mirage is good for a few hours of entertainment. If you time it right, you can take in the dolphins, white tigers, big aquarium behind the front desk, and rainforest lobby, then head outside at the right moment to see the volcano explode (all free except the dolphins).

Caesars Palace has Omnimax, a futuristic theater showing 45-minute movies that leave 50% of the audience with a slight touch of motion sickness. This attraction gets lots of ink but it's not that spectacular, and only fills about an hour of time.

The Gold Coast has a standard theater with $3.75 matinees and $1 popcorn and soda. Children under 5 years not permitted in theater.

The carnival-style games on the Circus Circus midway and at Excalibur's Fantasy Faire are great places to kill a few hours and a couple of rolls of quarters. As a rule, Excalibur's games are more expensive than Circus Circus; however, the quality of prizes is better at Excalibur. Excalibur also features the Magic Motion Machine, a popular three-minute thrill ride. There's a 42-inch height requirement.

If you're driving in from Southern California on I-15, the Primadonna at Stateline is a must. Though it's a barn of a casino, the ferris wheel out front and the merry-go-round in the basement (both free) are good for a 30-minute energy expender for the last stretch of road into Las Vegas.

Most casinos have video arcades. The largest are at Bally's (on the mall level across from *Catch a Rising Star*) and in the Riviera (next to the Mardi Gras food court); the most high-tech is at the Forum Shops mall at Caesars Palace (on the lower valet level).

Casinos with bowling centers are: Gold Coast, Sam's Town, Santa Fe, and Showboat.

Kids can ice skate year round at the Santa Fe Casino's indoor rink. Public skating begins at 11 am. There's also roller skating at three locations of the Crystal Palace (non-casino).

Less exciting for most kids is the Antique & Classic Auto Collection at the Imperial Palace. Though admission runs as high as $6.95, coupons for free entry are handed out right in front of the hotel.

Not in the Casinos

The Guiness World of Records Museum is located on the Strip one block north of Circus Circus. Though it's a bit expensive and only good for a half-hour at most, the exhibits are interesting and well-presented. The Riviera funbook also contains a $1 discount for this attraction.

The popular Lied Discovery Children's Museum features more than 100 hands-on displays for kids, good for several hours of entertainment-cum-education. It's located in North Las Vegas.

When you're done at the Lied, walk across the street to the Las Vegas Museum of Natural History. Hundreds of unusual stuffed birds and animals from around the world, plus a large exhibit on sharks and a room full of hands-on exhibits will keep you and the kids occupied for at least an hour.

For younger kids, there's a merry-go-round at the Meadows Mall. It costs 50¢ per ride and runs all mall hours.

Tours

Two tried-and-true excursions are the tours of Ethel M's Chocolate Factory and Cactus Garden and Kidd Marshmallow's marshmallow plant. At Ethel M's you view the chocolate-making through observation windows and get one free sample of candy in the showroom. The Kidd Marshmallow Factory is similar. Both facilities are located in Henderson so they can be done together, or in tandem with a trip to Hoover Dam.

Day Care

Most of the large hotel-casinos have in-room babysitting referral, which means you call the hotel operator, who either connects you with the service or gives you the phone number to call direct. Two day care companies dominate the business. Nanny's and Granny's, 3790 Redwood (off W. Flamingo near Torrey Pines), 362-9255, has a 24-hour drop-in service. They charge $3.50 an hour per child (5 weeks to 12 years or so). They appreciate a couple of hours notice to make sure there's an opening and enough staff. You can also have one of their babysitters come to your room: 4-hour minimum for $32, $6 for every hour thereafter. Vegas Valley Babysitters, 871-5161, provide a similar in-room service: 4-hour minimum for $28, $5.50 per hour thereafter, with a couple hours notice.

Guests of either Hilton can use the Las Vegas Hilton's Youth Hotel, 732-5111. It's $4 an hour for children 3-18, open Sun.-Thurs. 8 am-10 pm, Fri. and Sat. till midnight.

The Showboat, Gold Coast, and Sam's Town casinos offer three hours of free babysitting for kids 2-8 years old. The Gold Coast and Sam's Town require that the children be potty trained. You must remain on the premises. Combine the three for nine free hours of day care.

Shows

The best all-around Las Vegas production show for children is *King Arthur's Tournament* at Excalibur. Here, kids get to eat with their hands and pound on the tables and generally get a little crazy. They love it. They'll love you. You'll like it, too. Other kid-suitable shows (no topless) include: *Legends in Concert* at Imperial Palace, *Spellbound* at Harrah's, *Country Tonite* at the Aladdin, *Siegfried and Roy* and *Cirque du Soleil* at the Mirage, the *Jubilee* matinee at Bally's, and the early *Splash* show at the Riviera.

In search of other kid-suitable shows, we called all the main shows.

Aladdin—*Country Tonite*
"Children invited to all shows."
Imperial Palace—*Legends in Concert*
"Kids anytime."
Hacienda—*Lance Burton*
"Considered 'sensual,' but there's no nudity and children are welcome.
Mirage—*Siegfried and Roy* and *Cirque du Soleil*
"Suitable for the entire family."
Harrah's—*Spellbound*
"Ages seven and over."
Tropicana—*Folies Bergere*
"Ages seven and over."
Sahara—*Boy-lesque*
"18 and over."
Bally's—*Jubilee:*
"Adults only."
Flamingo—*City Lites*
"Adults only."
Sands—*Bare Essence*
"Adults only."
Stardust—*Enter The Night*
"Adults only."
Rio—*Brazilia*
"Racy, kids welcome at 8 pm show."
Riviera—*Splash*
"Early show is for family viewing."
Lady Luck—*Melinda, First Lady of Magic and her Follies Revue*
"Family show early, adult show late. "

LAS VEGAS AND SENIORS

Senior citizens are a powerful force within the travel industry. They control half of the nation's discretionary spending pool and account for more than three-quarters of all leisure travel. Despite these compelling statistics, special deals for seniors are not common in Las Vegas. The city's predisposition toward low prices for *everyone* is the reason. "Our prices are so low already, there's no room to cut further for seniors," is the line you hear over and over from casino publicity departments.

It's not just a Las Vegas phenomenon. In a 1990 *LVA* study, we sent 130 general form letters inquiring about senior discounts to casino public relations departments in Las Vegas, Atlantic City, Reno/Tahoe, and Laughlin. To be tricky, we followed with a second, personal mailing, identifying ourselves as senior customers about to embark on a casino vacation in an attempt to elicit non-official casino response (see the "Betty Bishop Mailing"). After tallying up the responses, the rule held true: senior discounts in gambling cities are the exception.

Have casino marketing departments fumbled the ball?

Demographics indicate that they haven't. Las Vegas and other casino cities remain extremely popular vacation choices with senior travelers. Apparently, there's more value *without* special concessions in casino towns than there is *with* them in most other vacation destinations. Of course, a few casinos *do* go out of their way for senior business. Number one in this category is the Four Queens.

Four Queens Club 55

Promotional material for Club 55 accurately describes it as "combining the advantages of a social club with the best aspects of a slot club." The Four Queens has set the standard for the casino industry. Members receive discounts on virtually everything in the casino: rooms (15%) seven days a week when available, food in all outlets except Hugo's (10%), and drinks at the bars (10%). They even have preferred status outside the casino. Card-carrying members can obtain discounts of 10-25% (usually the lower) at a growing number of Las Vegas businesses. The Club 55 merchant list includes beauty salons, bakeries, auto repair service, and more. There are more reasons to join:

- Members are invited to monthly free bingo sessions.
- Members are invited to special parties.
- Seminars, guest speakers, auctions, and other types of educational and social functions are routine.
- Who knows what else? *LVA* readers who are members have reported receiving the famous Four Queens free-money slot vouchers (of varying denomination) via the mail.

Other Casinos

Hilton Senior HHonors Club—An often overlooked source of discounts is the Hilton's "Senior HHonors" club. Members of the club can secure special rates at participating hotels throughout the Hilton chain, including both properties in Las Vegas and casinos in Reno and Laughlin. Discounts are substantial, but they're not always available. In addition to room-rate discounts, a membership card is good for 20% off meals in most Hilton restaurants. You must be 60 years old to become a member and then it's $50 to join and $35 yearly, or $265 lifetime (recently raised). Call 800-445-8667.

Santa Fe—Very senior-friendly due to its proximity to the Sun City retirement community. Santa Fe extends discounts for bowling, ice skating, and dining. They have a weekly Big Band night (Wednesdays), where an older crowd gathers to listen and dance. And they've recently hosted seniors-only video poker tournaments for a $10 entry fee.

Gold Coast—Discounts in the movie theater, and a Big Band night (Tuesdays) in the dance hall that's more popular than the Santa Fe's. Things get started about 7 pm and go until the place closes. There's always a big crowd—mostly locals, an even mix of singles and couples—and lots of dancing.

Other Discounts—A few casinos offer senior discounts on rooms, but they're really not important, since Las Vegas room rates are already rock bottom. This was borne out by a comprehensive comparison of casino and non-casino room rates that we conducted for the *LVA*. Neither the casino's discounted senior rates nor the most deeply discounted rates of the national non-casino chains (Best Western, Days Inn, Motel 6) could compete with the best standard rates at casinos like Fitzgeralds, Stardust, and Circus Circus. Senior discounts are available for the Caesars Palace Omnimax, Imperial Palace Auto Collection, Liberace Museum, and Guiness World of Records Museum. Finally, it's important to ask about senior discounts anywhere you go. Casinos institute new policies all the time.

Retiring to Las Vegas

It's the dream of many to eventually retire to Las Vegas. About 20% of the Las Vegas population is 55 years old or above. Besides the obvious allure of the action and excitement, there are solid financial reasons for those in the middle to high financial strata to consider such a move: no personal or corporate state income taxes; low property taxes and utility rates; inexpensive and varied dining and entertainment opportunities; desirable climate. New retirement communities are springing up throughout the city. Competing banks offer special perks designed to attract senior citizen accounts.

There's also a flip side. Las Vegas is lacking in the areas of good low-income housing, public transportation off the Strip, and reasonably priced health-care programs. If you are considering a move, a great source of honest, helpful information is the Cannon Center (702-366-1522). Their counselors can answer many questions. Another source is the Senior Citizens Information and Referral service, which is a service of HELP of Southern Nevada (702-369-4357).

Information

Prime Magazine—Carries some good coupons. Subscription only, $10 year for 12 issues. Send to 5300 W Sahara #100, Las Vegas, NV 89102 (702-871-6780). Free copies available at the Chamber of Commerce.

Senior Spectrum—Free all over the place: supermarkets, 7-11s, AM-PMs.

Las Vegas Golden Age—This is a new magazine that has just begun to show up on the freebie racks.

Local newspapers — Review-Journal "Living" section (Sundays) features "Action Seniors" column and weekly listing of local senior centers and support groups. *Sun* "Accent" section (Thursdays) features "50-Plus" column.

The Mature Traveler Newsletter — $4 per issue, $24.50 for 1-year subscription. Covers destinations all over the world. Because they are headquartered in Nevada, there's an increased likelihood that Las Vegas information will be included. Mature Traveler, Box 50820, Reno NV, 89513.

GAMBLING AND TAXES

Gambling necessitates the transferring of money, which necessitates the involvement of the Internal Revenue Service. The following is based on a 1991 interview with I. Nelson Rose, the recognized expert on all matters of law as they apply to the gambling business. Rose is the author of the book *Gambling and the Law*, and is a prolific writer on today's gambling scene. He is a full professor of law at Los Angeles' Whittier College. He is sought after as a gambling consultant and as an expert witness in litigation involving gambling.

There are two classifications of gambler for tax purposes: Casual and Professional.

The Casual Gambler

IRS treatment of winnings and losses for the casual gambler is remarkably straightforward.

- You are expected to report winnings as income.
- You may deduct gambling losses, but only up to the amount of your winnings.
- You may not carry losses forward to another year.
- You may not deduct associated expenses (travel, lodging, food) incurred while pursuing gambling activities.

Report Winnings—Gambling winnings are considered income. If you make a profit in any calendar year you are expected to report it under "Other Income."

Deduct Losses/No Carry Forward—You are allowed to offset your winnings with losses, but losses exceeding winnings may not be used to lessen your overall tax burden. Furthermore, this year's excess losses may not be used to offset winnings in subsequent years. Does this sound a little discriminatory? It should. If you had incurred net losses via investment in the financial markets—stocks, options, penny stocks, even highly speculative stock index futures—you would be allowed to deduct them, or carry forward if necessary.

The IRS does not allow you to "net out" winnings. For example, if you hit a video poker jackpot for $1,500, but have lost at least that much during other gambling sessions, you may not just call it even and ignore the $1,500 win. You can only deduct losses, under "Miscellaneous Deductions," if you itemize, not if you take the Standard Deduction.

Prove Losses—This is of paramount importance. You must be able to prove your losses to deduct them. From Nelson Rose:

> *It is best to keep a diary of gambling activity. The more complete, the better. [To accompany your diary] get a big manila envelope and throw in any receipts, money orders, cancelled checks, bank withdrawals, bills, markers or anything else related to the gambling session. Also include documents that prove you were where you say you were: hotel bills, airline tickets, and gasoline credit card slips. You don't have to be neat. And for big losses, get a statement from the pit boss or casino.*

In other words, don't wait until you hit a big jackpot then start scrambling to assemble your proof of losses. Rose cites examples of the IRS checking the age of ink used in diary notations, or looking for scuff marks on racetrack tickets. Record keeping is a little inconvenient, but necessary to protect yourself in the event that lightning strikes and you have a big win. Tournament players, in particular, should be keeping a detailed log and entry fee receipts for every event they play.

No Deducting Associated Expenses—This includes any portion of travel, meals, or educational materials like gambling books.

The Professional Gambler

The IRS began recognizing this classification only after the U.S. Supreme Court ruled that gambling can be defined as a "trade or business" in a 1987 decision. A professional gambler may claim losses in excess of winnings, he may carry losses forward, and he may deduct reasonable associated expenses. On the negative side, he will be liable for self-employment taxes levied on his gambling business.

What constitutes a professional gambler? The Supreme Court ruling holds that:

...the taxpayer must be involved in the activity [gambling] with continuity and regularity, and that the taxpayer's primary purpose for engaging in the activity must be for income or profit. A sporadic activity, a hobby, or an amusement diversion does not qualify.

Don't try writing off the cost of your Las Vegas vacation if you're a recreational gambler—even a successful one. There may be an opening to deduct some expenses as "expenditures for production of income" in rare cases involving tournament players or blackjack card counters who make and report a gambling profit year after year. Readers who feel they may fall into this category should seek the advice of a tax professional.

Jackpots

What can you expect when you hit a slot jackpot, or cash out big in bingo or keno? The magic number for slots or bingo is $1,200, $1,500 for keno. If you win a jackpot that nets this amount, you will have to sign a form W-2G, a copy of which will be sent to the IRS. You may have noticed video poker machines advertising royal flush jackpots of $1,199. This is so the reporting requirement can be avoided. No money will be withheld on a jackpot of any size if you are a US citizen.

Non-resident Aliens

Unfortunately, Canadians and other non-resident aliens must tolerate more restrictive rules. Non-residents are subject to a 30% withholding on jackpots of $1,200 or more. A portion of the money withheld can be recouped by filing a Form 1040NR.

In late 1991, Huntington Press was contacted by a Canadian reader who had hit a $4,000 royal flush. The caller was upset. The casino had withheld $1200 (30%) from winnings. This is standard IRS procedure for non-resident aliens who win slot jackpots of $1,200 or more. We suggested that the reader fill out and file a form 1040NR in an attempt to recover some of the money. The diligent reader did so, and attached a cover letter explaining the situation. The reader received a check from the IRS for the entire $1,200. Without filing, the $1,200 would have been lost.

Miscellaneous Questions

How, exactly, are gambling winnings taxed? Is it as ordinary income?
Rose: Yes, ordinary income which is taxed at the highest rate.

Is it likely that filing as a professional gambler will raise "red flags" with the IRS, and invite an audit?
Rose: Yes. Gamblers deal with large amounts of cash, which always interests the IRS. Such a filing could open you up [to an audit].

Sometimes lottery winners form agreements to split winnings for tax reasons. Is this a viable strategy? Should a husband and wife, or friends, form a partnership before gambling?

Rose: It makes sense from a tax standpoint, but more importantly, it preserves friendships. Many friendships have been destroyed by money disputes. An oral agreement is acceptable, but a written agreement is always better.

Conclusion

The overwhelming majority of readers will fall into the category of the casual gambler. Since this category is afforded no preferential tax treatment for losses, there's no reason to be overly concerned about every nuance of the law. Even though you are technically required to report all winnings and then deduct losses, it would be virtually impossible to do this for every winning and losing wager, and the IRS seems to concede this. Keep records to protect yourself in the event that you win enough to be sent a W-2G, and you will have covered the important bases.

Finally, it should go without saying that taxes are a technical (and touchy) subject. The purpose of this discussion is to provide insight into the current status of the gambling/tax relationship. Individual considerations vary, and the advice of certified tax professionals should be sought and followed.

17

TRAVEL & TRANSPORTATION

Travel Tip Contest

"If you have a great idea to save time and money while traveling, send it to the *Las Vegas Advisor.*"

We extended this invitation in March 1991 and provided some incentive by offering a one-year *LVA* subscription for each of the five best travel tips. We received 59 entries ranging from the best place to buy Ranch-style baked beans [Vons Supermarkets] to the best way to handle a traffic ticket [hand the officer a Monopoly "Get Out of Jail Free" card to ease the tension]. Most tips applied to travel in general, not just a Las Vegas vacation. They fell into four categories.

Air Travel

This was the most popular category. Several tips were of the common-sense variety: peruse in-flight magazines for coupons and bargain offers; be on the look-out for late-breaking discount fares. Two entries cited senior coupon books and both identified Delta as their favorite.

TIP—Get a Visa or Mastercard which gives frequent-flier mileage credit for credit card charges. I have an America West Visa, which credits me with one mile for each $1 in charges.

Credit cards with this frequent-flier affiliation are valuable if you do a lot of flying.

TIP—If time is close when arriving at the airport for departure, spring for five bucks and tip a redcap to check your ticket and tag your bags. Recently, a Delta redcap took care of everything, including checking the tickets. When you're late—don't panic, even if you see long lines. There's another way!

A related tip follows.

TIP—When traveling by air and having overweight and/or oversize luggage that the airlines charge extra for, use curbside check-in. For a tip far smaller than the charges, the porters will usually check your bags there.

Car Rentals

More common sense: verify the return route in case you are running late; refill tank yourself to avoid exorbitant agency gas charges; use credit cards that include free collision damage waivers.

TIP—When reserving a rental car at your destination, always request the least expensive category even if you want a larger car. You often will be given an upgrade at the same price. If not, you usually can get the larger car on the spot anyway.

Hotels/Casinos

TIP—Make advance credit card hotel reservations as soon as possible for summer and holidays. Lock-in early. Later, if a better deal shows, make the new reservation, cancelling the original with 48 hours notice.

Good. Hotel reservations are not like airline tickets where you are charged for cancellations. Take advantage of this flexibility.

TIP—Best buy in Las Vegas for car-to-room convenience is Stardust Motor Inn. It's nice to drive up to the door to load/unload.

TIP—A downtown (Las Vegas) trip is enhanced by using the Binion's Horseshoe parking garage...convenient to other casinos...open validation at [cashiers counter]...free parking.

Horseshoe parking is downtown's most convenient, though you can find a similar parking arrangement at any of several casinos downtown and on the Strip. If you run past your allotted "free parking" duration (usually 2-6 hours) you can have your ticket validated for an unlimited stay by playing a few hands of low-stakes blackjack. Hand your ticket to a pit boss as soon as you sit down. It's great when you win a few bucks, not so good when you lose. This strategy is commonly known as "playing for parking."

Miscellaneous Tips

TIP—Carry-on luggage is more convenient. Roll items of clothing to fit more snugly and avoid wrinkles.

TIP—I always bring 100-watt light bulbs with me to Las Vegas for better hotel room lighting.

TIP—Bed linens are changed but bedspreads are not. If smokers have stayed in the room prior to your stay, the smoke smell will remain in the spread. I always remove the bedspread before laying my clothes on the bed.

The Winners

TIP—In my experience, the cheapest car rentals in Las Vegas are, in order, Value (800-327-2501), General (800-327-7607) and Alamo (800-327-9633). It's a good idea to check their ads in the travel section of a newspaper like the NY Times since if you just call you will probably be quoted higher rates than their current "special".

The *LVA* has done several rate comparisons in which Value has always at or near the top.

TIP—Join all the larger airlines frequent-flier programs. The airlines send out promotions, dollar discount coupons on future flights, special air fares, etc. We have saved several hundred dollars on air fares with these promotions..

This is the same as joining slot clubs to get on a casino's mailing list. It doesn't cost anything and you never know what will materialize.

TIP—I don't know if the following will save time but it surely will save money. The best USA [air fare] discounter is Travel Avenue (800-333-3335) out of Chicago. You do your own background checking, then call Travel Avenue with the information. They refund from 7-10% of the (domestic) fare (minus a small ticketing charge), and they work quite rapidly. In a few days I have my tickets and my check..

This one teetered on the brink of not making the Top Five. The ticketing charge is $10 which means your refund check may be a scant $5. Many would rather not bother. However, another advocate of discount travel agencies wrote: "On two round-trip airline tickets of $288 each between Newark and Las Vegas I received a $26 rebate. It's a nice bonus for minimal effort." Most of these companies also offer other travel services that you may find useful.

TIP—Whenever traveling I take my own coffee pot. I can have coffee whenever I choose, and it's a money saver. I left it home once and was charged $7.50 for two cups of room service coffee..

I love this tip because I've been on the receiving end of the $7.50 (and more, especially in Atlantic City) charge. Even if coffee isn't your passion, the same concept can be applied in many ways to save money and time.

TIP—Your best money spent is on valet parking. Spring for a buck, then enjoy L.V. casinos. One should make every effort to save on rooms, car rentals, show tickets, free and half-price meals, etc. But then, drive to the front, tip the valet and enter with ease.

This strategy is so simple, so obvious...but rarely used. Other benefits include increased safety, easy access for handicapped and elderly, and better protection for your parked car.

Access Travel

Too Good To Be True

In late 1992 and early 1993, the following ad or a variation of it appeared in dozens of newspaper classifieds throughout the midwest and the south. The *LVA* had been hearing about "the Access Travel deal" for months, and decided it was time to find out what it was all about.

Red flags were everywhere. We could never get through to anyone in authority, nor did they return our phone calls. We sent a representative to their address and discovered that Access Travel was a mail drop at a commercial mail box storefront. Access Travel's "parent" company, Wholesale Travel Network, was located a block away from the mail drop in a cubby hole of an office. The windows were shuttered and there was no identifying sign.

We called consumer groups, regulating agencies, and reporting bureaus about Access Travel. Where they should have been, they weren't; where they shouldn't have been, they were. For example, 52 complaints had been filed with the Better Business Bureau in seven months, their Chamber of Commerce membership had been revoked, a Metro fraud investigation was in progress, etc.

Then we contacted people who'd been involved with Access Travel. We were told that, at first, Access accepted credit cards as payment. Then they didn't, and sent overnight couriers to your house to pick up a cashiers check. Customers were asked to choose three travel dates, then they were stalled until the third date or beyond. They were given a choice of 20 hotels, but our research turned up only one, Imperial Palace, with an open account. We also determined that no airline would do wholesale business with Access because they were not a member of the Airline Reporting Corporation.

The inevitable finally occurred on February 26, 1993, when postal inspectors, Metro detectives, and agents from the Nevada Consumer Fraud telemarketing unit raided the Access boiler room. And what did they find? Some old computers, telephones, and paperwork. No related arrests were made. At the time of the raid, the office had been closed for a week. None of the company officers have been found.

The Upshot

Do not do business with an unknown company like this unless you are willing to risk being hard sold, sucked in, relieved of your money, and stalled until who knows when, in exchange for the *possibility* of saving a few bucks on air fare and a hotel room. In the future, if you see a deal advertised that seems too good to be true, call the following agencies first. A few quick calls can save a lot of aggravation.

- Las Vegas Metro's Fraud Division at 702-229-3483
- Consumer Affairs at 702-486-7355
- Better Business Bureau at 702-735-6900.

CAT Scan

New Bus System

Las Vegas' public transportation was completely overhauled in late 1992. The new system is known as CAT (Citizens Area Transit).

The CAT system utilizes 128 buses that serve 29 routes all over the valley. They operate from 5:30 am to 1:30 am, except for the Strip service, which runs 24 hours a day. Nearly 100 of the buses are running at any given time during regular hours, stopping at over 2,000 locations, so you'll see them everywhere. All buses depart from and return to the Downtown Transportation Center (DTC), at Stewart St. and Casino Center.

From downtown to the Strip, the CAT local, #301, leaves the DTC every 10 minutes every hour of the day and night. The Strip shuttle, #302, leaves every 30 minutes around the clock, making a circular route beginning and ending at the Las Vegas Hilton; #302 connects the Strip to McCarran Airport and stops at various casinos along the Strip. By calling 228-7433, you can access CAT's automated information system for fares, times, detours, and routes, or talk directly to a customer service rep. The fares are $1 for adults, 50¢ for kids 5-17 and senior citizens over 65. Coupon books and monthly passes are available. Transfers are free, but only good for an hour.

Trolleys

These buses all stop at locations right at the curb on the street. The Strip trolley, however, pulls up to the front door of roughly 25 casinos from the Sahara to the Hacienda. Five trolleys run between 9:30 am and 2 am, passing each stop roughly every 30 minutes; $1.

Airport

The #109 local leaves the Downtown Transportation Center every half hour (on the hour and half hour) between 5:30 and 12:30 am. It travels down Maryland Parkway to the airport, and vice versa from the airport to downtown. You can get to the airport from the Strip by catching either the #302 mentioned previously, or taking the Strip #301 to the Tropicana, and then transfering to the #201, which runs east on Tropicana (once an hour); the bus stop is at the CAT sign in front of the Tropicana Hotel. Either ride costs $1. CAT requests that you board with no more than one suitcase and one handbag. Except for a free hotel shuttle, this is the cheapest airport transportation option.

To and from the airport, you can also take Bell Trans minibuses for $3.25 to the Strip and $4.50 to downtown; Gray Line for $3.25 to the Strip and $4.25 downtown; or Lucky 7 for $4 to the Strip and $5 downtown.

For taxicabs, the initial meter charge is $2.20. The cost for the first mile is $3.70, then $1.50 for additional miles. A cab ride to the south Strip should run roughly $8; to the center Strip $10; to the upper Strip $12; and to downtown $15-18.

Recommendations

The common experience of public transportation for visitors on the Strip—long waits for overcrowded buses—is a thing of the past. Now, the CAT and trolley systems provide ample options, with frequent buses and relative comfort. If you're not in a hurry, the local buses are a great opportunity for a cheap scenic cruise up or down the Strip, taking enough time for you to absorb the endless extravaganza. If you're hotel hopping, the trolley is hard to beat, stand at the main entrance of any hotel and within 30 minutes you're on the road. And if you just want to get to or from downtown in a hurry, or cover large chunks of the Strip in a single bound, grab the CAT shuttle.

18

ATLANTIC CITY

Ten riverboats in Illinois, more than 40 casinos planned for Mississippi, Indian casinos in more than a dozen states, and giant gambling-entertainment complexes destined for Chicago, New Orleans, St. Louis, Windsor, and other major cities across North America. Still, the two traditional gambling centers remain Las Vegas, Nev. (since 1931), and Atlantic City, NJ (since 1978). How do they compare?

Most noticeable in Atlantic City are the things that *aren't* there. There are no $25 hotel rooms. There are no sports books, and no keno (except video). There are no $1, $2 or $3 blackjack games, nor single or double decks. There are no bar-top video poker machines, and very few reasonable video poker pay schedules. There are no bars, at least not in the casinos (they're in the non-gambling areas). Despite a recent move to 24-hour gambling, there are no patrons at 6:30 am. And, horror of horrors, in 11 of 12 casinos, there are no nickel slots (Claridge is the exception).

High Minimums/Low Returns

If you're not careful, you can be eaten alive gambling in Atlantic City. At the 25¢ level, the most common Jacks or Better machines are 6/5s, and there are still a lot of two-pair machines around. Joker Poker is big, and the most common schedule returns only 97.2%, if you play perfectly. The most popular Deuces Wild schedule returns a paltry 91.4%. Things get a little better if you're playing the dollar machines. But an 8/5 non-progressive machine that pays $4,000 for a royal flush will beat you at a rate of $50-60 per hour. Cash rebates and perks from slot clubs help recoup some of this. Needless to say, you're out of your mind if you don't join slot clubs in Atlantic City. You can find 9/6 machines at the $1 level if you look hard.

Perhaps things will improve. Competition is a wonderful consumer ally, and if an Atlantic City casino wanted to separate itself from the pack, offering better video poker value would be the ticket.

Sticker Shock and Value

Everything is expensive relative to the bargains in Las Vegas. Expect to pay more in A.C. But there are ways around this, too. Most casinos have snack bars or food courts, and the boardwalk is a good source for low-priced food and drinks.

Even Atlantic City has deals. Trump's Castle's now famous prime rib buffet (under $5) can compete with any in Las Vegas for value. It was created in response to the first-ever bargain-priced buffet in Atlantic City, Resorts International's fabulously successful Beverly Hills Buffet. Low-priced buffets are such a rarity in Atlantic City you have to sign-up to eat almost two hours in advance on a weekday.

From an overall value standpoint—rooms, meals, gambling—Atlantic City's best is Trump's Castle, where a Las Vegas influence seems to be at work. Resorts is competitive. The Taj Mahal is surprisingly affordable and gambling options, at least by Atlantic City standards, are fairly liberal.

Random Observations

• Atlantic City has two things that Las Vegas will never have: the Atlantic Ocean and the boardwalk. On a beautiful day in October, this tandem is almost enough to make you forget about $2 steaks in Las Vegas. Almost.

• Some of the non-casino restaurants are terrific. Angeloni's II has received the *Wine Spectator's* Award of Excellence for their wine selection, although you might prefer the homemade red served by their competitor, Angelo's Fairmount Tavern. A submarine sandwich from the White House is a must, even though the locals insist that there are even better subs in Atlantic City. Seafood restaurants are plentiful in the beach cities just down the road. The Irish Pub on St. James is a great place for a beer.

• Join clubs, sign up for giveaways, get your name on lists! You'll get good things in the mail.

• Being a Player's Club member can save you money. While there's a big question-mark concerning the value of the club for Las Vegas visitors, there can be little argument that Atlantic City visitors will recoup their membership costs.

The Mirage vs. The Taj

Comparisons between Las Vegas' Mirage and Atlantic City's Taj Mahal are inevitable. Those who have seen both seem to favor The Mirage by about an 80% to 20% ratio. The Taj Mahal is enormous, and it's impressive, but it doesn't have a look of its own like The Mirage does. Walk from any Atlantic City casino into the Taj Mahal and you get the feeling that you're experiencing more of the same. Much of this has to do with excessive regulation in Atlantic City which forces casinos to operate almost identically.

From the standpoint of getting value for your gambling dollar, The Mirage is a clear winner, offering games that carry a lower casino edge in most cases.

Nevada Best Bet?

A 1990 Nevada Gaming Control Board study concludes that casinos in Nevada return a higher percentage of money wagered than Atlantic City casinos, by a margin of 92% to 88%. The report also states that the same 4% difference exists in the "payout rate" of slot machines. One can assume that the greater competition in Nevada forces casinos to provide gamblers with better odds.

Expert Rebutttal

Joel Friedman, a gambling expert based in the Atlantic City area, took issue with some of the contentions presented above. His response is printed below in its entirety.

Anthony Curtis has told you about all of the things that Atlantic City doesn't have. His view is somewhat biased, however, because of his expectations based on what Las Vegas has. This article lets you know about things Atlantic City has and Las Vegas doesn't.

One of A.C.'s negatives about A.C. is that, in general, the video poker pay scales are much worse than in Nevada. But this is really a positive feature in disguise. Casinos give out comps based on the idea that they are returning some fraction of what they expect to make from a player. A.C. casinos have much higher profit margins on slots and video pokers than Las Vegas casinos and can afford to be more generous to players. Thus, room and meal comps for slot players are much easier to come by than in Las Vegas.

A.C. casinos aggressively compete for customers, but their approach is a little different than Las Vegas casinos. Once you become a casino "regular," your mailbox is filled with entreaties to come to that casino. These come in various forms: 1) coupons exchangeable for cash; 2) special events; 3) drawings for cars, trips, etc. The scale for all this is much larger than in Las Vegas. Fifty-dollar coupons are fairly commonplace. On a recent trip to A.C., I cashed almost $350 worth of coupons. How does this compare to coupon runs in Las Vegas?

In the special-events category, my haul last year included a 27" color TV from a mini-golf tournament and $2000 from a stock-picking contest. I have so far won only minor prizes in drawings, but a friend who attends these more religiously has won a car and a trip to Aruba, among other things. One of the latest promotions is free bingo. Bingo is not a game approved in A.C., so they can't charge for it. All you have to do to participate in these things is show up.

Another major difference between A.C. and L.V. is the slot clubs.

Some A.C. slot clubs give cash back in excess of 1% of the action. (This is cash, not comps). To compare A.C. and L.V. payout structures without including the cashback is a big mistake. This is in addition to the cash coupons you get in the mail! Here, it pays to shop around. On poker machines you get anywhere from 0% to 1.33% back depending on the casino. In summary, it can pay to go to Atlantic City. But you do have to play.

Evolution of Atlantic City

For the on-going drama of Atlantic City, see Chapter 2, Evolution of Bargain City, 3/90, 2/91, 3/91, 7/91, 2/92, 3/92, 7/92, 7/93.

19

LAS VEGAS MISER

The Miser is our resident satirist. The Miser balances the Advisor. Here's a collection of the Miser's eccentric contributions, possibly the most irreverent Las Vegas writing anywhere.

April/May 1984

First let me say that I am pleased to be associated with a publication that provides tips on food bargains and gambling, due to the penuriousness (stinginess) of my nature. I am a miser, a tight-wad, guardian of those silver spondulicks, and I appreciate those who are sympathetic to my cause.

And now for my advice on tipping. You tip for "this," you tip for "that." Well, maybe *you* do—I don't. Sure, I tip cocktail girls, valets and cigarette girls—it helps their morale, but my pockets are filled with sand for show captains, dealers or desk clerks if they are unpleasant. As for tipping washroom attendants, remember:

tip if they smile
but not too much
tip if they help
but not if they touch.

Well, that's this issue's miserly tip. Next issue I promise to have the results of my survey that posed the question: At which casino can you find the most money on the floor?

October/November 1984

The first Couponomist Convention will be held at the Silver Star casino soon. We shall all get together and play coupon books, remembering to assume the Miser's posture: head down, eyes peeled, scouring for errant coupons and lost silver. Each attendee will receive the booklet "Five Best

Places to Find Coupon Books" and the Silver Star promises to have that Bucky guy play zany banjo music.

I have decided to gamble. But I have a strategy. Below is a basic strategy table for single deck blackjack.

BASIC STRATEGY FOR SINGLE DECK
(when playing vs. dealer 2 thru 5 only)

	2	3	4	5	
					H=Hit S=Stand G=Guess
12	H	S	Ah	Ah	Sp=split; take off, vamoos, see ya!
13	H	S	S	K	Ah=another Heineken please
14	G	G	D	K	D=don't know
15	Sp	Sp	D	D	K=kiss your chips goodbye

December/January 1985

A Miser's Christmas

Twas the night before Christmas when all through the house
the creatures were stirring, the Miser was soused
The slots were being pulled with patience and care
and the Miser was pie-eyed from Heineken beer
The fleas were nestled snug at the pits, ordering
drinks from cocktail waitresses, all with big . . . smiles
And Couponomists wore free Tropicana hats
while mapping their strategies for coupon attacks
Playing three-for-two bonus bucks, taking
free pulls for autos, mopeds and such
And the Miser is wandering the Golden Gate
finding loose coins at a phenomenal rate
He finds small fortunes due to serendipity
yet can't write Christmas poetry that rhymes
This season's for giving, so give it your best
join us at the Opera House for 25¢ draughts
Now Curtis! Now Michals! Now Rodman and Griffin!
On Gentile! On Wong! on Snyder and (your name here)!
To the Westward Hooo! To the Sands for Cashball!
Now dash away! Dash away! Dash away all!
We've hurt them with coupons, Couponomists all!
We're Advisors! We're Misers! So on, so forth and etc.!

February/March 1985

Miser's Dictionary of Casino Terms

ripped: Too many Heinekens.
deal: Anything 50¢ and under.
double down: Finding two nickels or two dimes or two quarters, etc.
flat-broke: What happens to your nose if you dare pick up a stray nickel near old women playing slots (see "kicker").
kicker: A form of retaliation against old slot women.
full house: Many, many people in the casino. An advantageous situation for finding money.
"H"-Bomb: A real knock-out cocktail waitress who brings Heinekens.
heads or tails: What to look for when scouring casino floors.
natural: The occurrence of finding any denomination coin when you're not even looking.
odds: The people who habituate Las Vegas casinos.
on the hop: Nabbing a stray and bouncing coin.
sure thing: Anything free (see "deal").
tip: ???

April 1992

I've learned many of life's lessons while on hiatus. For instance, I now know that the secret of life is gravity. Good gravity makes other people's silver coins drop to the casino floor so misers like myself can retrieve the lost dosh and drop them into special glass shekel jars. Bad gravity is unmeaningness, gaucherie, flap-doodle.

An example of good gravity is Bogie's nightclub in Las Vegas from 5-6pm on Fridays. Free food, free beer and wine, free clothing (i.e.. T-shirts, suspenders). Bad gravity is their Mr. Flap-doodle at the door who judges customer worthiness. (I wasn't wearing a shirt because I knew they would provide me with one inside!)

Good gravity is a matter of customer relations at the First Interstate Bank. A posted sign reads: "If you are dissatisfied with our service for any reason, we will give you $5, no questions asked." No coupon or ID required, they just hand over the cash. No bad gravity there. A long line has, thus far, been acceptable as a reason for dissatisfaction. Lunchtime on Friday is three for three.

May 1992

It finally arrived! I snagged my issue of the new and improved *LVA* from my smiling mailbox and rifled the pages like a boy with a wax-pack of baseball trading cards. I wasn't looking for anything in particular but felt warmed knowing I would soon be awash in the Advisor's exclusive up-to-date insider's knowledge. About time, you!

But here was the joy I found:

The Mint coupon book is #1... The Landmark has installed a hardwood Lambada floor... The Castaways is offering players free drinks and hobo sandwiches from 12-5 pm... The Silver Slipper burlesque show is free with a coupon... The Marina is paying 2-for-1 on all blackjacks...

What's going on here? What kind of dinosaurian *Las Vegas Advisor* is this? These casinos are extinct and the information as old as Paleolithic man!

Who's writing this stuff—Elvis?

Wait. The masthead reads "Volume 1, Number 1, 1987." Whoa! Guess that's what you get with the bulk rate. And I thought *I* was a miser!

June 1992

Everything is relative. . .

The Forum has opened at Caesars Palace. One of the designer boutiques has a cocktail dress in the window that costs $9,727. It's yellow and black and sort of stretchy and poofy. If I had $9,727, I sure wouldn't spend it on a yellowy, blacky, stretchy, poofy cocktail dress. With that kind of dosh I could:

- drink 97,270 beers at Vacation Village, or
- eat 9,825 breakfasts at King 8, or
- gobble 6,484 strawberry shortcakes at the Westward Ho, or
- see 329 Tom Jones shows at Bally's, or
- stay a year and a month at the Stardust, etc.

July 1992

The Miser's Convo With Stupak Parts I-VI:

The publisher of this newsletter is not so singularly privileged. I, too, have conversed with the enigmatic power-broker of Vegas World. I expected four to nine hours of the "Maverick's" time to discuss a serious money-grubbing business proposition to be located in his spinning, spiralling stratospheric tower.

I caught up to B.S. in the Vegas World parking lot and our conversation went something like this:

M: Excuse me, sir . . . What do you think of the idea of a Miser's Hall of Fame located at the very top of your smiling, swirling stratosphinctic tower, hm?

B.S.: Go away.

M: Oh. Okay, then . . . Got any free drink coupons on ya?

October 1992

Miser's 5 Reasons to Attend the LVA Party at Harrah's

5. Eats. I like food. Free food is best, I don't care what it tastes like.
4. Swigs. Candy is dandy, but liquor gives me the courage to play without coupons! (I don't know if this is such a good thing.)
3. A free room ... indoors.
2. No mimes allowed.
1. I will sign autographs. (For a small donation.)

December 1992

The White Elephant Tour

Forget the Mirage volcano, Caesars Forum shops, Stupak's Stratosphere Tower. While in Las Vegas, take the "White Elephant" tour. It's historical and free!

Start at the Dunes, which is soon to be rubble. A mile east you'll find a purposeless pirate boat in an empty dirt lot. Behind the San Remo sits a gutted cartoonish pink airplane. The Landmark, though dead, still stands as the ultimate memorial to the sex life of Howard Hughes, also dead. You can't go to the El Rauncho, either, former home of the world's oldest cocktail waitresses. Near downtown you can view the Minami hole, a proposed office tower turned fenced-off sink-tank. Finally, see Main Street Station, a turn-of-the-century styled locked-up cardboard box.

Coupons and out-of-state ID required.

March 1993

1) What do the following casinos have in common: Landmark, Dunes, El Rancho, Caesars Palace?

a) All are defunct.
b) All are on the Strip.
c) Mirage owner Steve Wynn wants to turn them all into lakes.
d) I found stray quarters on the floor of each.

2) Which headline are you most likely to see first?

a) "Stupak's Tower Completed"
b) "Sinatra Plays King 8"
c) "Miser Says Coupons No Good"
d) "Hell Freezes Over"

3) Which show am I most likely to attend?
   a) *Siegfried and Roy* ($72.85)
   b) *Cirque du Soleil* ($38.50)
   c) *Crazy Girls* and buffet ($16.45)
   d) Comedy Express ($0)

4) For which comp would I play at a $10 minimum blackjack table for one hour?
   a) A line pass to the Mongolian grill at the Rio buffet.
   b) The wrist watch at Fitzgeralds.
   c) Airfare, lanai suite, private chef.
   d) None.

Editor's Note: When we asked the Miser why he submitted a quiz without any answers, he replied, "The correct answers are obvious—although that complimentary wrist watch sounds pretty good."

May 1993

I recently talked to MGM board members to discuss in detail the economic impact of the Boardwalk promotions on the long-term viability of their soon-to-open megaresort.

MSR: Do you have chicken dinners?

MGM: No. We're not even open yet.

MSR: If you did have chicken dinners, would you charge 59¢? The Boardwalk did for more than a month. And though the Boardwalk doesn't have Oz World (or whatever), it does have a plaster-of-paris Elvis greeter out front. And though the Boardwalk doesn't have a lion's-mouth entrance, the Boardwalk does have Hobo stew, tiny Castle burgers, and a 12-inch pizza for $3.49. And though the Boardwalk doesn't have rides and movie-studio tours, the great difference is—correct me if I'm wrong—the Boardwalk is open and you're not!

MGM: You're right about that . . . would you like a green balloon?

MSR: Yes please.

July 1993

Opening Ceremonies

Soon, the Dunes will be sand. Blown away by a ceremonial Treasure Island cannon shot, sailing benignly over the Mirage, with a Long John Silver salute to Caesars Palace, and plop.

Other opening ceremonies . . . Circus Circus' Grand Slam Canyon will squirt a giant water-pistol across the street at Wet 'n Wild . . . The gargantuan Luxor sphinx will cough hairballs at the Tropicana's Polynesian heads . . . The MGM Grand lion will tap dance and sing "Born Free", then gobble up every Boardwalk 59¢ roast beef dinner . . . and the Vegas World Stratospheric Tower will simply fall down.

APPENDIX

These books, computer software, newsletters, and magazines are recommended for further study. All are available at Gambler's Book Club, the world's largest specialty bookstore on the subject of gambling. A visit while in town is time well spent. The store is located at 630 S. 11th St. (corner of 11th and Charleston). Or you can call 800-522-1777 to order a free catalog listing more than 1,000 books covering casinos and just about anything else remotely associated with gambling.

These products also available from Huntington Press, 702-597-1884.

BLACKJACK

Books

Theory of Blackjack, by Peter Griffin, $9.95, Huntington Press
Basic Blackjack, by Stanford Wong, $14.95, Pi Yee Press
Blackjack Secrets, by Stanford Wong, $14.95, Pi Yee Press
Blackbelt in Blackjack, by Arnold Snyder, $12.95, RGE Press

Software

Blackjack Analyzer (IBM), by Stanford Wong, $29.95, Pi Yee Press
Blackjack Count Analyzer (IBM), by Stanford Wong, $79.95, Pi Yee Press
Blackjack Trainer (Mac, system 6.0 or higher), $75, ConJelCo

Newsletters

Current Blackjack News, by Stanford Wong, 12 issues, $145, contact: Pi Yee Press, 7910 Ivanhoe #34, La Jolla, CA 92037, 619-456-4080
Blackjack Forum, by Arnold Snyder, 4 issues, $40, contact: RGE, 414 Santa Clara Ave., Oakland, CA 94610, 510-465-6452
Blackjack Review, by Michael Dalton, 4 issues, $25, contact: Spur of the Moment Publishing P.O. Box 541967, Merritt Island, FL 32954

VIDEO POKER

Books

Professional Video Poker, by Stanford Wong, $14.95, Pi Yee Press
Winning Strategies for Video Poker, by Lenny Frome, $15.95, Compu-Flyers
America's National Game of Chance: Video Poker, by Lenny Frome, $19.95, Compu-Flyers
Mastering Joker Wild Video Poker, by Bradley Davis, $14.95
Fundamentals of Video Poker, by Mason Malmuth and Lynne Loomis, $3.95

Software

Stanford Wong Video Poker (IBM and compatibles with at least 120K), $29.95, Villa Crespo Software
JACKPOT!, $29.95, (IBM at least 128K RAM, 5 1/4" or 3 1/2" disks, Amiga, and Macintosh), Above Average Software

OTHER GAMBLING

Books

Tournaments

Casino Tournament Strategy, by Stanford Wong, $14.95, Pi Yee Press

Pai Gow Poker

Optimal Strategy for Pai Gow Poker, by Stanford Wong, $14.95, Pi Yee Press

Sports Betting

Sports Betting 101, by Arne K. Lang, $19.95, GBC Press
SuperBookie, by Art Manteris, $18.95, Contemporary Books
Race and Sports Book Management, by Michael Roxborough and Mike Rhoden, $29.95

Race Betting

Betting Cheap Claimers, by Stanford Wong, $14.95, Pi Yee Press
Money Secrets at the Racetrack, by Barry Meadow, $27.95, TR Publishing

Poker
The Theory of Poker, by David Sklansky, $29.95, Two Plus Two Publishing
Fundamentals of Poker, by Mason Malmuth and Lynne Loomis, $3.95, Two Plus Two Publishing

General Gambling
Extra Stuff, by Peter Griffin, $11.95, Huntington Press

Software

Craps
CrapSim (IBM), by Ken Elliott, $60, ConJelCo

Newsletter

Gambling Prospector (Colorado Casinos) 12 issues, $40, contact: Token Press, 8174 S. Holly, Ste. 112, Littleton, CO, 80122, 800-227-6465.

Magazines

Casino Player, 12 issues, $24, Contact: Casino Player Magazine, 2524 Arctic Avenue, Atlantic City, NJ 08401, 800-637-9992.
The Card Player, published bi-weekly, available free in most casinos, subscription: 6 months $21, one year $39. Contact: The Card Player Magazine, 1455 E. Tropicana Ave. #450, Las Vegas, NV 89119, 702-798-5170.

GUIDES

Las Vegas, by Deke Castleman, $14.95, Compass American Guides
Nevada Handbook, by Deke Castleman, $13.95, Moon Publications
The Casino/Resort Riverboat & Fun Book Guide, $6.95, contact: Casino Vacations, P.O. Box 703-A, Dania, FL, 33004
The Unofficial Guide to Las Vegas, by Bob Sehlinger, Prentice Hall Travel (Available at most bookstores)

INDEX

ABOUT THE AUTHOR

Anthony Curtis is the publisher of the *Las Vegas Advisor* newsletter. An authority on Las Vegas and gambling, he has appeared in more than 100 national newspapers, including the *Los Angeles Times* and *USA Today*, and on CNN's *Moneyline* and *Your Money*. He is the consultant to the Nevada Motion Picture Division for movies and television sequences incorporating casino gambling. His gambling tournament wins and winnings include:

—Blackjack ("Matchplay"), $76,000, Las Vegas Hilton, 1986
—Craps, $125,000, Caesars Palace (Atlantic City), 1990
—Keno, $50,000, Caesars Palace, 1990
—Keno, $35,000, Caesars Palace, 1991
—Craps, $30,000, Imperial Palace, 1992

THIS BOOK IS DISTRIBUTED BY:

Sunbelt Publications
8630 Argent St., Suite C
Santee, CA 92071
(619) 258-4911

Baker & Taylor
All divisions nationwide

LAS VEGAS ADVISOR

$5

Couponomy

Bargain City

LAS VEGAS' TOP TEN VALUES

Free Rooms At Harrah's

If you liked Bargain City, you're going to love the

Las Vegas Advisor

The 12-page *Las Vegas Advisor* newsletter is the ultimate up-to-the minute insider's guide to Las Vegas. Included in every issue: Las Vegas' Top Ten Values, the lodging, dining, entertainment and gambling scenes, current gaming news, reviews of gambling promotions, an Advance Planner (featuring key dates, tournaments, entertainment schedules, sample room rates and weather forecasts for the upcoming three months), and much more. All new subscribers receive a complimentary *LVA Reference Guide.*

And that's not all . . . your subscription fee is immediately recouped! *LVA's* Subscriber Benefit Package consists of exclusive coupons with a value ranging from a minimum of $113 to a maximum of over $350. If you use only two coupons during your next Las Vegas vacation, you'll recover the cost of your newsletter subscription!

And it makes a great gift for that person on your list who is impossible to buy for, but loves coming to Las Vegas.

Huntington Press
5280 S. Valley View Blvd., Suite B, Las Vegas, NV 89118
(702) 597-1884 • (702) 597-5208 Fax

YES! I want to buy a subscription to the Las Vegas Advisor!

(Nevada residents add 7% sales tax)

❑ I am enclosing $45 for one year of the LVA at 2nd class postage.

❑ I am enclosing $50 for one year of the LVA at 1st-class postage.

Paying by: ❑ check/money order ❑ Visa/MasterCard

Acct# ____________________ Exp. ________

Signature (req'd) ____________________

Name ____________________ Phone # ________

Address ____________________

City ____________________ State ______ Zip ________